||| || ||||||||||| | |||| | ||||||||||||| ||| ||| |||

⬨ **W9-AYC-316**

TEACHER'S GUIDE AND ANSWER KEY

LATIN: Our Living Heritage (Book I)

PREFACE

The purpose of this guide is to provide the teacher with background knowledge of the principles involved in the grammatical sections and exercises and with a more complete treatment of derivatives than the text can present. Such a depth of knowledge, while necessary for effective teaching, can often be attained only through hours of research. This guide makes such information readily accessible.

The guide follows the order of presentation of material that is used in the text. It is keyed to the text by section numbers. Unless otherwise indicated, the section references are to *Latin: Our Living Heritage,* Book I.

In the case of both Latin and English readings, the guide provides specific references to original sources and to correlated material in the books listed as reference works. Only material that has actually proven useful has been recommended. The large number of references is intended to insure that teachers in schools with limited library facilities may have some choice. In the bibliography, some evaluation of the various references has been given.

The guide contains information concerning the mottoes that introduce each lesson and a key to word-study sections, readings, drills, and sentences. In both readings and exercises, the key frequently suggests alternate versions of wording or of style, but these are by no means exhaustive. In the translations from Latin to English, an attempt has been made to keep the language idiomatic. Where it seems advisable, a literal version has been inserted.

Throughout the guide, suggestions for teaching devices and procedures are offered quite tentatively with the realization that most teachers prefer to develop their own methods and to adapt them to the needs and abilities of their students. The following are a few suggestions for use of the text:

1. Use the motto, which is an integral part of each lesson, to introduce the lesson.

2. Throughout the early lessons, read the Latin to the students. As soon as the students learn the sounds, have them read the Latin aloud daily. Without overemphasis on rules, insist on correctness of pronunciation, accent, and length of syllables. At this stage, the students will learn most easily by imitation.

ISBN 0-675-01997-4

Published by
CHARLES E. MERRILL PUBLISHING CO.
A Bell & Howell Company
Columbus, Ohio 43216
Toronto • London • Sydney

Copyright © 1982, 1968 by Bell & Howell

3. Try to complete as much as possible of the first eight lessons within the class session. Assign for homework only what has been mastered. Teach the pupils to find in the sample sentences, in the Latin exercises, and in the reading selections, the words, phrases, and constructions they need to use in the English-Latin exercises. Emphasize the principle that homework is practice and that bad practice is worse than none. Avoidance of error at this stage will save both teacher and student trouble later.

For the average class it will be advisable to spend two class periods on most lessons; with a slower class many lessons will require three periods. This, of course, will vary depending on the length of the period, the ability of the class, and the preference of the teacher.

4. Use every possible means to vary and to reinforce drill. The overhead projector is an effective means of teaching vocabulary. Tapes, prepared in advance, can be used for vocabulary and for drill of grammar in class and in the language laboratory. Rapid oral drill and chalkboard drill in class can be equally effective. In all drill, emphasize the necessity for a swift response.

5. Encourage the students to use their newly acquired knowledge to advance their knowledge of English. Most students find derivative study fascinating and undertake it enthusiastically. It may, however, be necessary often to impress upon them the need for accuracy. A good English dictionary should be available at all times to check every new hypothesis and to temper imagination with fact.

6. In the readings, encourage the students to strive for a free and idiomatic English translation, within the bounds of accuracy. In the exercises, encourage imitation of the text.

7. Keep all projects within the realm of the students' various abilities. Book reports and oral reports on background material are to be encouraged. Compilations of derivative notebooks and of scrapbooks of clippings from newspapers and magazines illustrating the use of Latin in English can be a valuable learning aid. Free composition, letter writing, storytelling (except by imitation), and attempts to produce a Latin newspaper should be discouraged during this first year. Such work may have adverse results if undertaken before students have attained a reasonable degree of facility.

8. Blank pages are provided on pp. 27-28, 75-76, 125-126 for Teacher's Notes.

It is hoped that the use of the guide will conserve time within the classroom, and, by so doing, will make possible greater emphasis upon the needs of the individual student.

Mary A. Barrett

LESSON 1

Motto

Read the motto in Latin. Comment on the word order "Twice he gives who quickly gives," mentioning that the verb commonly, but not always, comes last in a Latin clause. Ask whether anyone has an idea where, in Latin, the *he* of the English translation is. It may be possible to introduce the grammar of this lesson by means of a correct answer to this question. Ask the class to think of English words related to **bis** (for example, *biennial*).

1 Call attention to the use of inflection to express the person doing the action. Note that the inflection is not actually the pronoun but is a means of indicating person without necessarily using the pronoun. Refer to **dat** in the motto.

Point out that one form in Latin contains all the present ideas expressed in English by three forms. Illustrate the form *do carry* by a question (*Do you carry?*) and by a negative (*I do not carry*). Mention also that the common English expression *I do* is an ellipsis of this form.

3 Mention the fact that in some tenses the first person singular ending is **-m**. It is not necessary for the student to concern himself with this fact at present but mentioning it here will avoid confusion later.

4-5 Students will remember the meanings of the verbs better if they can relate an English word to each: for example, *amiable, arable, data, inhabitant, applaud, portable, vocation, tenacious, timid, evident.*

Point out the similarities in the present tense of first and second conjugation verbs: means of translation, endings, long vowels; then point out the difference, the stem vowels **a** and **e.**

Explain that such terms as *first conjugation* and *second conjugation* are merely convenient names to apply to a group of verbs which have the same characteristics.

Emphasize the importance of learning the first two principal parts of the verbs in Sections 4 and 5. Students should be made to realize in the beginning the necessity of memorizing vocabulary thoroughly: pronunciation, spelling and meaning.

1

7 In addition to the questions in Section 7, others may be added which require a change of subject in the answer.

Question.	**Amāsne?**	*Answer.*	**Amō** *or* **Nōn amō.**
Question.	**Amātisne?**	*Answer.*	**Amāmus** *or* **Nōn amāmus.**
Question.	**Videōne?**	*Answer.*	**Vidēs** *or* **Nōn vidēs.**
Question.	**Habitāmusne?**	*Answer.*	**Habitātis** *or* **Nōn habitātis.**

8   EXERCISES

A.   The first verb might be done in class with open book, following the model closely; the second, with closed book. Two students might serve as secretaries for the class, one writing the Latin forms and one the English meanings at the board, as they are given by the other class members.

	Singular
vocō	I call, am calling, do call
vocās	you call, are calling, do call
vocat	he calls, is calling, does call
	Plural
vocāmus	we call, are calling, do call
vocātis	you call, are calling, do call
vocant	they call, are calling, do call
	Singular
videō	I see, am seeing, do see
vidēs	you see, are seeing, do see
videt	he sees, is seeing, does see
	Plural
vidēmus	we see, are seeing, do see
vidētis	you see, are seeing, do see
vident	they see, are seeing, do see

NOTE: Such forms as are done in class should be done with the text open to p. 7. Emphasize here and in the succeeding lessons that the exercises are designed to set permanently in the student's mind the grammar presented in each lesson and that they are, therefore, absolutely valueless unless done accurately.

If parts of these exercises are assigned as homework, the pupils should be told that the text is intended to serve as a teacher at home and should be consulted at every step of the preparation.

B.   1. You carry, are carrying, do carry; I carry, am carrying, do carry; we move, are moving, do move; they move, are moving, do move.   2. He (She, It) loves, is loving, does love; you plow, are plowing, do plow; I see, am seeing, do see; they have (hold), are having, do have.   3. He (She, It) sees, is seeing, does see; I live, am living, do live; he (she, it) holds, is holding, does hold; we love (like), are loving, do love.   4. I give, am giving, do give; we praise, are praising, do praise; you move, are moving, do move; you call, are calling, do call.   5. They obey, are obeying, do obey; he (she, it) plows, is plowing, does plow; you see, are seeing, do see; you give, are giving, do give.

C.   1. Dat, habēmus, vocant, amātis.   2. Movent, laudās, habitāmus, pāret. 3. Portāmus, timeō, arant, tenētis.   4. Dās, timet, pāretis, habent.   5.Portās, moveō, habitant, vocat.

D.   1. Amō.   2. Portat.   3. Tenēmus *or* Habēmus.   4. Timētis.   5. Vocant.   6. Dās.   7. Pāreō.   8. Habet.   9. Habitāmusne?   10. Vidēs. 11. Laudant.   12. Arō.   13. Tenet *or* Habet.   14. Portāmusne? 15. Timētis.   16. Dantne?   17. Habeō.   18. Laudat.   19. Vident. 20. Arās.

E.   1. Arant *or* Nōn arant.   2. Vocat *or* Nōn vocat.   3. Pārēmus *or* Nōn pārēmus. Also Pāretis *or* Nōn pāretis.   4. Timet *or* Nōn timet.   5. Vocant *or* Nōn vocant.   6. Movent *or* Nōn movent.

LESSON 2

Motto

Comment on the fact that English *experience* is directly derived from Latin **experientia.** Mention one or two other nouns of this type (for example, *patience,* **patientia;** *grace,* **grātia**), noting briefly the change from Latin **-tia** to English *-ce.* Although this is an item of later word study, it can profitably be mentioned here.

Call attention to the person and the number of the verb **docet** and ask whether anyone can explain why that ending is used. This discussion may introduce the subject-verb agreement of this lesson.

9   The Island Britain

Britain is an island. Is Britain a small island? Britain is not a small island; it is large. Britain is in Europe. On the island (there) are sailors. Farmers also live in Britain. In Britain lives a family: a sailor, a woman and a girl. The woman and girl don't sail with the sailor; they are afraid. They are plowing with the farmer.

NOTES: Point out the *do* form for the negative in the next to the last sentence. Suggest that the present progressive of English be given as a translation for at least some of the verb forms, and insist on this form in sentences where the pure present would be awkward in English.

Students' questions concerning the final **-ā** in certain words can be answered briefly, but in such a way as to simplify greatly the presentation of the ablative in Lesson 4.

3

Respondē Latinē:

1. Britannia nōn est parva (īnsula). 2. Fēmina et puella nōn nāvigant. 3. Nauta nāvigat. 4. Britannia est in Eurōpā. 5. Agricolae in īnsulā habitant.

10 Comment on the term *first declension* applied to a group of nouns similarly inflected. Point out that this declension may be considered the **a** declension, just as the *first conjugation* may be considered the **a** conjugation.

11 Explain the term *finite verb* by contrasting a finite form with an infinitive. For instance, *he sails* may be contrasted with *to sail,* showing that *he sails* limits the sailing (person, number, tense) while *to sail* is not so limited.

12 Explain the fact that a noun subject of a sentence always requires a third person verb by relating the noun to its corresponding pronoun: the sailor (he); the woman (she); the island (it); farmers (they).

13 Explain the difference between the verb *to be* used as an intransitive verb and as an auxiliary verb in the progressive in the English sentence.

Agricola in Eurōpā est.	The farmer is in Europe.
Agricola arat.	The farmer is plowing.
In īnsulā sum.	I am on the island.
In īnsulā habitō.	I am living on the island.

Call attention to the fact that a form of *to be* used as an auxiliary verb is omitted in the Latin sentence and the idea expressed by use of the present tense.

14 Make certain that the difference between subject and predicate nominative is clearly understood and that the distinction is not seen merely as a matter of word order. Show how in Sec. 9 **Īnsula Britannia** in 1. 1, **īnsula** is a predicate nominative, while **nautae** in 1. 3, is the real subject.

17 EXERCISES

A.

	Singular		Singular
sum	I am	**sum agricola**	I am a farmer
es	you are	**es agricola**	you are a farmer
est	he (she, it) is	**est agricola**	he is a farmer
	Plural		Plural
sumus	we are	**sumus agricolae**	we are farmers
estis	you are	**estis agricolae**	you are farmers
sunt	they are	**sunt agricolae**	they are farmers

B. 1. We are, they give, he is moving, you praise. 2. You love *or* like, he is, he hurries, I see. 3. I am, I am carrying, you do hold, they are plowing. 4. You are, they obey, you are, you have *or* hold. 5. We love *or* like, they are, they are holding, he is living.

4

C. 1. Agricola 2. agricolae 3. Puellae 4. Īnsula 5. puella 6. Nauta
7. Puella 8. Nautae 9. nauta 10. Īnsula 11. īnsula 12. Agricolae
13. īnsula 14. femina; puella

D. 1. Britannia est īnsula. 2. Īnsula est parva. 3. Agricolae arant. 4. Sunt
puellae in īnsulā. 5. Fēmina et puella properant. 6. Nauta nāvigat. 7. Est
agricola in īnsulā. 8. Fēminae nōn arant. 9. Nautae nāvigant. 10. Agricolae sunt.

NOTE: Limitation of space does not permit all possible answers to be
given. It is assumed that the teacher will accept any correct answer for a
particular item.

SUPPLEMENTARY VERB DRILL

1. Sumus, amat, properant, habitāmus. 2. Timēs, nāvigō, sunt, pāret.
3. Sum, portō, habētis, vocāmus. 4. Habent or tenent, estis, est, laudat.
5. Es, dās, vident, amāmus.

LESSON 3

Motto

The students may be familiar with the expression **terra firma.** Write it on
the board and ask for a literal translation of the expression. Point out that the
motto **Dēscende ad terram** has a literal meaning for parachutists (it is the
motto of the 507th Parachute Infantry Regiment). It can be used as a warning to others as well. Ask for what type of student **Dēscende ad terram** would
be good advice.

19 The Island of Britain

Britain is an island. Once upon a time there were in Britain many Roman
roads. The Roman roads were good. The island of Britain has many inhabitants. The inhabitants are both sailors and farmers. The sailors often sail
to Europe and (to) America. The farmers stay in Britain and plow the fields.

In Britain there is a queen. The queen is a good woman. The inhabitants
of Britain do not fear the good queen; they love their queen. The queen has
a daughter. The daughter of the queen also is good.

NOTE: Although possessive adjectives are usually omitted in Latin unless
required for clarity or emphasis, they are usually expressed in English.
Notice the translation of **rēgīnam** in 1. 7: *They love their queen.*

Respondē Latīnē:

1. Britannia est īnsula. 2. Britannia multōs incolās habet. 3. Nautae ad
Eurōpam et ad Americam nāvigant. 4. Agricolae nōn nāvigant. 5. Agricolae agrōs arant. 6. Agricolae in Britanniā manent. 7. Rēgīna est fēmina
bona. 8. Incolae Britanniae rēgīnam amant. 9. Incolae Britanniae rēgīnam nōn timent. 10. Fīlia rēgīnae est bona.

5

21 Point out the advantages an inflected language has over an uninflected one. Since meaning depends on inflection, word order can be varied to achieve emphasis or another desired effect. Compare the following as regards emphasis: **Agricola puellam videt. Puellam agricola videt. Videt puellam agricola.**

22 Refer to the motto of this lesson for an example of the accusative case as the object of a preposition.

23 WORD STUDY

It would be worthwhile to bring an unabridged dictionary to class to show the students how to determine the derivation of words. Students should be encouraged to check all English derivatives in this way.

24 EXERCISES

A.

Singular	Singular
Nautam videō.	**Puellās laudō.**
Nautam vidēs.	**Puellās laudās.**
Nautam videt.	**Puellās laudat.**
Plural	Plural
Nautam vidēmus.	**Puellās laudāmus.**
Nautam vidētis.	**Puellās laudātis.**
Nautam vident.	**Puellās laudant.**

B. 1. Puellae ad īnsulās nāvigant. 2. Rēgīnae fīliās habent. 3. Fēminās agricolae timent. 4. Nautae trāns viās puellās portant. 5. Fīliās bonās fēminae laudant.

C. 1. Fēmina bona agricolam vocat. 2. Puella in viam properat. 3. Nauta ad īnsulam nāvigat. 4. Fīliam rēgīna amat. 5. Fēmina agricolam videt.

D. 1. puella 2. fīliās 3. nautae 4. Agricolam 5. Nautae 6. īnsula 7. fēmina

E. 1. Agricola puellās vocat. 2. Rēgīna fīliam amat. 3. Properatne trāns viam? 4. Agricolae arant. 5. Quō nāvigant? 6. Ad īnsulās nāvigant. 7. Puellae nautam timent. 8. Britannia est īnsula. 9. Puella aquam trāns viam portat. 10. Agricolae ad fēminās properant.

SUPPLEMENTARY DRILL

A. 1. We are calling the girls. 2. Do they fear the sailor? 3. The queen praises the farmer. 4. The sailor loves his daughters. 5. The women are calling the inhabitants. 6. She praises her daughter. 7. I am afraid of the farmers. 8. The daughter loves a sailor. 9. An inhabitant is carrying the water. 10. Does he praise the girls?

B. 1. Manent, vocāmus, videt, nāvigō. 2. Dās, habet *or* tenet, laudant, pārēmus. 3. Timeō, arant, estis, amat. 4. Sum, laudāmus, pārēs, habitō. 5. Habent, est, nāvigat, portātis.

25 The vocabulary will suggest many related English words such as: *aquarium, aquatic, filial, via, bonus, multiple, transport.*

26   ROMAN ROADS

References: Johnston, p. 307 and pp. 328-338; Robathan, pp. 14, 19, and pp. 25-29; Showerman, *Rome and the Romans,* pp. 485-498; Treble and King, p. 20 and p. 153. See also the map on p. 157 of the text.

LESSON 4

Motto

Mention the omission of the verb in the motto as an example of ellipsis. Ask for English derivatives of **periculum** and **mora.** If *moratorium* is not suggested, use the word in a sentence and let students deduce the meaning.

27   Roman Provinces

There are in Italy large Roman forces. The forces hurry from Italy (in)to Gaul, a Roman province. The Romans are stationing forces in many provinces. The Gauls attack the Roman province with spears. In Gaul Roman forces are fighting with (the) Gauls. They fight with the Germans also. The Romans do not recall the(ir) troops from the provinces.

The Roman sailors sail to many islands. They are sailing to the island (of) Britain. In Britain live many farmers. The farmers live with women and girls in Britain. The farmers plow the fields. Daily the Roman forces fight with the farmers. Roman forces are attacking the farmers with spears and arrows. The Romans kill many farmers. The forces do not stay in Britain. After the(ir) victory the Romans recall the troops from Britain to Italy.

NOTE: A map of ancient Gaul will help to make the reading lesson meaningful to the students. Locate the countries mentioned on the map and explain that these areas will become very familiar when Caesar's **Commentāriī dē Bellō Gallicō** are read.

Respondē Latīnē:

1. Cōpiae ex Italiā properant. 2. Cōpiae in Galliam properant. 3. Rōmānī cōpiās multīs in prōvinciīs collocant. 4. Gallī prōvinciam Rōmānam oppugnant. 5. Cōpiae Rōmānae cum Gallīs pugnant. 6. Rōmānī cōpiās ā prōvinciīs nōn revocant. 7. Nautae Rōmānī ad multās īnsulās (Britanniam) nāvigant. 8. Agricolae in Britanniā cum cōpiīs Rōmānīs pugnant. 9. Rōmānī multōs agricolās necant. 10. Cōpiae Rōmānae in Britanniā nōn manent.

28 Emphasize the importance of the macron in the ablative singular ending in the first declension since it is the only distinguishing feature between the nominative singular and the ablative singular.

30 Note that one of these place constructions in the ablative, the ablative of *place where* or *in which,* is already familiar from the Latin readings of the previous lessons.

31 Point out that the ablative of means (*with* or *by what*) is the only use of the ablative case learned in this lesson which omits the preposition.

35   EXERCISES

NOTE: Exercises A and B could be used for drill after the principles of the lesson and the vocabulary have been learned. Send some students to the board to translate from dictation. Let the rest of the class detect errors and correct.

A.   1. from Italy   2. into the street   3. on the way *or* in the road   4. after victory   5. across the island   6. through the room   7. with the queen   8. to Gaul   9. from (out of) Italy   10. with a spear   11. from the streets   12. on islands   13. into the islands   14. with the girls   15. across the streets   16. with a woman   17. through the streets   18. to(ward) the sailors   19. out of the streets   20. by (with) spears

B.   1. ab īnsulā   2. ex Italiā   3. per cameram   4. sagittā   5. cum rēgīnā   6. in aquam   7. in aquā   8. aquā   9. ad Galliam   10. trāns īnsulam   11. post victōriam   12. per īnsulās   13. ab incolīs   14. hastīs   15. cum fēminīs   16. in viīs   17. in viās   18. ē viā   19. trāns viās   20. ad agricolās

C.   1. The sailor is killing an inhabitant.   2. After victory the queen recalls the troops.   3. Daily the women recall their daughters from the street.   4. They are moving the troops from Gaul (in)to Germany.   5. Many Roman forces stay in Britain.   6. There are both sailors and farmers on the island.   7. Girls don't fight with spears and arrows.   8. With whom is the woman hurrying from the room?   9. Where are the inhabitants stationing the Roman forces?   10. Sailors are sailing to the island with the farmers.

D.   1. Properatne trāns viam cum puellā?   2. Cōpiae dē Galliā ad Italiam properant.   3. Est via in īnsulā.   4. Incolās hastīs et sagittīs oppugnant.   5. Post victōriam cōpiās revocant.   6. Quō nauta cotīdiē nāvigat?   7. Puella aquam ad nautam portat.   8. Quibuscum (Quōcum) fēminae pugnant?   9. Rēgīnā cōpiās in īnsulā collocat.   10. Portatne agricola aquam ad viam?

SUPPLEMENTARY DRILL

1. in viam   2. trāns īnsulam   3. cum fēminā   4. ad īnsulam   5. ab Italiā   6. per viam   7. hastā   8. ē Galliā   9. post victōriās   10. in cameram   11. sagittīs   12. trāns viam   13. ad Britanniam   14. cum incolīs   15. aquā

LESSON 5

Motto

After reading the motto in Latin, repeat it in the so-called Italian pronunciation, **"Glōria in** *ekchelsīs* **Deō"** and remark that this is the correct pronunciation for this phrase. Ask whether anyone can explain why this is so and whether anyone can identify the source of the phrase. Some will recognize it from the Christmas story (Luke 2:14) or from the Christmas hymns.

37 Farmers

From Italy to Sicily sailors sail daily. Farmers do not sail with the sailors; they stay in Italy. Women and their daughters do not sail with the sailors. Daily the women plow the fields with the farmers. The little girls do not plow; they carry (the) water to the women and farmers. They give the women and farmers water. The farmer often gives the girls money; he brings (*lit.* carries) the money to the girls. The girls like the farmer. The farmer gives orders to the girls; good girls obey the farmer.

Respondē Latīnē:

1. Nautae ad Siciliam nāvigant. 2. Cum agricolīs fēminae arant. 3. Fīliae nōn arant. 4. Puellae aquam (ad agricolās et fēminās) portant. 5. Fēminīs et agricolīs aquam dant. 6. Agricola puellīs pecūniam dat. 7. Agricola puellīs imperat. 8. Puellae agricolae pārent.

38 Contrast the datives **puellae, rēgīnae, nautae** with the dative of the motto (**Deō**). If the pupils are asked to account for this difference, the teacher may draw from them the answer that the word **Deō** must belong to a different, or second, declension.

39-40 Both of these sections may need special emphasis. It may be well to go over in class some of the prepositional phrases introduced by *to* in exercises C and E before any homework is assigned. Have the students decide what thought the phrase conveys and the Latin case required by the idea of the phrase.

42 EXERCISES

A. 1. Puellīs sagittās dant. 2. Rēgīnīs victōriās nūntiant. 3. Nautīs respondent. 4. Quibus hastās dant? 5. Incolīs rēgīnae imperant.

B. 1. Cui incola pāret? 2. Fēminae pecūniam dat. 3. Incolae victōriam nūntiat. 4. Agricolae fīlia respondet. 5. Rēgīna puellae imperat.

C. 1. puellae 2. ad silvam 3. Nautae 4. ad incolās 5. rēgīnae 6. incolīs 7. ad prōvinciam 8. cōpiīs 9. fēminīs 10. agricolīs

D. 1. We are announcing the victory to the queen. 2. He gives the farmers money. 3. The sailor is killing the farmer with a spear. 4. He gives orders to the provinces. 5. Sailors are hastening across the island with the troops.

6. Girls are bringing (carrying) money to the woman. 7. The girls give the woman money. 8. The inhabitants see the sailor. 9. The daughters are walking through the forest; they do not see the women. 10. The troops announce victory to the inhabitants.

E. 1. Fēmina puellae pecūniam dat. 2. Fēmina aquam ad puellam portat. 3. Agricolae incolīs respondent. 4. Cōpiae rēgīnae victōriam nūntiant. 5. Fēminam ad cameram vocat. 6. Rēgīna cōpiīs imperat; cōpiae rēgīnae pārent. 7. Nautās ad prōvinciam revocant. 8. Incolae hastīs et sagittīs pugnant. 9. Fēminae patriam amant; pugnam nōn amant. 10. Nautae ab Italiā ad īnsulam cotīdiē nāvigant.

SUPPLEMENTARY DRILL

1. Nautae pecūniam 2. rēgīnae 3. Incolīs victōriam 4. Hastās . . . nautās 5. cōpiīs 6. nautīs pecūniam 7. Puellae 8. Agricolae 9. fīliās . . . cameram 10. puellae sagittam

43 Related English words suggested by the vocabulary: *pecuniary, impecunious, pug(ilist), Pennsylvania, terrestrial, perambulator (pram), imperative, retain.* Have students suggest others. Note the spelling changes in the English words *Pennsylvania* and *retain*.

LESSON 6

Motto

Note the case of **mora** and ask who can explain the use of the nominative case. Point out that **maximum** came into English unchanged in spelling and **ira** with only a slight change. Discuss the application of the motto to human behavior. Is it a universal truth?

44   The Inhabitants of Italy

There are in Italy many inhabitants. The inhabitants are farmers. The people of Italy love the(ir) native land; they do not like fighting.

Sailors sail from Africa to Italy; they are looking for booty. The sailors make ready (collect) a supply of spears and arrows; they are preparing for battle. The sailors frighten the inhabitants of Italy; they lay waste the land. With spears and arrows they fight with the Roman forces. They kill many inhabitants. The sailors terrify the farmers' daughters but do not kill them because the women and girls do not fight.

The women are standing around the gates. An inhabitant sees them. He calls the women and farmers' daughters together; he gives orders to the women. The women and girls obey the inhabitant. The inhabitant points out a road through the forest. The women and girls hasten to(ward) the forest. They remain in the woods. Finally an inhabitant announces the victory of the Roman forces to the women and girls.

Respondē Latīnē:

1. Incolae Italiae pugnam nōn amant.   2. Nautae ab Āfricā cōpiam hastā-rum et sagittārum comportant.   3. Nautae cum cōpiīs Rōmānīs pugnant.
4. Nautae fīliās agricolārum terrent.   5. Nōn necant quod fēminae et puellae nōn pugnant.   6. Fēminae circum portās stant.   7. Incola fēminīs imperat.
8. Fēminae et puellae incolae pārent.   9. Fēminae et puellae ad silvam pro-perant.   10. Incola fēminīs et puellīs victōriam nūntiat.

46   Two students might act as secretaries to write at the board sentences contributed by class members to illustrate the nominative plural, genitive singular and dative singular in the samė sentence. A fairly large number of examples will show that, while ambiguity is possible in an isolated sentence, it is rare.

48   Emphasize the importance of learning declensions for quick recall. Drill on the first declension endings. To help the students memorize them, have them repeat them first with open, then with closed books; then have them write the endings. Rapid, smooth declension should follow naturally. Re-view by asking for case endings out of order: accusative singular; dative plural; ablative singular; etc.

49   WORD STUDY

advocāre, *to summon;* **convocāre,** *to call together;* **ēvocāre,** *to call out;* **revocāre,** *to call back*

Mention English derivatives *convoke, evoke, revoke.* Note the change in spelling of **c** to *k,* a rather common change.

50   EXERCISES

A.

Singular	Plural	Singular	Plural
nauta	nautae	porta	portae
nautae	nautārum	portae	portārum
nautae	nautīs	portae	portīs
nautam	nautās	portam	portās
nautā	nautīs	portā	portīs

B.   1. Ad silvās ambulant.   2. Cum agricolīs sunt fīliae.   3. Incolae insulā-rum sunt nautae.   4. Nautae puellīs sagittās dant.   5. Puellae sunt fīliae agricolārum.

C.   1. Fēminae viam mōnstrat.   2. Puella est fīlia rēgīnae.   3. Nauta hastam portat.   4. Est via in īnsulā.   5. Fēmina cum puellā ambulat.

D.   1. rēgīnae   2. nautārum   3. fīliā   4. Nautīs   5. Fossam   6. Porta
7. Incolās   8. sagittīs   9. Incolae   10. Fēminae

E.   1. Is there a lack of money?   2. They are making ready a supply of arrows and spears.   3. On the large island lives a farmer.   4. We are hurry-ing from the gate to the forest.   5. The sailor's daughter obeys the queen.

11

6. We fill the ditch with water daily. 7. They are killing many inhabitants with arrows and spears. 8. An inhabitant is pointing out the way to the women. 9. The inhabitants of Italy love their native land. 10. The queen praises good girls.

F. 1. Incolae Italiae patriam amant. 2. Cūr fīliās agricolārum amās (amātis)? 3. Puellīs victōriam cōpiārum nūntiat. 4. Multōs incolās sagittīs et hastīs necant. 5. Agricola cōpiam aquae ad fīliās portat. 6. In viās saepe ambulāmus. 7. Incolae pugnam parant quod cōpiās timent. 8. Nautae dē Italiā ad Āfricam nāvigant. 9. Sunt multae fēminae in īnsulā. 10. Rēgīna fēminae imperat sed fēmina rēgīnae nōn pāret.

SUPPLEMENTARY NOUN DRILL

1. cum fēminīs 2. trāns viam 3. aquā 4. ad īnsulam 5. inopia pecūniae 6. Nautīs pāret. 7. circum portās 8. cōpiam hastārum 9. Rēgīnae respondent. 10. in silvīs

REVIEW LESSON ONE

Most of the work of this lesson can best be done as rapid oral review in class. Section II (Forms), however, lends itself well to written work at the board. If, during the class review, the pupils make a note of those words, forms, or constructions in which errors are made, they will have a fairly small number of specific items on which to concentrate when they are reviewing at home.

II. A.

	Singular	Plural
Nom.	agricola	agricolae
Gen.	agricolae	agricolārum
Dat.	agricolae	agricolīs
Acc.	agricolam	agricolās
Abl.	agricolā	agricolīs

B.

	Singular
laudō	I praise, am praising, do praise
laudās	you praise, are praising, do praise
laudat	he (she, it) praises, is praising, does praise
	Plural
laudāmus	we praise, are praising, do praise
laudātis	you praise, are praising, do praise
laudant	they praise, are praising, do praise

	Singular
moveō	I move, am moving, do move
movēs	you move, are moving, do move
movet	he (she, it) moves, is moving, does move

	Plural
movēmus	we move, are moving, do move
movētis	you move, are moving, do move
movent	they move, are moving, do move

	Singular		Plural
sum	I am	**sumus**	we are
es	you are	**estis**	you are
est	he (she, it) is	**sunt**	they are

C. 1. incolae 2. hastā 3. nūntiat 4. rēgīnae 5. agricolārum 6. habēmus 7. parās 8. pārēs 9. terram 10. terrent

D. 1. We walk, are walking. 2. Do they live? Are they living? 3. He removes, is moving back. 4. She hurries, is hastening. 5. You do not see. 6. They are. 7. I fear, am afraid of. 8. They kill, are killing. 9. Do you sail? Are you sailing? 10. He shows, is pointing out.

E. 1. Videt. 2. Portant. 3. Pārēmus. 4. Habēs *or* Tenēs. 5. Pugnantne? 6. Nōn parat. 7. Estis. 8. Arō. 9. Dant. 10. Manet.

III. A. 1. feminine; masculine 2. nominative 3. dative 4. accusative 5. ā, ab; ē, ex; dē; ablative 6. ablative 7. **cum**; ablative 8. **ad**; accusative 9. ablative; accusative 10. genitive 11. nominative; subject 12. interrogative (a question) 13. subject

B. 1. indirect object; dative plural 2. direct object; accusative plural 3. subject; nominative plural 4. governed by preposition **ad**; accusative singular 5. noun describing or classifying another noun; genitive singular 6. ablative of means; ablative singular 7. governed by preposition **cum** (in company with); ablative singular 8. indirect object of verb **pārēmus**; dative singular 9. governed by preposition **ex**; ablative singular 10. predicate nominative; nominative singular

IV. 1. D 2. B 3. E 4. A 5. C 6. F

V. 1. financial (pertaining to money) 2. belligerent (eager for fighting) 3. ample, full (plenty of) 4. of a daughter 5. shut off from heat and cold (made an island) 6. doors (gates) 7. the Archer (carrier of arrows) 8. vicarious ruler 9. dwelling place 10. tending to hold fast 11. capable of being plowed 12. praiseworthy 13. destruction 14. canceled by recalling or taking back 15. capable of walking

13

VI.   1. The Appian Way, the queen of roads, in Italy between Rome and Capua and later between Rome and Brundisium   2. Steps in road building: earth leveling, foundation stones, a layer of broken stones, flat stones laid close together for pavement, curbstones, footpaths. Some of these roads, used throughout the Middle Ages, can be seen today.   3. 65 miles (**mīlia passuum**) from Rome   4. paid chiefly in cattle (**pecus**); later paid with coins

LESSON 7

Motto

Read the Latin and give the literal meaning: *a measure of land not so large*. Ask what case **agrī** must be. Note the ending **-ī** for the genitive singular and identify as a second declension noun, thus introducing the grammar of the lesson. Ask which word means *large* and why the student connects **magnus** with *large*. Ask for several derivatives from **magnus**.

52   The Roman School (Conversation)
                Vir, a man   **Puer,** a boy

V.   Who are you, boy?
P.   I am Lucius, the son of Publius.
V.   Are you a Gaul, Lucius?
P.   No, I am a Roman boy but Cotus is a Gaul.
V.   Who is Cotus, Lucius?
P.   Cotus is a slave and a pedagogue.
V.   What does a pedagogue do?
P.   Pedagogues take the boys to school; they carry the boys' books.
V.   Where is the school?
P.   Our school is near the walls of Rome. I walk to the walls daily with (my) friends.
V.   Who is the teacher?
P.   Our teacher is not a Roman. He is a slave but a good man.
V.   What does the teacher teach the boys?
P.   The teacher teaches the boys the Latin language; he also teaches Latin literature.
V.   Are the schools public?
P.   Schools at Rome are not public. Boys bring money to school; they give the teacher money. The teacher praises the boys; he gives good boys a prize.
V.   Are there girls in the Roman schools?
P.   There aren't often girls in the Roman schools. There were never girls in our school. Roman girls stay at home.

Respondē Latīnē:
1. Lūcius est fīlius Publiī.   2. Lūcius est puer Rōmānus.   3. Cotus est

servus et paedagōgus. 4. Paedagōgī puerōs ad scholam dūcunt. 5. Paedagōgus librōs portat. 6. Puer ad mūrōs cum amīcīs ambulat. 7. Magister puerōs docet. 8. Puerōs linguam Latīnam (et litterās Latīnās) docet. 9. Puerī magistrō pecūniam dant. 10. Nōn saepe sunt puellae in scholā Rōmānā.

53 The student may find it helpful to know that, just as first declension nouns are a nouns, second declension nouns can be called o nouns. Mention the old spelling of **servus (servos)** and **servum (servom)** and show how the short o underwent change, while the long o resisted it, as in the accusative plural **servōs.**

54 Exceptions to the rule of gender of second declension nouns ending in **-us** should be mentioned. Feminine nouns are: 1. Cities and islands (**Corinthus**). 2. Most trees (**ulmus,** *elm*). 3. Many Greek nouns (**atomus,** *atom*) and a few isolated words, among which **humus,** *ground,* is the most common.

56-57 English derivatives of nouns ending in **-er** will help the student remember whether the spelling keeps or drops the **e** throughout the declension; for example, *agrarian, library, magistrate* but *puerile.*

59 The familiar phrase **"Et tū, Brūte"** is a good illustration of the vocative ending **-e.** The name of a famous Roman orator, **Mārcus Tullius Cicerō,** shows all three forms of the vocative: **Mārce Tullī Cicerō.**

60   EXERCISES

A. 1. agrī, incolae, mūrī 2. victōriae, amīcī, librī 3. servīs, rēgīnīs, magistrīs 4. fēminae, puerō, amīcō 5. agricola, mūrus, nauta 6. amīce, rēgīna, fīlī 7. silvās, magistrōs, mūrōs 8. virō, puellā, amīcō 9. viam, īnsulam, agrum 10. virōrum, librōrum, sagittārum

B. 1. Puerī magistrīs librōs dant. 2. Servī fīliās portant. 3. Erant agricolae in agrīs. 4. Librōs puellae habent. 5. Ubi, fīliī, sunt hastae?·

C. 1. Nautam servus timet. 2. Incola īnsulae magistrō pāret. 3. Vir incolam sagittā necat. 4. Ad mūrum fēmina properat. 5. Quōcum, amīce, ambulās?

D. 1. The teacher is teaching the boys the Latin language. 2. There were many men in the fields. 3. Do the boys walk to school? 4. The slaves fill the ditch with water daily. 5. The(ir) daughters are hurrying through the large forest but they do not see their sons. 6. On the island there was a scarcity of men. 7. Often we carry books to the queen. 8. A slave is announcing the victory to the teacher. 9. Is there a supply of books in the school? 10. I am walking with my friend to the gate.

E. 1. Erant servī in prōvinciā. 2. Cui puerī pecūniam dant? 3. Agricolae agrōs cotīdiē arant. 4. Virīs viam mōnstrāmus. 5. Est in īnsulā inopia librōrum. 6. Cūr incolae fīliōs nautae timent? 7. Fēminae prope mūrum stant. 8. Rēgīna bona fīlium vocat. 9. Cōpiam aquae ad virum pòrtat. 10. Fīliī servī in agrīs manent.

61 Ask the students to explain such words as *servile, virile, agrarian, docile, amicable* basing their explanations on the vocabulary of this lesson.

LESSON 8

Motto

Point out to the class that **facta** and **verba** are plural nouns and not first declension. Explain that they are second declension neuter nouns which have slightly different endings from the masculine nouns learned in the last lesson.

62   A Roman Boy and a Helvetian Boy (Conversation)
                    Dīvicō   Mārcus

D. Who are you?

M. I am Marcus, the son of a Roman, and I live in a small town in (of) Italy.

D. I am Divico, the son of Moritasgus. I live in the land of Helvetia.

M. Where is the land of Helvetia?

D. The land of Helvetia is near Gaul. The land of Helvetia is bounded by Gaul, Germany and Italy. Helvetia is a small country.

M. Are there many inhabitants living in the land of Helvetia?

D. Oh, yes. Many (inhabitants) live there, and they often wage war with the Germans.

M. Where is Moritasgus?

D. He is in the Roman camp with the Helvetians. I see the gate of the camp. How many gates has a Roman camp?

M. A Roman camp has four gates. It also has a ditch and a rampart. The ditch is wide; the rampart, high.

D. Is there a garrison in the camp?

M. Yes, there is a large garrison in the camp.

D. Do the Gauls fight with the Romans?

M. The Gauls often fight with the Romans because the Gauls dislike the Romans. Now the Gauls are preparing for war.

D. Have you a spear?

M. No, but I have an arrow.

D. I have a long spear, a gift of Moritasgus.

M. Let's go into the Roman camp.

NOTE: It would be well to refer to a map of Gaul again to locate **terra Helvētia** and **Germānia.**

16

Respondē Latīnē:

1. Mārcus est fīlius Rōmānī. 2. In parvō oppidō Italiae habitat. 3. Dīvicō in terrā Helvētiā habitat. 4. Dīvicō nōn est (puer) Rōmānus. 5. Helvētia est prope Galliam. 6. Incolae Helvētiae cum Germānīs pugnant. 7. Castra Rōmāna quattuor portās habent. 8. Castra fossam et vāllum (quoque) habent. 9. Mārcus hastam nōn habet. 10. Mārcus sagittam habet.

63-64 Since only the nominative and accusative of neuters of the second declension present any problem, it would be well to drill on these, asking first for the accusative singular and then for the accusative plural of a series of nouns (for example, **rēgīna, mūrus, bellum, fīlia, vāllum, servus, agricola, oppidum**). An intensive drill of this type here will do much to prevent errors in the exercises.

When students are thoroughly familiar with first and second declension endings, mention some words coming into the English language from Latin which retain the Latin spelling for the plural form: *larva, alga, alumnus, bacillus, stimulus, datum, memorandum, curriculum.* Then ask for the correct plural form of the noun in parentheses in the following sentences:

1. (*alumna*) The sorority girls had an annual Christmas tea for their _____.
2. (*datum*) These _____ were fed into the computer.
3. (*stimulus*) He responded to all _____.
4. (*larva*) We studied all the _____ that hatched last night.
5. (*memorandum*) He referred to those _____.

67 Be certain to make the students aware of the plural form and singular meaning of **castra;** the word is frequently a source of error.

68   WORD STUDY

(c) Germany, injury, Italy, luxury, Sicily, victory
(d) grace, innocence, silence, space

69   EXERCISES

A. 1. rēgīnam; puerum; oppidum 2. vālla; mūrī; camerae 3. virō; amīcō; praesidiō 4. iniūria; proelium; servus 5. fīliī; bellī; agricolae

B. 1. ad oppida; ad viās; ad agrōs 2. cum puerō; cum nautā; cum praesidiō 3. ex castrīs; ex camerīs; ex silvīs 4. prope mūrum; prope oppidum; prope prōvinciam 5. cōpia frūmentī; porta oppidī; fīlius agricolae

C. 1. Praesidia in oppidīs collocant. 2. Ā portīs virī properant. 3. Magistrī amīcis librōs mōnstrant. 4. In īnsulīs hastīs sagittīsque pugnant. 5. Incolae prōvinciārum oppida oppugnant.

D. 1. Pictūram rēgīnae fīliaeque video. 2. Oppidum portam et vāllum habet. 3. Quōcum, amīce, agrum arās? 4. Incola īnsulae proelium nōn amat. 5. Cui magister imperat?

E. 1. Because of the need for (of) grain we are working in the fields 2. The boy, a farmer's slave, is carrying grain to the town. 3. The troops of the Gauls are preparing for war. 4. We see the gate of the Roman camp. 5. The queen gives orders to the slaves every day; the slaves obey the queen. 6. After battle, the men bring together the loot, a large amount of money. 7. The Roman camp is large; there is a garrison in camp. 8. The inhabitants of Italy love their fatherland; they do not like (the) fighting. 9. A man remains near the rampart with his daughter. 10. Both boys and girls praise the teacher.

F. 1. Rōmānī bellum parant. 2. Cōpiae rēgīnae castra oppugnant. 3. Erat in oppidō cōpia frūmentī. 4. Post proelium (pugnam) incolīs victōriam nūntiant. 5. Vidēsne portās castrōrum? 6. Praesidia in oppidō superāmus. 7. Rēgīna, fēmina bona, fīliam docet. 8. Incolās hastīs sagittīsque vulnerant. 9. Nautae agrōs prōvinciae vāstant. 10. Propter Gallōs timēmus.

SUPPLEMENTARY EXERCISE
1. in oppidum; in castra; in viam 2. dē vāllō; dē portā; dē mūrō 3. cum amīcō; sagittā; frūmentō 4. ā castrīs; ab oppidō; ab īnsulā 5. inopia aquae; inopia frūmentī; inopia librōrum

LESSON 9

Motto

Questioning will draw from the class the fact that the word **Rōmānus** here must be an adjective, although it has been met only as a noun. Compare *an American* and *the American people, a Roman* and *the Roman people* to show that, in English also, the same word can be both adjective and noun.

71   Roman Slaves (Conversation)
     Viātor, a traveler   **Rōmānus,** a Roman
V. Who is that tall man with the little boy?
R. He (It) is my friend Marcus.
V. And who is the little boy (who is) walking with your friend?
R. He is the son of a Briton. The Briton is Marcus' slave and he works in the fields.
V. Are there many British slaves in Rome?
R. Yes. The Roman people have a large camp in Britain. Our forces are fighting with the Britons. Many Britons are now slaves of the Romans.

V. Do your friends have many slaves?

R. Yes, my friends have broad fields and many slaves. Men work in the fields. They carry grain from the fields into the towns.

V. Are the men unhappy?

R. Our friends' slaves aren't unhappy. Marcus' slaves are not unhappy because my friend is a good man. However, a few slaves are wretched because they obey evil masters.

V. Are the daughters of the Britons free?

R. No, the daughters of the Britons aren't free; they obey Roman women.

V. Are the girls also unhappy?

R. A few girls are unhappy because of the great injustices of their mistresses.

V. Are the British girls beautiful?

R. They are large and beautiful, but Roman girls also are beautiful.

Respondē Latīnē:

1. Longus vir cum parvō puerō est (amīcus meus) Mārcus. 2. Mārcus est vir Rōmānus. 3. Servus Mārcī est Britannus. 4. In Britanniā populus Rōmānus magna castra habet. 5. Multī Britannī sunt servī Rōmānōrum. 6. Virī frūmentum ex agrīs in oppida portant. 7. Servī Mārcī nōn sunt miserī quod vir bonus est. 8. Servī miserī dominīs malīs pārent. 9. Paucae sunt miserae propter iniūriās dominārum. 10. Puellae Britannicae sunt pulchrae.

75 Point out that, as in previous cases where variation in word order has occurred, change of position of the adjective may indicate a shift in emphasis or may simply be made to obtain a more euphonious phrase or sentence. It would be wise for beginners to use either the word order of the text or that suggested by the teacher, until they become more accustomed to the sound of the language.

80 WORD STUDY

1. **Āfricānus, -a, -um,** African; **Āfricānus, -ī,** *m.,* an African; **Āfricānī, -ōrum,** *m. pl.,* the Africans

2. **Italicus, -a, -um**

81 EXERCISES

A. 1. malus; pulchra; magnum 2. parvam; lātum; līberum 3. meō; Rōmānō; līberō 4. paucīs; parvīs; vestrīs 5. magna; nostrae; miserī

B. 1. Servī miserī agrōs arant. 2. Agricolae bonī puellīs bonīs librōs dant. 3. Fīliās fēminārum pulchrārum in camerīs tuīs vidēmus. 4. Per agrōs longōs lātōsque properant. 5. Fīliī nautārum in parvīs īnsulīs habitant.

NOTE: Draw attention to A. 5, **agricolae miserī** and B. 2, **agricolae bonī** to point out once more that agreement emphatically does not mean that the endings must look alike.

19

C. 1. Librum meum puer malus habet. 2. Magistrō bonō viam mōnstrat. 3. Cum fēminā ex agrō parvō incola ambulat. 4. Magnum proelium fīlius vester amat. 5. Oppidum nostrum parvam portam et mūrum longum habet.

D. 1. fēminam malam; fīlium meum; multum frūmentum 2. multās portās; viās lātās; magna vālla 3. amīcō bonō; puellae pulchrae; populō Rōmānō 4. ex magnīs castrīs; ā longō virō; cum rēgīnā bonā 5. virōrum bonōrum; parvārum hastārum; paucōrum puerōrum.

E. 1. Fēminae virō bonō nōn parvō puerō pārent. 2. Rōma erat parvum oppidum; populus Rōmānus erat līber. 3. Propter iniūriam agricolārum servī sunt miserī. 4. Paucīs incolīs victōriam cōpiārum nūntiat. 5. Prōvinciam nostram, parvam īnsulam, vāstant. 6. Virī puerīque multum frūmentum ex agrīs comportant. 7. Regīna bona multōs servōs ad cameram vocat. 8. Cōpiae, Rōmānī, oppidum vestrum oppugnant et agrōs vestrōs vāstant. 9. Fīlium malum nautae timēmus; cum amīcō nostrō pugnat. 10. Ubi, Mārce, sunt librī tuī?

NOTE: Call attention in E. 8 to word order used in a sentence containing a compound verb.

SUPPLEMENTARY EXERCISES

A. 1. tuam; tuōs 2. vestrōs; vestram 3. tuā; tuīs 4. tuum; tuōs 5. vestrae; vestrīs

B. 1. Hasta est longa; mūrus est longus; vāllum est longum. 2. Oppida sunt lībera; prōvinciae sunt līberae; magistrī (dominī) sunt līberī. 3. Multōs amīcōs vidēmus; multās sagittās vidēmus; multa praesidia vidēmus. 4. in patriā meā; in mūrō lātō; in parvō oppidō 5. cum paucīs servīs; cum puellīs pulchrīs; hastīs longīs

LESSON 10

Motto

These are the famous words with which Julius Caesar in 47 B.C. reported his victory over Pharnaces, King of Pontus in Asia Minor. Point out the similarity to the message "Sighted sub, sank same," sent in March, 1942, during World War II by David Francis Mason, U.S.N. chief aviation machinist's mate. Mason, who was on patrol duty in the South Pacific, saw a Japanese submarine below him, loosed his depth charges, radioed his base this laconic message, and resumed his patrol. Ask the students whether they think this officer may have studied Latin. Draw attention to the effectiveness of the alliteration in each of the messages. Make mention of the fact also that Caesar is considered by literary critics the master of the "plain style."

83   The Gauls (Part 1): The Children See a Gaul

Rome was once a small town on the bank of the Tiber (River). Around Rome there was a long high wall. In the fields close to the Tiber were many Roman men and women with their children.

The Gauls are free inhabitants of Gaul. They are large men and they fight with spears and swords. The Gauls are not friendly to the Romans.

In the Roman land is a camp of the Gauls. The Gauls have assembled large forces in(to) the camp and there they have placed a garrison. They have gathered grain from the fields into the camp.

A farmer's sons often wander in the fields far from town. They saw a black horse near the forest and on the horse a large Gaul. Although the boys were greatly afraid, one of them cried, "Who are you? Why have you frightened us?" The Gaul did not answer.

The boys hurried home. Their father said, "Where have you been?" They answered, "We have been in the fields. We saw a black horse in the fields and a big Gaul on the horse. The Gaul scared us."

NOTE: The adjective **Rōmānī** in line 4 refers to both *men* and *women*. It is in agreement with the nearer noun.

Respondē Latīnē:

1. Circum Rōmam erat mūrus altus et longus. 2. Gallī hastīs gladiīsque pugnant. 3. Castra Gallōrum in agrō Rōmānō sunt. 4. Gallī magnās cōpiās in castra convocāvērunt. 5. Gallī in castrīs praesidium collocāvērunt. 6. Fīliī agricolae magnum Gallum vīdērunt. 7. Puerīs nōn respondit. 8. Puerī domum properāvērunt. 9. Puerī (magnopere) timuērunt.

85 Stress the importance of this section. Use every means possible (for example, oral and written class drill, spell-downs, completion-type exercises) to insure that the students learn thoroughly the last two parts of those verbs of which they already know the first two parts. Left to themselves, they may be inclined to think that the knowledge of the first two parts will insure their knowing the rest of the verb without their actually learning it.

90-92 Emphasize the absence of an auxiliary verb in the Latin perfect tense. Caution against the use of **habeō** in forming the tense. Contrast *The men have fought with swords* and *The men have swords:* **Virī gladiīs pugnāvērunt** but **Virī gladiōs habent.** Contrast *Marcus has seen a black horse* and *Marcus has a black horse:* **Mārcus equum nigrum vīdit** but **Mārcus equum nigrum habet.**

93   EXERCISES

A. 1. monuit 2. complēvimus 3. nāvigāvistī 4. retinuērunt 5. dedērunt 6. mānsistī 7. mōvērunt 8. respondimus 9. terruistis 10. clāmāvistī

B. 1. Gladiōs lātōs tenuimus. 2. Agrōs vāstāvērunt. 3. Nautās malōs timuērunt. 4. Oppida oppugnāvimus. 5. Vīdistisne vālla alta?

C. 1. Ubi, puer, fuistī? 2. Equum nigrum vīdī. 3. In prōvinciā mānsit. 4. Hastā et gladiō pugnāvistī. 5. Incola servum laudāvit.

D. 1. The inhabitants of the town were on the high wall. 2. I gave (have given) grain to the wretched men. 3. Because of the wrong, the children feared the sailors. 4. We announced the victory to the queen immediately. 5. He is stationing a garrison in the Roman camp. 6. The Gauls (have) prepared for a long war. 7. Where are you hurrying, friend? 8. After the battle we collected a large amount of booty. 9. The teacher's beautiful daughter stood on the wide (river) bank. 10. My friend teaches many children.

E. 1. Agricolae in agrīs labōrāvērunt. 2. Rēgīna cōpiīs imperāvit. 3. Quibuscum in castra errāvistī (errāvistis)? 4. Quō parvī līberī (puerī) tuī (vestrī) properāvērunt? 5. Gallus, quamquam parvus est, multōs virōs gladiō necāvit. 6. Victōriam cōpiārum rēgīnae nūntiāvimus. 7. Frūmentum ex agrīs ad castra comportāvērunt. 8. Parvōs līberōs (puerōs) meōs terruistī. 9. Equum nigrum in agrō vīdimus. 10. Populus Rōmānus est amīcus incolīs īnsulārum or Rōmānī sunt amīcī incolīs īnsulārum.

SUPPLEMENTARY EXERCISE

1. Vocant; vocāvērunt. 2. Laudāmus; laudāvimus. 3. Movetne? mōvitne? 4. Sum; fuī. 5. Terrēs; terruistī. 6. Dat; dedit. 7. Pārēmus; pāruimus. 8. Nōn vident; nōn vīdērunt. 9. Moneō; monuī. 10. Arātis; arāvistis.

94 The vocabulary suggests many English words of which the student should now have a better understanding: *riparian, equitation, amity, errant, admonish, premonition.*

LESSON 11

Motto

The idea of glory or fame as a spur to action is frequently expressed by Latin authors. Ovid presents this thought in several ways: **Ardua per praeceps glōria vādit iter,** *Tristia,* IV, 3, 74, *Glory scales the heights by steepest paths.* . . . **immēnsum glōria calcar habet,** *Ex Ponto,* IV, 2, 36, *Renown possesses a mighty spur.* **Nōn parvās animō dat glōria vīrēs,** *Tristia,* V, 12, 37, *Desire for fame lends no small strength to the mind.*

The teacher might use the lesson motto as a means to pinpoint the difference between *where,* indicating place *to which* (**quō**) and *where,* indicating place *at rest* (**ubi**).

The father takes the women and children into a building. He collects the animals from the fields. He is angry because the Gauls have frightened the children.

At night the father and Marcus, the children's brother, come to the other farmers; they try to warn (them) about the danger. But the farmers do not hear because they are asleep. Therefore they don't reply.

Marcus, angry, loudly cries: "Don't you hear (Aren't you listening)? Why are you asleep? We are warning you of great peril. The Gauls have reached our lands. They have frightened our children. Your buildings and families are in great danger. You have waited too long."

At length the farmers answer: "We aren't asleep. We hear you." They collect the animals from the fields at once. With the children and women they flee to Rome. They take with them their goods and their slaves. They stay inside the walls of Rome. Because they have escaped the danger, they are happy.

Respondē Latīnē:

1. Pater in aedificium līberōs fēmināsque dūcit. 2. Est īrātus quod Gallī līberōs terruērunt. 3. Pater et Mārcus, frāter līberōrum, ad cēterōs agricolās veniunt. 4. Agricolae nōn respondent quod dormiunt. 5. Agricolae cum līberīs fēminīsque fugiunt. 6. Sēcum bona portant. 7. Agricolae intrā mūrōs Rōmae manent. 8. Laetī sunt quod perīculum effūgērunt.

96 A considerable amount of time spent in a careful development of this new step in grammar will pay dividends later.

Have the pupils pay particular attention to the difference between -ēre and -ere in infinitives. Give orally several infinitives and have the students classify the verbs according to conjugation. Have the present of **moveō** and that of **dūcō** written on the board in parallel columns and discuss the differences.

Contrast **dūcō** and **capiō** in Section 96. Point out that the two verbs are identically inflected in forms where **dūcō** has an **i** (2nd and 3rd person singular and 1st and 2nd person plural) and that in the other two forms (1st person singular and 3rd person plural) the insertion of the **i** in **capiō** and **capiunt** is the only difference.

97 Have **capiō** and **audiō** written in parallel columns at the board. Note the similarity of formation except for the long vowel in the 2nd person singular, and 1st and 2nd person plural, of **audiō**. To clarify this point of difference, compare the present indicative of **portō** and of **moveō** and show that when the stem vowel of the present infinitive is long, the vowel remains long in these three forms.

Have the present active of **portō, moveō, dūcō, capiō** and **audiō,** written in parallel columns at the board and trace each person and number through all five verbs.

98 Note the general statement regarding formation of the perfect indicative active in this section. Review the perfect tenses of first and second conjugations learned in Lesson 10: **vocō, dō, timeō, videō** and of the irregular **sum.** Then study the paradigms of Section 98. This drill will highlight the statement that all verbs are conjugated alike in the perfect indicative active.

99   EXERCISES

A.   1. Virī perīcula effugiunt.   2. Agricolās īrātōs audīmus.   3. Cūr, puerī, clāmātis?   4. Servōs nostrōs in aedificia dūcunt.   5. Intrā agrōs manēmus.

B.   1. Vidēsne, amīce, in agrō Gallum?   2. Ex oppidō fugiō.   3. Equum nigrum dūcit.   4. Cūr, puella, dormīs?

C.   1. dūxērunt   2. vēnērunt   3. tenuistī   4. monuimus   5. terruī   6. audīvērunt   7. effūgistis   8. coēgit   9. pervēnimus   10. Vīdistīne

D.   1. vident   2. Audiuntne   3. cōgunt   4. respondēs   5. dūcit   6. dormīmus   7. venit   8. timet   9. clāmāmus   10. monētis

E.   1. The farmer is taking the women and children into the building.   2. The angry boy doesn't answer the slave.   3. The Gauls arrived at (reached) the gates of the town.   4. What did you hear (have you heard), my son?   5. The sailors stayed on the bank with the slaves.   6. With whom are the inhabitants of the island fleeing?   7. The Roman people gathered forces.   8. We warned the men of (about) the great danger.   9. He led large forces (many troops) against the Romans.   10. The Gauls are capturing many inhabitants but the inhabitants are not afraid.

F.   1. Quibuscum agricolae fugiunt?   2. Ad portās castrōrum (per-)vēnimus.   3. Puellae incolās dē perīculō monuērunt.   4. Agricola īrātus līberōs in aedificium dūcit.   5. Ubi dormiunt servī?   6. Cēpitne vir malus amīcum meum?   7. Quamquam fortiter clāmāvī, nōn respondērunt.   8. Incolae cōpiās intrā alta vālla collocāvērunt.   9. Audīsne amīcōs tuōs?   10. Magister puerō bonō librum dedit.

SUPPLEMENTARY EXERCISE

1. *Pres.,* they move, are moving.   2. *Perf.,* we (have) heard.   3. *Perf.,* he (has) frightened.   4. *Perf.,* I seized, have captured.   5. *Pres.,* he hears, is listening to.   6. *Perf.,* we (have) fled.   7. *Pres.,* they catch, take.   8. *Perf.,* you (have) remained, stayed.   9. *Pres.,* you lead, are leading.   10. *Pres.,* he comes, is coming.   11. *Perf.,* he has come, came.   12. *Perf.,* I (have) led.

100 Ask the students to explain the derivation and meaning of the following words: *edifice, irate, cogent, (in)audible, auditory, audition, dormant, dormitory, intramural.*

References: Becker, pp. 195-198, Johnston, p. 147; Showerman, *Rome and the Romans,* pp. 103-105; Treble and King, pp. 63-65.

LESSON 12

Motto

Identify Martial as a writer of the first century remembered for his short and witty epigrams. Note the motto as a good example of his stinging satire in which he is poking fun at one of his contemporaries. Explain that Martial usually invented names for those who were the victims of his biting sarcasm.

102   The Gauls (Part 3): The Sacred Geese Save Rome

The Gauls had led (their) troops out of Gaul and had pitched camp near the Tiber. They had terrified the farmers, had taken or killed many animals and (had) burned the buildings. Because of the danger the farmers had collected free men and slaves; they had fled from the fields to Rome. The Gauls now were reaching the walls of Rome.

Soon the Romans hear the Gauls around the walls of Rome. Because there is a great scarcity of grain in Rome, the children are hungry.

In the Roman citadel near the walls is a big coop. In the coop are the sacred geese of Juno, a goddess and the queen of the gods. Although there is a great need for (of) grain, the Romans give the geese grain daily because the geese are sacred.

At night the Gauls are preparing to climb onto the citadel; the Romans are asleep. The geese are not sleeping because they are eating grain. Stealthily the Gauls hurry to the walls. Gaul stands on Gaul and soon the first Gaul is ascending the wall. The geese hear the Gauls; they arouse the Romans. Marcus Manlius, a Roman soldier, is near the wall. Manlius hears the geese and with his spear kills the Gaul. Many men come and fight bravely with the Gauls. The Gauls flee.

Thus have the geese saved (did . . . save) Rome.

NOTE: The historical present tense has been used in much of the reading lesson for the sake of vividness. It seems advisable to translate most historical present tenses into the English past tense and, if the teacher prefers, the entire story may be rendered in the past tense.

Reference: Livy, V, 35-49

Respondē Latīnē:

1. Gallī castra prope Tiberim posuerant.   2. Gallī agricolās terruerant.
3. Agricolae līberōs servōsque coēgerant.   4. Quod Rōmae est magna inopia frūmentī (Propter inopiam frūmentī Rōmae), līberī sunt iēiūnī.   5. Ānserēs

sunt in caveā. 6. Rōmānī ānseribus frūmentum dant. 7. Rōmānī dormiunt. 8. Ānserēs nōn dormiunt. 9. Mārcus Mānlius ānserēs audit. 10. Post pugnam Gallī fugiunt.

105   EXERCISES

A. 1. Cēpit, he (has) captured; cēperat, he had captured. 2. Clāmāvistis, you (have) shouted; clāmāverātis, you had shouted. 3. Dormīvērunt, they (have) slept; dormīverant, they had slept. 4. Dūximus, we (have) led; dūxerāmus, we had led. 5. Tenuit, he (has) held; tenuerat, he had held. 6. Portāvērunt, they (have) carried; portāverant, they had carried. 7. Dedī, I gave, have given; dederam, I had given. 8. Vēnimus, we came, have come; vēnerāmus, we had come. 9. Laudāvī, I (have) praised; laudāveram, I had praised. 10. Posuistī, you (have) placed; posuerās, you had placed.

B. 1. Although the Gauls had pitched camp near the Roman fields, they had not killed the inhabitants. 2. Our children did not have good books. 3. The sailors and their sons are frightening the inhabitants of the town. 4. The little boy had climbed the high rampart. 5. Where are the men hastening with the large forces? 6. Do you have a large amount of money? 7. The Gauls fought many battles against the Romans; they captured many inhabitants. 8. The wicked men had killed the wretched slaves with a long sword. 9. The angry farmer warned the boys and girls of the great danger. 10. Did you listen to my friend?

C. 1. Gallī (in) vāllum altum ascenderant. 2. Servī agricolaeque in agrīs labōrāvērunt. 3. Amīcī nostrī saepe fuerant in parvā īnsulā. 4. Fēmina pulchra cum puellīs in silvam properāvit. 5. Propter perīculum agricolae frūmentum comportāverant. 6. Quod est inopia frūmentī, līberī sunt miserī. 7. Castra in agrīs Rōmānōrum posuerāmus. 8. Rēgīna bona fortiter clāmāvit; fīliam terruit. 9. Magna porta fuerat in rīpā; Gallī portam incendērunt. 10. Magister miser virō malō nōn respondit. 11. Rōmānī praesidia prope vālla castrōrum posuerant. 12. Dormiuntne servī?

107   WORD STUDY

1. **accipiō, -ere, accēpī, acceptum,** take to oneself, receive, accept; **afficiō, -ere, affēcī, affectum,** do anything to someone or something, influence, work upon; **attineō, -ēre, attinuī, attentum,** hold to, keep, pertain to

2. **concipiō, -ere, concēpī, conceptum,** lay hold of, take in; **cōnficiō, -ere, cōnfēcī, cōnfectum,** make completely ready, finish, accomplish; **contineō, -ēre, continuī, contentum,** hold together, contain

3. **excipiō, -ere, excēpī, exceptum,** take out, receive; **efficiō, -ere, effēcī, effectum,** make out, work out, do, produce

4. **recipiō, -ere, recēpī, receptum,** take back, regain; **reficiō, -ere, refēcī, refectum,** make again, restore, repair; **retineō, -ēre, retinuī, retentum,** hold back, detain

26

TEACHER'S NOTES

I.   For students who enjoy the spur of competition, the class may be divided into even-numbered and odd-numbered teams. The teacher or a very competent student who obviously does not need this review can be scorekeeper, chalking up the number of correct answers given by members of each team. A spell-down type of vocabulary review is not advisable, because it eliminates too soon the students who need the competition most.

If there is opportunity for students to use the language laboratory, the teacher may prepare, in advance, a tape for vocabulary review. This will permit the students who need extra work on the words to have such work outside class; at the same time they will be able to check the correctness of their responses against the tape. Unless the teacher is very familiar with the way in which such tapes are prepared (the proper spacing, etc.), it will be wise to ask for help from someone in the school system who uses the audio-lingual method and who knows the procedures and how to operate the equipment.

NOTE: Be sure to require all principal parts for the verbs.

II.   This drill may be done either orally or at the board.

A.

magister meus

	Singular	Plural
Nom.	magister meus	magistrī meī
Gen.	magistrī meī	magistrōrum meōrum
Dat.	magistrō meō	magistrīs meīs
Acc.	magistrum meum	magistrōs meōs
Abl.	magistrō meō	magistrīs meīs

nauta bonus

Nom.	nauta bonus	nautae bonī
Gen.	nautae bonī	nautārum bonōrum
Dat.	nautae bonō	nautīs bonīs
Acc.	nautam bonum	nautās bonōs
Abl.	nautā bonō	nautīs bonīs

magna castra

Plural

Nom.	magna castra
Gen.	magnōrum castrōrum
Dat.	magnīs castrīs
Acc.	magna castra
Abl.	magnīs castrīs

29

B.

	dō	videō	faciō	dormiō

Singular

dedī	vīdī	fēcī	dormīvī
dedistī	vīdistī	fēcistī	dormīvistī
dedit	vīdit	fēcit	dormīvit

Plural

dedimus	vīdimus	fēcimus	dormīvimus
dedistis	vīdistis	fēcistis	dormīvistis
dedērunt	vīdērunt	fēcērunt	dormīvērunt

C.

doceō

Singular	Plural
docueram	docuerāmus
docuerās	docuerātis
docuerat	docuerant

D. 1. vēnimus; vēnerāmus 2. dedit; dederat 3. fuērunt; fuerant 4. cēpit; cēperat 5. servāvī; servāveram 6. vīdimus; vīderāmus 7. incendistī; incenderās 8. audīvit; audīverat 9. coēgimus; coēgerāmus 10. interfēcistis; interfēcerātis

E. Interficiunt; audīs; servat; doceō; effugimus

F. They (have) wandered, they did wander; he moves, is moving, does move; he (has) moved, did move; I came, have come, did come; had he seen?

III. 1. vocative 2. four 3. ā-; ē-; e-; ī- 4. perfect 5. the case of the word to which it is appositive 6. -e; -ī; nominative 7. nominative 8. case, number; gender 9. singular 10. nominative; accusative; -a

IV. 1. vir miser 2. amīcōs nostrōs 3. habent 4. fīlī 5. gladiīs 6. magistrī 7. magnō perīculō 8. equus niger 9. multa oppida 10. vestrīs

V. A. 1. childish, immature 2. friendly 3. with large numbers of people 4. the science of soil cultivation and field-crop production 5. advice, warning 6. capable of being injured 7. sound; picture 8. wrong, mistaken 9. marked by a suspension of activity 10. made a god

B. Greece; injury; picture; edifice; patience

VI. 1. by a wall and a ditch
2. a feast on the seventeenth of March chosen to celebrate the coming of age of a Roman boy
3. Similarities:
   the fundamentals of education: reading, writing, arithmetic
   foreign language studied (in Rome, usually Greek)
   tools of learning: tablet and stylus in Rome; tablet and pen or pencil today

Differences:

no public schools in Rome

extremely strict discipline in the Roman schools

great emphasis on speaking and oratory in the Roman curriculum

the role of the **paedagōgus** important to a Roman boy

long school day in Rome

many holidays in the Roman school calendar

girls taught by the Roman mothers at home

4. bravery, endurance, patriotism, respect for elders, reverence for the gods, sense of duty to the state

LESSON 13

Motto

This frequently quoted saying is found in Juvenal, *Satires,* 10, 356-357:
> **Ōrandum est ut sit mēns sāna in corpore sānō;**
> **Fortem posce animum mortis terrore carentem.**

Bernard Shaw, in "Maxims for Revolutionists" (appended to *Man and Superman*), takes exception to the proverb by commenting thus, **"Mēns sāna in corpore sānō** is a foolish saying. The sound body is a product of a sound mind."

Call attention to the fact that concern for good mental health is not just a modern concept, since it was considered a desirable objective by the ancients.

108   The Colosseum

Many people are gathering at the Colosseum today. The Colosseum is a large building in which Romans, both men and women, watch the contests of the gladiators. (The) men (people) love to look at the gladiators in the arena.

The gladiators are not Romans but miserable slaves and captives. Roman leaders have marched into Gaul and Spain; they have taken soldiers with them. The Roman legions have waged many wars in Gaul. They have killed many Gauls; they have captured many. After victory the Roman leader (general) has led the prisoners to Rome. The Gauls have large bodies and they fight well in the arena with spears and swords. Many Gauls are now gladiators.

Donnataurus is a gladiator. Once he was a free Gaul. A leader of Roman soldiers pitched camp near the village of Donnataurus. There he stationed two legions.

Although the forces of the king of the Gauls were not ready for war, they marched with the(ir) king through the forest to the Roman camp. They waged war with the Roman soldiers. Soldiers, both Roman and Gallic, gave many wounds and received many. On the body of Donnataurus were many wounds when a Roman soldier captured him. The Roman commander took Donnataurus captive to Rome. Because the Gaul has a large body he has become a gladiator. He often fights in the arena with men, often with animals. Today Donnataurus is fighting in the Colosseum.

Respondē Latīnē:

1. Ad Colossēum multī hominēs conveniunt. 2. Colossēum est magnum aedificium (in quō Rōmānī pugnās gladiātōrum spectant). 3. Gladiātōrēs nōn sunt Rōmānī. 4. Ducēs Rōmānī iter in Galliam et Hispāniam fēcērunt. 5. Post victōriam imperātor Rōmānus captīvōs Rōmam dūxit. 6. Donnataurus est gladiātor. 7. Dux mīlitum Rōmānōrum prope vīcum Donnataurī castra posuit. 8. Cōpiae rēgis Gallōrum bellum cum mīlitibus Rōmānīs gessērunt. 9. Mīles Rōmānus Donnataurum cēpit. 10. Donnataurus magnum corpus habet. 11. Saepe pugnat cum hominibus, saepe cum animālibus.

Interesting topic for class discussion or student reports: **Origin of Gladiatorial Combats. References:** Johnston, p. 283; Showerman, *Rome and the Romans,* pp. 333-334.

113   EXERCISES

A. 1. mīles 2. mīlitēs 3. mīlitis 4. mīlitum 5. Mīlitī 6. Mīlitibus 7. Mīlitēs 8. Mīlitem 9. mīles 10. Cum mīlite

B. 1. Vulnus 2. Corpora 3. corpus 4.vulnera 5. corpore; vulnerum

C. 1. captīvīs; puellīs; hominibus 2. bellum; vulnus; proelium 3. itinera; proelia; corpora 4. imperātōre; virō; incolā 5. rēgis agricolae; magistrī 6. incolārum; ducum; virōrum 7. Mīlitī; amīcō; fēminae 8. Rōmānīs; rēgīnīs; imperātōribus 9. Imperātor; amīcus; puer 10. Corpora; legiōnēs; captīvī

D. 1. Men fear the evil god because he is not friendly to people. 2. They threw the bodies of the Germans down from the rampart. 3. The leader at once marches through Gaul with his (the) soldiers. 4. What does a Roman give his children? 5. Why aren't the sacred geese asleep? 6. The Gaul, a large man, (has) led a black horse to the camp. 7. The Roman soldiers obeyed the(ir) good leader. 8. Where are the king's daughters, Marcus? 9. He is hurrying into Italy by a long march; he is stationing soldiers in Italy. 10. He had often fought in the arena with gladiators.

E. 1. Cōpiae rēgis ad silvam properāvērunt. 2. Propter vulnera mīlitēs sunt in magnō perīculō. 3. Incolae Britanniae sunt amīcī ducibus bonīs. 4. Legiōnēs Rōmānae bellum cum cōpiīs Britannicīs gessērunt. 5. Parvī līberī (puerī) mīlitum dormiunt. 6. Dux noster, bonus vir, multa vulnera habet. 7. Hominēs malum deum timuērunt quod equōs interfēcit (necāvit). 8. Quamquam multī captīvī iter fēcerant, paucī imperātōrēs ad castra ambulāvērunt. 9. Propter perīculum rēx gladiōs et hastās (hastāsque) spectat; bellum parat. 10. Castra prope oppidum posuimus; incolās nōn oppugnāvimus.

114 Ask the students to suggest English words derived from these nouns: **corpus, homō, iter, mīles, vulnus.** Mention the fact that the genitive case, which provides the stem, often gives the derivative.

115   WORD STUDY

navigator, one who sails, fr. **nāvigāre;** liberator, one who sets free, fr. **līberāre;** spectator, one who watches, fr. **spectāre;** captor, one who captures, fr. **capere;** auditor, one who hears, fr. **audīre;** demonstrator, one who points out, shows, fr. **dēmōnstrāre (dē + mōnstrāre)**

LESSON 14

Motto

Call attention to the verb **dubitābant,** noting the imperfect tense sign **-ba-** used in the quotation to describe a situation in past time. Identify Tacitus as an illustrious Roman historian.

116   Proserpina (Part 1)

Ceres, the sister of the god Jupiter, was the goddess of grain. Ceres had one daughter, a beautiful maiden. The maiden's name was Proserpina. Although Ceres loved many islands, she lived with her daughter Proserpina on the island of Sicily. Because Ceres was friendly to (the) farmers, the inhabitants of Sicily had a large supply (an abundance) of grain.

Once Proserpina was walking through the Sicilian fields with several girls (maidens). The girls were gathering many kinds of beautiful flowers near the river bank and were making garlands for their heads. Proserpina wandered far away from the girls.

In Orcus there lived a great god, brother of Jupiter, named Pluto. Because he was king of the underworld, all men feared Pluto. (On) that day the god was driving his black horses through Sicily. Meanwhile the goddess Venus with her son was watching the island.

Venus saw Pluto and Proserpina and said to her son, "Cupid, shoot an arrow into the body of Pluto." Cupid obeyed Venus. He shot the arrow. Pluto saw Proserpina and, because of his wound, he fell in love with the girl (maiden) at once, and he desired to have her as his wife.

At once the god seized Proserpina and carried her off. The girl shouted, "Who are you? Why have you frightened me?" The god did not answer the maiden; he placed her in his chariot. Proserpina kept on shouting, "Girls, where are you?" But because the girls were not near Proserpina and did not hear her, they did not save the maiden. And so Pluto carried the poor girl to the lower world.

NOTES: Mention the distinction between **puella,** usually a little girl, and **virgō,** a young unmarried woman (girl).

Ask the students if they know the Greek names of the divinities in the story. Those who have read stories based on mythology may be familiar with some of these:

Jupiter—Zeus   Proserpina—Persephone   Venus—Aphrodite
Ceres—Demeter   Pluto—Hades (Pluton)   Cupid—Eros

Explain that the name **Orcus** is synonymous with **Hades** and that both these words, as well as the name **Dīs,** are used as synonyms for **Plūtō.**

Respondē Latīnē:

1. Cerēs ūnam fīliam habēbat. 2. Nōmen virginis erat Prōserpina. 3. Quod Cerēs erat amīca agricolīs, incolae Siciliae magnam cōpiam frūmentī habēbant. 4. Per agrōs Prōserpina cum complūribus virginibus ambulābat. 5. Multa genera flōrum pulchrōrum virginēs legēbant. 6. Plūtōnem omnēs hominēs timēbant. 7. Plūtō equōs nigrōs agēbat. 8. Statim virginem amāvit. 9. Quod neque prope Prōserpinam erant neque audiēbant, virginem nōn servāvērunt. 10. Plūtō puellam miseram ad Orcum portāvit.

117 Have the imperfect tense of the model verbs of each conjugation put on the board in parallel columns, so that all five examples can be seen at once. Point out the **-ba-** tense sign and similar endings of all conjugations. Note the stem vowels preceding the tense sign.

Discourage the use of the simple past as a rendition of the Latin imperfect, except in cases where such phrases as *continued to, kept on,* and *used to* are really awkward. A pupil who uses the simple past to translate the imperfect will gradually lose sight of the real meaning of this tense and will have difficulty in making the proper distinction between perfect and imperfect.

118 To distinguish **nōnne** from **num,** compare **nōnne** with the English *aren't you,* the French *n'est-ce pas,* or the Italian *non è vero,* all of which contain a negative and anticipate an affirmative answer.

Have the students memorize the words which may translate *yes* or *no.*

119   EXERCISES

A. 1. Properant; properābant; properāvērunt. 2. Dūcit; dūcēbat; dūxit. 3. Sunt; erant; fuērunt. 4. Effugiunt; effugiēbant; effūgērunt. 5. Pervenīmus; perveniēbāmus pervēnimus. 6. Respondēs; respondēbās; respondistī. 7. Nūntiat; nūntiābat; nūntiāvit. 8. Mittitis; mittēbātis; mīsistis. 9. Dō; dabam; dedī. 10. Capiunt; capiēbant; cēpērunt.

B. 1. Pugnat; pugnābat; pugnāvit. 2. Manēmus; manēbāmus; mānsimus. 3. Audiunt; audiēbant; audīvērunt. 4. Ascendō; ascendēbam; ascendī. 5. Facis; faciēbās; fēcistī.

C.   1. With the rest of the maidens Proserpina was wandering through the fields.   2. Near the riverbank the maidens (girls) were picking many kinds of beautiful flowers.   3. Ceres, the goddess of grain and the sister of the god Jupiter, lived in Sicily.   4. Neither brother nor son has fled from the town.   5. The commander wasn't looking at the gladiators, poor captives, was he? No, he was not.   6. Both Roman legions and troops of Gaul were marching toward the camp.   7. Because of the great danger the Roman soldiers had prepared for war.   8. Men fought with men, didn't they? Yes.   9. Few rivers of Italy are long.   10. The Gaul has a wound on his body; the Roman, on his head.

D.   1. Imperātor Rōmānōrum in Germāniam, patriam Germānōrum, iter faciēbat.   2. Praesidium multa genera hastārum habēbat.   3. Ubi sunt cōpiae? Quō iter faciunt? Quibuscum bellum gerunt?   4. Nōnne legiōnēs Rōmānae trāns flūmen fugiēbant? Vērō.   5. Mīlitēs ducibus pārēbant neque rēgī.   6. In castrīs erat parva cōpia frūmentī.   7. Puer pecūniam prope flūmen āmīserat.   8. Num gladiātōrēs sunt (virī) līberī? Minimē.   9. Dux mīlitibus imperābat.   10. Iūnō, dea bona, uxōrēs līberōsque Rōmānōrum servat.

SUPPLEMENTARY EXERCISES

A.   1. Where were the soldier's arrows?   2. The girls were picking beautiful flowers.   3. Juno is both sister and wife of Jupiter.   4. Many Romans had three names.   5. The rest of the inhabitants were friendly to the sailors.

B.   1. Frūmentum comportābāmus.   2. Cōpiās removēbant.   3. Magister puerōs docēbat.   4. In īnsulā habitābam.   5. Veniēbātisne ad oppidum cotīdiē?

120   Mention the phrase *per capita* frequently used in English. Ask the students to explain a *per capita* tax. Compare the expressions *per person* and *poll tax*. This might be a good place to discuss briefly the fact that, although the greater number of words which we have in English today are derived from Latin, the basis of our language is Teutonic in origin. (*Poll* and *head* are words of Teutonic origin.)

Give the following English words connected with the Latin of this vocabulary and ask the students to suggest the meaning, showing the relationship between the Latin and English: *nominate, nominee, decapitate, (il)legible, uxorious, mission(ary)*.

The students are familiar with the abbreviation **etc.,** *and so forth.* Point out that it is the shortened form of **et cetera,** *and other things.*

Explain the term *itinerant teacher* as one who travels from school to school. Special teachers such as teachers of art, music, and physical education are sometimes *itinerant.* Compare the expression *migratory* workers (fr. **migrō, migrāre,** to move).

abigō, drive away, banish; **adigō,** drive to, force to; **exigō,** drive out, complete, determine (*perf. part. pass.* **exāctus,** accurate, precise, exact); **dēligō,** pick, choose, select; **dīligō,** choose, prize, esteem; **colligō,** gather, bring together, collect

LESSON 15

Motto

If time permits, an introduction to the *imperative* could be achieved very simply here and would pave the way for the grammar of Section 129. The student will easily recognize *guard* as an imperative. If the teacher writes on the board the words **servāre, vidēre, mittere, iacere, dormīre,** and then, by erasing the **-re** of **servāre,** shows how the command *guard* is the result, it will be easy and stimulating for the student to see how he can immediately form the commands *see, send, throw,* and *sleep.*

Since the imperative is not emphasized in this lesson, it probably would not be advisable to take the discussion further.

122 Proserpina (Part 2)

Ceres, Proserpina's mother, immediately hurried to Sicily. When she saw the other maidens, she asked, "Girls, where is my daughter? Have you seen her?" The girls replied, "We saw her before she wandered far away. Now we do not see her."

Angry because she had lost her daughter there, the goddess decided to punish the inhabitants of the island. She said, "In the fields of Sicily there will be neither flowers nor a crop (*lit.* supply) of grain."

Through woods and across rivers Ceres roamed (kept wandering); always she kept asking, "Have you see my daughter?" Finally she saw the (a) girl's belt in the water of a river.

In the river lived a nymph named Arethusa. After Ceres saw her daughter's belt, she called the nymph. As soon as Arethusa saw the goddess, she cried out, "Oh great goddess, I am unhappy because there is a scarcity of food (grain) in Sicily. We who live in Sicily love you; for the sake of our children give us grain."

But Ceres said, "I love you; I love the people of Sicily. Now they have no grain because my daughter has been lost. Where is my daughter? Have you seen Proserpina?"

"Your daughter is not lost," said the nymph. "Pluto saw your daughter and kidnapped her. Now Proserpina is the queen of Orcus."

At once Ceres, angry because of Pluto's wrongdoing, flew to Greece to Mount Olympus and stood before Jupiter, father of the gods. She said, "My daughter is with Pluto in Orcus. Oh great father, give me my daughter. I despair of Proserpina's safety."

Jupiter, holding the balance between his brother and his unhappy sister, divides the year into two equal parts. Now Proserpina spends part of the year with her mother on earth, part with Pluto under the earth.

NOTES: Several interesting points of grammar are to be noted in this lesson.

Āmissa est in lines 19-20 can be clearly seen in the English expression "(she) is lost." The agreement of **āmissa** corresponds to the rule previously learned for adjective agreement and so "(she) is lost" = "(she) has been lost." Attention given to this point here will make the entire perfect system passive much clearer later.

The use of the emphatic **tū** in line 26 should be considered. Point out the awkwardness of the English "give you me" but also mention Kipling's "Come you back to Mandalay." Ask for suggestions for a good English equivalent for the **Dā tū.** (Emphasize with the voice alone, the expressions *do give me, I beg you to give me,* etc.)

References: Bulfinch, *Bulfinch's Mythology*, pp. 47-52; Coolidge, *Greek Myths,* pp. 28-35; Gayley, pp. 159-164 and Commentary §§ 114-117; Hamilton, *Mythology,* pp. 57-64; Hertzberg, pp. 160-165; Larousse, pp. 174-176 and p. 190; Rose, pp. 91-92.

Respondē Latīnē:

1. "Ubi, puellae," rogāvit, "est fīlia mea?" 2. Incolās īnsulae pūnīre cōnstituit. 3. In flūmine habitābat nympha, Arethūsa. 4. Zōnam virginis in aquā flūminis vīdit. 5. Est misera, quod in Siciliā est inopia frūmentī. 6. Cerēs ad Graeciam ad Olympum volāvit. 7. Plūtō est frāter Iovis. 8. Nunc Prōserpina partem annī cum mātre in terrā agit.

123 If the teacher has used the expression, **"Et tū, Brūte"** as an illustration of the vocative, and has told the story of the assassination of Julius Caesar, it could be mentioned here that Caesar is said by some sources to have expressed his sorrow at Brutus' betrayal in the words, **"Et tū, mī fīlī."** This observation will have the double effect of reviewing the vocatives **Brūte** and **fīlī** (-us and -ius nouns) and of focusing attention on the vocative form of **meus.**

If a student asks about the third person pronoun, or if the teacher feels that this question should be considered, it is sufficient to say that the pronouns used for the third person will be studied later. The problem of **hic, ille, is, īdem, iste,** and **quī,** all of which may at some time or other be equated

37

with the English third person pronoun, is too complicated to be considered here.

Appending the preposition **cum** will need to be emphasized frequently. If the expression **Dominus vōbīscum** or **Pāx vōbīscum** from the Latin liturgy is known to some of the students, it can serve as a familiar point of departure for this rule.

124 EXERCISES

A. 1. meus 2. tuā 3. mea; mēcum 4. nostrī; nōs 5. vestrum 6. Mihi 7. nōbīscum 8. vestrum 9. ad nōs 10. Ego; tū

B. 1. Nōs vōs laudāmus. 2. Vōbīs equōs pulchrōs damus. 3. Amīcī nostrī nōs amant. 4. Nōbīscum sorōrēs vestrae ambulant. 5. Librōs vestrōs habēmus.

C. 1. Dux meus mē laudāvit. 2. Pugnatne gladiātor tēcum? 3. Mihi viam mōnstrāvit. 4. Fīlia tua longē errāvit. 5. Amīcus tuus mē terrēbat.

D. 1. We who live in Sicily love you; you have given us grain. 2. I have given orders to you; be obedient to me. 3. Did the Roman soldiers fight with you? 4. As soon as our leader heard about the injustice (wrongdoing) of the Gauls, he immediately hastened into Gaul. 5. What were you throwing into the river, boy? 6. The mother despaired of the safety of her beautiful daughter. 7. He has not reported the victory of the queen's forces to you, has he? 8. After the rest of the girls had wandered far away, Pluto seized the maiden. 9. Many of us scaled the high walls. 10. He is calling the soldiers into camp because they have many kinds of wounds.

E. 1. Equum tuum (vestrum) nōn vīdī; vīdistīne (vīdistisne) equum meum? 2. Ubi tē (vōs) vīdimus? Quis tēcum (vōbīscum) erat? 3. Cum patre meō in castrīs Rōmānīs fuī; ubi fuistī (fuistis)? 4. Ibi mīlitēs vestrōs (tuōs) cum imperātōre vestrō (tuō) vīdimus. 5. Pater meus magnam pecūniam habet; pater tuus (vester) multās terrās habet. 6. Multī nostrum ante portās cum mātribus nostrīs stābant. 7. Quod puerī bonī fuistis, vōbīs pecūniam dō. 8. Propter inopiam frūmentī, incolae Siciliae miserī erant.

SUPPLEMENTARY EXERCISE

1. ubi; vīdit 2. simul atque; cēpit 3. Priusquam; errāvit 4. postquam; vēnit 5. simul atque; vīdit

125 A short drill to emphasize the difference in idiom in English and Latin would be useful here and would also serve as a verb drill on the perfect tense: for example, *after they had come, seen, stood, obeyed,* etc., **postquam vēnērunt, postquam vīdērunt, postquam stetērunt, postquam pāruērunt;** *as soon as she had been, given, warned,* etc., **simul atque fuit, simul atque dedit, simul atque monuit;** *when we had reported, moved, filled, replied,* etc., **ubi nūntiāvimus, ubi mōvimus, ubi complēvimus, ubi respondimus.**

NOTE: Insist on the repetition of the conjunction with each verb.

abripiō, snatch away, drag off; **corripiō,** seize violently, attack, rebuke; **dē-ripiō,** snatch away, tear down; **dīripiō,** snatch apart, tear to pieces, pillage; **ēripiō,** snatch away, tear out

127 GIRLHOOD AND MARRIAGE

References: Becker, pp. 153-169 (esp. p. 167); Johnston, pp. 125-137; Showerman, *Rome and the Romans,* pp. 112-123; Treble and King, pp. 73-75.

LESSON 16

Motto

Identify Catullus c. 84-54 B.C. as the first great Latin lyric poet, here addressing a beloved lost brother whom he laments. Call attention to the imperative verb forms used in combination with the vocative case for the noun of direct address.

128 The Greatest Treasure of the Roman State

Although the Romans had waged many wars, they had never been in such great danger. For, because of a sudden earthquake, a great fissure had appeared in the Roman Forum. As soon as the Romans saw the fissure, they threw a large amount of earth into the chasm but they could not fill it (up). Because the Romans had not been able to fill it up, they were afraid and began to despair of the safety of Rome.

Because the danger was very great, the Roman people sought aid from a prophet. The Romans asked, "What are we to do? Give us help. Tell (us) the will of the gods." The prophet replied, "If you wish to save Rome, throw your greatest treasure into the chasm. Do not hesitate." "What is our greatest treasure?" the Romans asked.

While they were hesitating, a Roman soldier named Curtius said, "The greatest Roman treasure is the arms and courage of the Roman soldiers. For the safety of our country I shall dedicate myself and my weapons to the gods. I am happy because I give my life for my fatherland. Romans, be joyful also." While he was saying these things he spurred his horse into the chasm. The crowd of men and women threw offerings of fruit over him. Soon the gods filled the chasm.

NOTES: **Subitō** in line 2 is the ablative form of the adjective **subitus.** Observe the translation of **neque,** *but . . . not* in line 5. **Neque (nec)** is often nearly equivalent to **nec tamen.**

Notice also the intensive force of the prefix **com-** in **complēvērunt,** line 6, translated by the *up* of English *fill up.*

Respondē Latīnē:

1. Magna vorāgō in Forō Rōmānō appāruerat. 2. Rōmānī multam terram in vorāginem iēcērunt. 3. Quod eam nōn complēverant, Rōmānī dēspērābant *or* dē salūte Rōmae dēspērābant. 4. Quod perīculum erat maximum. auxilium ā vāte petīvērunt. 5. "Quid," rogāvērunt, "faciāmus?" 6. Respondit, "Iacite in vorāginem maximum bonum vestrum." 7. Curtius erat mīles Rōmānus. 8. Equum in vorāginem incitāvit. 9. Multitūdō virōrum et mulierum frūgēs in vorāginem iēcērunt. 10. Maximum bonum Rōmānum est arma virtūsque mīlitum Rōmānōrum.

129 Use the motto of Lesson 15 as a familiar point of departure for learning the imperative. To illustrate the vowel change from short **-e** to **-i** in the stem of the third conjugation verbs (before the addition of the ending **-te**), compare the imperative with the present indicative of verbs of this conjugation. By saying aloud the forms of the present indicative and the present imperative, the teacher can demonstrate to the class that the vowel weakening from **-e** to **-i** to **-u** is a natural consequence, for example: **dūcere, dūcis, dūcunt; cape, capite.** Point out the tendency in English to mispronounce a short *e* in a similar position in a word: biz' nĕs becomes biz' nis and hĕv' ĕn becomes hĕv' un.

Tell the students that **fer,** *carry, bear,* is another imperative of the type of **dīc, dūc,** and **fac,** which they will meet later.

130 The use of **dum** in subordinate clauses needs frequent emphasis. Each time a sentence similar to sentence 2 occurs in the exercises, particular attention should be given to it.

132 EXERCISES

A. 1. Abl., from the field 2. Acc., to Greece 3. Acc., before (in front of) the building 4. Acc., among the gods 5. Acc., around the camp 6. Acc., against the Britons 7. Abl., with our sister 8. Abl., with us 9. Abl., down from the wall 10. Abl., concerning the king's name 11. Abl., out of the water 12. Acc., outside the rampart 13. Abl., in the forest 14. Acc., into the earth 15. Acc., across the river 16. Acc., between (among) the ramparts 17. Acc., within the walls 18. Acc., because of the wrong 19. Acc., through Sardinia 20. Acc., through the wars 21. Acc., after victory 22. Acc., except the farmers 23. Abl., in front of the ditch 24. Abl., in behalf of (for) the children 25. Acc., near the town gate 26. Acc., because of the booty 27. Abl., without your mother 28. Abl., under the ground 29. Acc., close (up) to the rampart 30. Acc., above the earth

B. 1. Ad castra; ad vālla castrōrum; in castra 2. trāns fossam; per portam; inter flūmina 3. in Italiā; prope aquam; nōbīscum 4. circum oppidum; sub aedificium; trāns flūmen 5. Sine hastīs; circum agrōs; prō mulieribus (fēminīs)

C. 1. Este amīcī meī (nostrī). 2. Iacite flōrēs in flūmina. 3. Nōlīte dēsperāre. 4. Laudāte, Rōmānī, deōs. 5. Dīcite nōbīs nōmina vestra.

D. 1. Nōlī esse miser. 2. Dūc, amīce, ad oppidum uxōrem fīliumque. 3. Rēgī tuō pārē. 4. Es bonus mīles. 5. Age equum sub vāllum.

E. 1. As soon as the soldier (had) announced the victory, the brothers came to the king. 2. You were leading the forces across the river against the Germans. 3. Without the legions we hastened through the province into Gaul. 4. Attack the camp of the Gauls, soldiers. 5. The sailors (have) sailed from Greece to Italy. 6. Because he had heard about the wrongdoing of the Germans, he was angry. 7. Place a garland on the head of the maiden. 8. The Romans despaired of the safety of the women and children. 9. Before the battle he stationed the legions between the forest and the river. 10. The Gauls killed the leader while he was leading the soldiers through the forest.

F. 1. Patrēs nostrī agrōs trāns flūmen in Galliā habēbant. 2. Postquam legiōnēs ex prōvinciā dūxit, ad īnsulam Britanniam nāvigāvērunt. 3. Patrēs prō fīliīs fīliābusque semper labōrant. 4. Dum māter mea mēcum prope portam stat, pater meus nōs vīdit. 5. Dūc, imperātor, cōpiās tuās sub vāllum. 6. Quod puerī bonī fuistis, vōbīs pecūniam dō. 7. Quid est maximum bonum tuum (vestrum)? 8. Fēminae (mulierēs) dē salūte līberōrum dēspērābant. 9. Rōmānī numquam fuerant in tantō perīculō. 10. Dīc nōbīs voluntātem deōrum.

SUPPLEMENTARY EXERCISE
1. legunt 2. legunt 3. pugnant 4. spectat 5. iaciunt

134 WORD STUDY

antepōnō, place before, prefer; **circumdūcō,** lead, move, drive around; **circummittō,** send around; **circumveniō,** come around, surround; **impōnō,** put, set, place in or upon; **interdīcō,** forbid, prohibit, make an injunction; **interpōnō,** put, place between or among; **postpōnō,** put after, esteem less; **submittō,** send under, let down; **trānsmittō,** send across or over, pass through

To emphasize the effect of a preposition used as a prefix, ask the students to explain the difference between the *intramural* and *interscholastic* programs of the school. Note the effect of the prefix in these two italicized words and also in the following words: *circumnavigate, contradict, extracurricular, postponement, transcontinental.*

LESSON 17

Motto

Identify the Venerable Bede as an English priest and historian of the eighth century who had a profound influence as a scholar on his own and succeeding generations. Explain that his many-sided literary activity included "The Ecclesiastical History of the English Nation" and verse in both Anglo-Saxon and Latin.

Draw attention to the use of **habeō** to mean *consider, regard as,* and compare the English "We hold these truths to be self-evident" (Declaration of Independence). Tell the pupils that **dūcō,** as well as **habeō,** often means *consider.*

To avoid confusion in the mind of the pupil, it would be wise to state that **dulce** is really an adjective meaning *sweet, pleasant,* but that it may be translated here as a noun. An observant pupil may question the spelling of this adjective, because it differs from those already studied. It is sufficient to state that it is the neuter of a third declension adjective and to have the students refer to **ācre** and **forte** on p. 175 of the text, telling them that **dulce** is the neuter of an adjective of the type of **forte.**

135   Romulus and Remus (Part 1)

Once upon a time Numitor was king of Alba Longa. Numitor's brother, named Amulius, wanted to be king. And so, when he had collected many friends, he got ready to drive Numitor out. After he drove his brother out, he seized the kingdom; but he was not happy, for he feared Romulus and Remus, the little sons of Rhea Silvia, Numitor's daughter. Although it was wrong for Amulius to kill the boys, he ordered his slaves to throw them into the Tiber River.

The slaves carried the boys in a cradle toward the river. But the good gods prevented the slaves from throwing the boys into the Tiber, for the slaves could not approach the river bank because the river had flooded the fields. And so they decided to leave the cradle in the water near the bank of the river because the king had forbidden them to bring the boys back. Soon, a she-wolf saw the boys while they were sleeping; she carried the boys to her den; there she cared for them with her cubs.

Finally a shepherd, named Faustulus, found the children near the wolf's cave; he decided to carry the boys with him to his wife, a good woman. For (Through) many years Faustulus and his wife cared for Romulus and Remus.

Respondē Latīnē:

1. Amūlius rēx esse volēbat.   2. Amūlius, postquam frātrem expulit, rēgnum occupāvit.   3. Inīquum erat Amūlium puerōs necāre.   4. Servī puerōs ad

flūmen portāvērunt. 5. Bonī deī servōs puerōs in Tiberim iacere prohibuē-
runt. 6. Servī ad rīpam adīre nōn potuērunt quod flūmen agrōs inundāverat.
7. Rēx eōs puerōs redūcere vetuerat. 8. Lupa puerōs, dum dormiunt, vīdit.
9. Pāstor puerōs ad uxōrem portāre cōnstituerat. 10. Faustulus uxorque
Rōmulum Remumque cūrābant.

137 The use of the infinitive as object presents no problem whatsoever.

138 The accusative as subject of the infinitive may be illustrated by com-
paring the English "I believe that she is the one" with "I believe her to be
the one." The students will recognize the second construction as correct in
English, even though it is far less common.

139 The translation of **prohibeō** + accusative + infinitive as *to stop
someone from doing something* needs particular emphasis. This construction
should be thoroughly understood before the student studies the gerund.

140   EXERCISES
A. 1. Bonum est . . . 2. Malum est . . . 3. Aequum est . . . 4. Bonum
est . . . 5. Inīquum est . . . 6. Malum est . . .

B. 1. Bellum gerere 2. Fugere 3. mātrī pārēre 4. puellās terrēre
5. pugnāre

C. 1. līberōs cūrāre; tē līberōs tuōs cūrāre 2. patriam amāre; nōs patriam
nostram amāre 3. agrōs vāstāre; mīlitēs agrōs vāstāre 4. iniūriās facere;
vōs iniūriās facere 5. statim respondēre; puerōs statim respondēre

D. 1. Captīvōs effugere; Nōs effugere 2. Puerōs venīre; Mē venīre
3. Puellās flōrēs legere; Tē flōrēs legere 4. Servōs auxilium petere; Mulierēs
auxilium petere 5. tē esse laetum; mātrem tuam (vestram) esse laetam

E. 1. (Subject) It is bad for us to leave the boys; (Object) We are not
preparing to leave the boys. 2. (Object) I am afraid to drive my brother
away; (Subject) It is wrong for me to drive my brother away. 3. (Object)
They force the soldiers to fight; (Subject) It is right for soldiers to fight,
isn't it? 4. (Subject) It was good for you to send auxiliary forces but (Object) he kept you from sending auxiliaries. 5. (Object) We forbade you
to seize your brother's kingdom; (Subject) It was wrong for you to seize
the kingdom.

F. 1. Mulierēs servāre cōnstituerat. 2. Captīvī ā castrīs effugere parant.
3. Propter perīculum dormīre timēmus. 4. Mīles victōriam nūntiāre properāvit. 5. Rēx servōs puerōs ad flūmen portāre coēgit. 6. Pāstor parvōs puerōs longē errāre vetuit. 7. Cūr nōs ibi relinquere cōnstituerās? 8. Mē cūrāre
tē (vōs) iusserat. 9. Bellum cum Rōmānīs gerere nōn timent. 10. Inīquum
erat Amūlium frātrem ab rēgnō expellere.

141 Mention *pastoral, (in)equitable, sinecure, relinquish, relic, invent(ion)*
as English words related to this vocabulary. Use the English word in a
sentence and ask students to suggest the meaning.

43

dispellō, drive in different directions, scatter; **expellō,** drive out, expel; **prōpellō,** drive before one, drive away; **repellō,** drive back, banish, repel

143 THE KINGS OF ROME

If the teacher has time to reread even a little Livy, several interesting items can be added here. Pupils are always interested to know that some suspicion was attached to Romulus' miraculous ascent into heaven. There were those who felt that the **patrēs** had done away with him under cover of the storm during which he supposedly was carried off by Mars. Pupils are also interested in the miraculous circumstances of the adoption of Servius Tullius by the elder Tarquin and in the dramatic story of Lucretia.

If time permits, some work on Etruscan contributions to Roman civilization might be done by interested pupils, who afterward would report to the class.

References: For Etruscans see, Hus; Lissner, pp. 365-370; Robinson, pp. 440-445.

LESSON 18

Motto

The translation of the couplet given here is one which Thomas Brown, a student at Christ Church, Oxford, worked out under unusual circumstances. Brown, having aroused the displeasure of the Dean of the college, was threatened with expulsion unless he could translate this Martial epigram at sight.

Point out the infinitive **dīcere** and, by giving the literal translation "I am not able to say," show its use to complete the meaning of **possum.** This will serve as an introduction to the grammar of the lesson.

144 Romulus and Remus (Part 2)

After many years Faustulus called Romulus and Remus to him. He said, "You are not my sons, but the sons of Rhea Silvia, Numitor's daughter." Then, angry because Amulius had driven Numitor from Alba, Romulus and Remus hurried to Alba with many men and sought Amulius. They killed the wicked king and restored Numitor to his kingdom.

Then the brothers decided to found a new city. And so they led a large number of shepherds to the bank of the Tiber and got ready to build walls.

They also decided to name the new city. Each brother wanted to call it from his own name. For a long time they hesitated. Finally they sought the advice of the gods through augury. Remus stood on the Aventine Hill, Romulus (stood) on the Palatine. First Remus saw six vultures; Romulus afterward saw twelve.

And so Romulus as victor could call the city Rome.

While Romulus and his friends were working, Remus dared to laugh at (mock) their walls because they were not high. Soon there was a fight; then the angry Romulus killed Remus. Thus Romulus founded the Roman state and he alone held the royal power.

One day Romulus had called his citizens together; suddenly there was a great storm; a black rain-cloud hid the king; from that time on Romulus could not be seen on earth.

NOTE: **Ibi** (line 23), which normally means *there,* may mean *then* or *thereupon* when it refers to time.

Reference: Livy, I, 4.

Respondē Latīnē:

1. "Nōn estis fīliī meī," inquit Faustulus. 2. Fīliī Rheae Silviae erant. 3. Cum multīs virīs Albam properāvērunt. 4. Rēgem malum interfēcērunt. Numitōrem ad rēgnum redūxērunt. 5. Novam urbem condere cōnstituērunt. 6. Uterque frāter urbem dē nōmine suō appellāre volēbat. 7. Cōnsilium deōrum petīvērunt. 8. Rōmulus novam urbem appellāre potuit. 9. Rōmulus īrātus Remum interfēcit. 10. Rōmulus nōmen Rōmam urbī dedit.

146 **Potis** is an indeclinable adjective.

By placing the paradigms of **sum** and **possum** on the board in parallel columns, the teacher can easily show that **possum** is a combination of **pot(is)** and **sum** (principles of assimilation apply here) and is so conjugated in the present, imperfect and future tenses. Although the two verbs are irregular, point out that they are conjugated regularly throughout the perfect tenses.

Show that *can* is a possible translation for the future and *could* for the imperfect (or perfect) tense by sentence illustration: Can you help us tomorrow? Could Remus name the city?

148   EXERCISES

A. 1. fortiter pugnāre 2. Inīquus esse 3. Forō *or* Ad Forum appropinquāre 4. Pecūniam invenīre 5. agrōs vāstāre 6. Līberī esse 7. mātrī meae pārēre 8. laetus esse 9. Līberōs nostrōs relinquere 10. Capita equōrum vidēre

B. 1. sum; possum 2. eris; poteris 3. fuit; potuit 4. erāmus; poterāmus 5. erat; poterat 6. sunt; possunt 7. fuerant; nōn potuerant 8. poterant; erant 9. fuistis; poteritis 10. poterat; erit

C. 1. A good Roman ought to fight for his fatherland. 2. You had kept us from pitching camp on the riverbank. 3. You ought to be friendly to my sister. 4. He dared to fight with the gladiators also. 5. At last Romulus could found a city.   6. While the Romans were asleep, the Gauls dared to scale the walls.   7. A commander ought to keep (his) prisoners from escaping.   8. Do not hesitate to tell the names of your friends.   9. The mother despaired of the safety of her children.   10. We shall soon be free, shall we not? Surely we shall be able to have a free state?

D.   1. Quamquam potestās Etrūscōrum est maxima, cīvitātem nostram dēfendere dēbēmus.   2. Este amīcī nostrī. Nōlīte dubitāre auxilium petere.   3. Frātrēs cīvitātem novam condere cōnstituerant.   4. Postquam Amūlium necāvērunt, Numitōrem ad rēgnum redūxērunt.   5. Rōmānī cōnsilium deōrum petere audēbant.   6. Rōmulus Remum urbī nōmen dare prohibuit.   7. Mulierem līberōs cūrāre iusseram.   8. Voluntātem deōrum scīre nōn poteritis.   9. Nōlīte, amīcī, tempestātem timēre.   10. Deī nōs servāre possunt.

SUPPLEMENTARY EXERCISES

A.   1. He is able (can)   2. To be able   3. He was   4. He had been able   5. He will be able (can)   6. He has been able (could)   7. They will be able (can)   8. They have been (were) 9. Is he able (Can he)   10. You are able (can)

B.   1. Possunt (Poterunt)   2. Sumus   3. Possumus   4. Poterat (Potuit)   5. Poterat (Potuit)   6. Posse   7. Erunt   8. Poterunt   9. Poterāmus (Potuimus)   10. Possumus (Poterimus)

150   WORD STUDY

aequitās, state of being fair, fairness, justice; bonitās, state of being good, goodness, kindness; inīquitās, state of being unfair, unfairness, injustice; lībertās, state of being free, freedom, liberty; servitūs, condition of being a slave, slavery, servitude; virginitās, state of being a virgin, maidenhood, virginity

aequitās, equity; cīvitās, city; inīquitās, inequity; lībertās, liberty; virginitās, virginity

REVIEW LESSON THREE

II.   A.   1. infinitive   2. imperfect   3. -ne; nōnne; num   4. present   5. command; present; -te; present; i   6. infinitive   7. -is   8. nominative   9. accusative   10. tuus; vester   11. -am, -um, -em; -ārum, -ōrum, -um; -ās, -ōs, -ēs   12. perfect

B.   1. capitis; cōnsiliī; multitūdinis   2. flūmina; arma; rēgēs   3. captīvō; mihi; tibi   4. ducēs nostrī; maxima corpora; mātrēs laetae   5. audēbam; sciēbam; rogābam   6. mitte; dūc; iace   7. cūrāte; este; iubēte   8. erunt; poterunt   9. cōnstituistī; gessistī; fuistī   10. rapiēbat; vetābat; poterat

III.   A.   1. While the maidens were gathering flowers, the king saw the daughter of the goddess and fell in love.   2. The king kept the general from sending the soldiers into Gaul without the auxiliaries.   3. We ought never to despair of the safety of our legions.   4. Marcus, flee with me from the fields; the farmers are seizing many little children.   5. Romulus in anger killed his brother; then he founded a new state.   6. The little boys were wandering among the buildings of the town but couldn't reach the gate.   7. I was the wife and you were the sister of a good man. Often he used to walk with us in the streets of Rome.   8. It is not good to look at the poor gladiators, women, for you see the wounds of many men.   9. Because of (his) wrongdoings the Roman people banished the unjust king. The king marched with many soldiers to Rome.   10. After the storm many mothers found their children near the river. They were joyful, were they not? Yes, they certainly were.

B.   1. parva capita   2. tēcum   3. mittere   4. Aequum est   5. Effugere   6. posuit   7. āmittere   8. vestram   9. petēbant   10. flūmen; rīpā

IV.   A.   1. requiring little work; carefree   2. existing in name only   3. probationary period of a religious order   4. of the body; by death   5. gave up   6. healthful; desirable   7. name   8. ministry; new ideas, methods   9. formal written request   10. route of the journey

B.   1. one who watches or looks at   2. one who looks after a museum, art gallery, zoo or other place of exhibit   3. one who does or performs   4. one who does wrong or evil   5. one who leads

C.   1. carry across   2. put off until a later time   3. hem in; defeat by ingenuity or stratagem   4. admit as a member   5. resist or oppose in argument

V.   A.   4; 3; 8; 10; 2; 9; 12; 6; 5; 11; 1; 7

B.   1. Roman girls were commonly given the **nōmen** or **praenōmen** of the father in its feminine form or given a name indicating order of birth.   2. Customs similar to those of modern times: marriage was often preceded by a formal engagement; June was a popular month for weddings since it was considered lucky; the bride wore white; a feast followed the ceremony; the bride was carried over the threshold of her new home by her husband. Customs different from those of modern times: girls usually married young, between the ages of fourteen and sixteen; marriage was usually arranged by the parents; no priest or public official to perform the ceremony was necessary; a wedding procession escorted the newly married couple to their home.   3. During the reign of Romulus, Sabine warriors, invited to participate in the Roman games, had their young maidens kidnapped by the Romans.   4. A monarchy or kingdom.

VI. Once upon a time, a frog was walking in a meadow; a cow also was walking there. The frog saw the cow, and touched by envy of such size, she blew herself up. She asked her sons, "Am I as broad as a cow?" They said no. Again she blew herself up and again she asked, "Am I as tall as a cow?" "No, no," answered the little frogs. And while she was blowing herself up once more, the jealous frog burst and lay dead.

NOTES: Comment on the use of the historical present in the last two sentences.

Notice **sē rumpit,** *she burst,* in the last sentence. Some verbs that require a reflexive direct object in Latin may be intransitive as well as transitive in English, for example: **sē abdere, sē cēlāre,** English intransitive, *to hide;* **sē iungere, sē coniungere,** English intransitive, *to join.* (**Sē lavāre,** English intransitive, *to wash,* and **sē vertere,** English intransitive, *to turn,* are also found as intransitive verbs in Latin.)

LESSON 19

Motto

Identify the quotation as the motto of Canada: **Et dominābitur ā marī usque ad mare: et ā flūmine usque ad terminōs orbis terrārum.** *'He shall have dominion also from sea to sea, and from the river unto the ends of the earth,' Biblia Sacra,* Psalmus lxxii.

Also point out the difference between **ad,** *to* and **usque ad,** *all the way to.* Mention **ab ōvō usque ad māla,** *from eggs to apples,* as the Roman equivalent of the modern expression *from soup to nuts.*

151   Horatius

Tarquin the Proud, the last king of the Romans, was an unjust man. Because of the king's great wrongdoing, the Roman people banished him from the city. Then Tarquin sought aid from Lars Porsena, king of the Etruscans. When Tarquin came to Porsena, he said, "O Porsena, you are the greatest of the Etruscans; your lands stretch from the sea to the mountains; you know that I too am an Etruscan. The Romans have driven me from my city. You ought to restore (*lit.* lead back) me to my kingdom. Gather a large number of soldiers and take them to Rome. Do not delay. Do this at once."

Great was the power of the Etruscans and great was the reputation of Porsena. And so Porsena led large forces against the city, and with fire and sword he laid waste the lands of the Romans. At Rome there was a large garrison. While the Etruscans were approaching the gates of Rome, the Romans carried weapons into many parts of the city and closed the gates.

The Tiber River protected part of the city but there was a bridge over the Tiber. Soon the Etruscans were approaching the bridge.

Then one man saved the city, for Horatius shouted, "The Etruscans are frightening many of you; citizens, do not fear the enemy. I shall defend the bridge; meanwhile, destroy (*lit.* break) it." Nor did Horatius advance against the enemy single-handed, but two companions, Spurius Lartius and Titus Herminius, came with Horatius.

NOTE: Tell the students that this hero of early Rome is given his Latin name **Horātius,** even in English, but that the poet, **Quīntus Horātius Flaccus,** is called *Horace* in English.

Respondē Latīnē:

1. Tarquinius auxilium ā Larte Porsenā petīvit. 2. Populus Rōmānus eum expulit. 3. Etrūscī portīs Rōmae appropinquant. 4. Arma in multās partēs urbis portāvērunt. 5. Flūmen Tiberis partem urbis mūniēbat. 6. Horātius et duo sociī urbem servāvērunt. 7. "Nōlīte," inquit Horātius, "hostēs timēre. Ego pontem dēfendam; interim vōs pontem rumpite."

152 If the students learn thoroughly these rules for distinguishing **i**-stem nouns, they will save themselves a great deal of time in checking vocabulary later.

Since **mare** and **animal** are the two most commonly used neuter nouns of this type, it is sufficient for the student to memorize only these two. The student should be told that there are other nouns declined like **mare** and **animal** which he is not required at present to know; for example, **īnsigne, tribūnal.** (There are about 44 nouns of this type).

153   EXERCISES

A. 1. mortem 2. hostibus 3. animālia 4. Hostibus 5. montēs 6. hostium 7. flūmine; mare 8. Cīvis; urbem 9. cīvium 10. marī

B. 1. rīpam; gladium; perīculum; pāstōrem; mare 2. prōvinciā; rēgnō; virō; colle; animālī 3. equī; corpora; ducēs; animālia; partēs 4. incolae; annī; vulneris; virtūtis; mentis 5. auxilia; vulnera; maria; nōmina; genera 6. sagittās; agrōs; mulierēs; patrēs; itinera 7. agricolārum; captīvōrum; cīvium; mīlitum; animālium 8. magistrō; mātrī; sorōrī; flōrī; nōminī 9. servīs; aedificiīs; legiōnibus; flūminibus; hostibus 10. rēgīnīs; servīs; corporibus; hominibus; cīvibus

C. 1. A citizen of Rome ought to fight for his native land. 2. He had kept us from pitching camp on a high mountain. 3. We were destroying the fields of the enemy with fire. 4. The sailors didn't fear the dangers of the sea, did they? 5. Many of us have defended the city. 6. It is right for us to banish an evil king. 7. He collected warships from the provinces. 8. The Roman soldiers fought with the enemy and the slaughter was great. 9. He had forbidden a few of us to approach the walls. 10. Although the power of the enemy is very great, citizens, do not despair of safety.

D. 1. Hostēs arcem cēperant. 2. Nōlīte, cīvēs, dē salūte dēspērāre. 3. Post tempestātem magnum ignem in colle fēcērunt. 4. Mēns nōn est pars corporis. 5. Necā animal et iace corpus in mare. 6. Paucī nostrum mare timent. 7. Este amīcī nostrī. 8. Cīvēs cōnsilium deōrum petere vetuit. 9. Iter ab fīnibus hostium ad montēs fēcerāmus. 10. Nautae perīcula maris nōn timent.

SUPPLEMENTARY EXERCISES

A. 1. The citadel had high walls and in the citadel were many soldiers. 2. It is not right to force the provinces to give you warships. 3. What do small animals fear? 4. Pitch camp near the Tiber, soldiers. 5. A large forest stretches from the Tiber River to the sea.

B. 1. Mīlitēs, ubi marī appropinquāvērunt, castra posuērunt. 2. Aequum nōn (Inīquum) erat nōs cum auxiliīs venīre prohibēre. 3. Mīlitēs Rōmānī mortem timēre nōn dēbent. 4. Propter inopiam nāvium cīvēs pontem facere iussit. 5. Post caedem et mortem multōrum cīvium in arcem vēnerant.

154 Ask the students to suggest the meaning of the italicized words in these phrases: a musical composition entitled *Nocturne;* a *nocturnal* prowler; *non compos mentis;* an *impartial* opinion; *urban* population; an *urbane* manner; belief in *immortality;* "the foe's haughty *host* in dread silence reposes"; a *hostile* attitude; study of *marine* life

155   THE DRESS OF A ROMAN CITIZEN

References: Becker, pp. 409-430; Evans, pp. 21-24; Houston, pp. 86-100 (military dress, pp. 100-108); Johnston, pp. 186-201; Lester, pp. 67-70 and pp. 75-77; Showerman, *Rome and the Romans,* pp. 56-64; Wilcox, pp. 28-39.

LESSON 20

Motto

Ask the students to suggest the gender of the adjective **omnēs** and **omnia.** Showing that the masculine means *all men* and the neuter, *all things* will pave the way for a much later lesson which deals with adjectives used as nouns.

156   Horatius (Part 2)

With his brave comrades, Horatius was watching the enemy's troops; they withstood a first attempt; they wounded many soldiers of the powerful king, they killed many too.

When the Romans had almost broken the bridge down, Horatius told his two daring friends to flee across the bridge to the city.

"I shall defend the bridge alone now," he said; "flee to the city; leave me here." Horatius' danger was grave; he stood on the part of the bridge nearest to the enemy and single-handed, without help, for a long time held off the fierce enemy soldiers.

Finally, the Romans had broken down all the parts of the bridge. Horatius looked at the river, he looked at the enemy. Then he shouted, "O Father Tiber, take me and these arms of mine." Burdened with his heavy arms, he jumped down into the river and through a barrage of (*lit.* many) Etruscan spears, he swam across unharmed to his friends on the riverbank.

Thus, because of the bravery of Horatius, the Etruscans did not capture the city of Rome. The Roman citizens set up a statue of Horatius in the Forum, because he had defended the city so bravely.

NOTES:　Comment on the meaning *attempt* given for **perīculum** in line 2. This is the first meaning of **perīculum,** which more commonly means *danger.* Compare **perītus,** *experienced,* **experior,** *put to the test,* and other words having the same stem.

Notice the difference in the English and the Latin idiom in lines 16-17, **ad rīpam ad amīcōs,** *to his friends on the riverbank.*

This reading affords an excellent opportunity for contrasting the imperfect as a past descriptive tense with the perfect. This may be done graphically in two ways: 1. Consider the imperfect as a continuous line and the perfect as an individual point *x* on the line. Thus, "The sun was shining, the grass was green, and the birds were singing" could be the continuing factors represented by the continuous line, while a clause such as "when I awoke" or "when he returned" could represent the event which took place, considered as a definite and single act occurring at some point *x* along the line.　2. Make the same contrast by representing the descriptive circumstances as a circle (the imperfect), while representing the individual act (the perfect) as a single point *x* within the circle.

Students may inquire why *he was afraid* is sometimes **timēbat** and sometimes **timuit.** Although this is a distinction which the students find difficult to understand, the teacher should try to make clear that the *continuance* is in the mind of the narrator, and that it has nothing to do with the *absolute duration* of the action. The fear might have lasted for hours or for seconds in either **timēbat** or **timuit,** but in the former the narrator dwells on the *process* of fearing; in the latter, he merely states the *result.* For example, *She stayed in Rome two years* would be **Rōmae duōs annōs mānsit,** unless the speaker wished to dwell on the process of remaining.

The teacher may like to read the excerpt dealing with Horatius' exploits from Macaulay's stirring *Lays of Ancient Rome*. This sections begins:
"Lars Porsena of Clusium by the Nine gods he swore
That the great house of Tarquin should suffer wrong no more."

Reference: Livy, II, 10.

Respondē Latīnē:

1. Horātius cum fortibus sociīs cōpiās hostium spectābat. 2. Multōs mīlitēs potentis rēgis vulnerābant; multōs quoque interficiēbant. 3. Horātius duōs amīcōs audācēs trāns pontem in urbem fugere iussit. 4. Grave erat perīculum Horātiī. 5. In parte pontis hostibus proximā stābat. 6. Sōlus mīlitēs ācrēs hostium diū sustinēbat. 7. "Ō Tiberīne pater," clāmāvit, "cape mē et arma mea." 8. Ad rīpam ad amīcōs incolumis trānāvit. 9. Ob virtūtem Horātiī urbem Rōmam nōn cēpērunt. 10. Statuam Horātiī in Forō posuērunt.

158 The adjectives that have not already been learned should be memorized. The students will find that using the dative with these adjectives will be natural, except in the case of **similis** and **dissimilis.**

159   EXERCISES

A. 1. grave; fortem; grave; fortem 2. potentium; ācrium; ācrium; potentium 3. omnēs; omnia; omnēs omnia 4. ūtile; ūtile; ūtile; ūtile 5. audācī; audācī; audācī; audācī

B. 1. Iacite, mīlitēs, sagittās ūtilēs. 2. Imperātōrēs proelia ācria parāvērunt. 3. Cīvēs audācēs nōn fugiunt. 4. Gladiātōrēs vulnera gravia habent. 5. Servīs fortibus gladiōs novōs dedimus.

C. 1. Dux noster virum fortem laudat. 2. Tibi grave tēlum dō. 3. Cīvis audāx perīculum nōn timet. 4. Cum mīlite ācrī pugnāvit. 5. Rumpe pontem lātum.

D. 1. nōbīs 2. gladiīs 3. fīnibus 4. tibi 5. omnibus (hominibus)

E. 1. We cannot break down the gates of the neighboring city. 2. I know that you are a brave man. 3. Your plan will be dangerous for the Roman people. 4. He stationed all the troops in the citadel. 5. Before the fierce battle he asked the commander for auxiliary forces. 6. Do not hesitate to banish evil citizens. 7. Many of us defended our borders for a long time. 8. The brave sailors did not fear the dangers of the sea, did they? 9. While the leader was collecting warships from the provinces, the enemy attacked our camp. 10. The bold gladiator, a wretched captive, has sustained many wounds.

F. 1. Multōs ācrēs mīlitēs in omnēs partēs prōvinciae dūxerat. 2. Hominēs fortēs cōnsilia audācia amant. 3. Arx omnibus nōbīs ūtilis fuit. 4. Rēx potēns erat inimīcus populō Rōmāno. 5. Dēfende, Horātī, patriam tuam. 6. Nōlīte iter in fīnēs populī amīcī facere. 7. Agricola nōn est similis (est dissimilis) nautae et nautae non sunt similēs (sunt dissimilēs) pāstōribus. 8. Post mortem virginis salūtem petere cōnstituimus. 9. Multitūdō cīvium audācium vālla arcis ascendēbant. 10. Propter vulnera gravia mīlitēs in castrīs diū mānsērunt.

160 The vocabulary will suggest related English words: *acrid, fortitude, grave, gravity, omnibus, omnipotent, audacity, rupture, disrupt.* Ask the students to explain the meaning of the English word and/or use it in a sentence.

161 WORD STUDY

regal, from **rēx,** belonging to a king; *floral,* from **flōs,** pertaining to flowers; *mural,* from **mūrus,** pertaining to a wall; *capital,* from **caput,** belonging to the head; *fraternal,* from **frāter,** pertaining to a brother; *maternal,* from **māter,** pertaining to a mother; *paternal,* from **pater,** belonging to a father; *corporal,* from **corpus,** of the body; *nominal,* from **nōmen,** in name; *mental,* from **mēns,** of the mind; *ducal,* from **dux,** belonging to a duke (a leader); *provincial,* from **prōvincia,** of a province.

LESSON 21

Motto

Ask the students' opinions of this observation of Julius Caesar. Point out the fact that his keen understanding of human nature was a contributing factor to Caesar's notable success as a leader of men.

162 Achilles

Teacher. Have you heard of that youth who was the greatest of the Greek soldiers?

Boys. No, master (sir), that young man is unknown to us. Tell us about him.

Teacher. Once there was in Greece a young man named Achilles. His mother, the goddess Thetis, forbade him to fight against the Trojans.

Marcus. Why didn't Thetis want him to wage war with the Trojans?

Teacher. Because she feared for her son.

Lucius. What plan did the goddess form?

Teacher. She sent her son to an island near Greece to king Lycomedes.

Marcus. How was the king able to protect Achilles?

Teacher. The king adopted this plan. He gave Achilles women's clothing and kept him among his daughters.

Lucius. Did Achilles remain with that king long?

Teacher. No, indeed. The Greek fleet was assembling for war and Agamemnon, overlord of the Greeks, sent envoys to Lycomedes. They asked the king for Achilles.

Marcus. Did Lycomedes give up Achilles to them?

Teacher. At first the king kept denying that Achilles was on the island. Meanwhile, however, Ulysses, who was among the (those) envoys, had devised a clever plan.

Lucius. What was his plan?

Teacher. Ulysses was showing all the king's daughters many things which are of interest to women. Among these things, however, he had placed a spear and a shield.

Lucius. When he saw these (the) weapons, what did Achilles do?

Teacher. As soon as Achilles saw them, he seized the shield and spear. At once he made ready to sail with the Greek fleet to Troy. With his companions he fought bravely against the Trojans.

NOTE: Identify the **īnsula Graeciae fīnitima** of king Lycomedes as Scyros, a small barren island of the Aegean Sea not far from Thessaly.

Respondē Latīnē:

1. Thetis erat māter Achillis. 2. In īnsulam Graeciae fīnitimam ad rēgem Lycomēdem fīlium mīsit. 3. Eum inter fīliās suās servābat. 4. Agamemnon erat prīmus Graecōrum. 5. Rēx Achillem lēgātīs Graecīs nōn trādidit. 6. Omnibus fīliābus rēgis multa quae ad mulierēs pertinent mōnstrābat. 7. Inter ea, hastam clipeumque posuerat. 8. Simul atque ea vīdit, clipeum et hastam rapuit. 9. Contrā Trōiānōs fortiter pugnāvit.

163-164 The topics presented in these sections are exhaustively handled and will require little amplification. Section 163c will need some emphasis, and perhaps a little additional drill on the eight **cum** phrases will be required.

165　　　　　　　　　　EXERCISES

A. 1. **Is.** That boy is bad. 2. **Is.** He doesn't have a book. 3. **eam . . . ea.** The teacher doesn't like that girl because she doesn't work. 4. **eīs** *or* **iīs; eī** *or* **iī.** The teacher gives money to these slaves because they are good. 5. **eō.** I used to walk to town with him. 6. **eō.** I did not walk with that man. 7. **eōs** *or* **eās.** We used to see them in town. 8. **ea.** I give those weapons to my companion. 9. **eōrum.** Their forces are very large. 10. **Is . . . eum.** This soldier is brave. The leader praises him.

NOTE: The Latin as well as the English of the sentences in Exercise A should be done *in full*.

B. 1. Is 2. eius 3. eī 4. eum 5. eō 6. Eī *or* Iī 7. eōrum 8. eīs *or* iīs 9. eōs 10. eīs *or* iīs.

NOTE: The sentences in which the above forms are to be substituted should be done *in full* by the student.

C. 1. suīs; eius 2. suīs; eōrum 3. suō; eius 4. suōs; eius 5. suīs; eōrum 6. suum; eius 7. suōs; eōrum *or* eārum 8. suōs; eōrum 9. suam; eius 10. suō; eōrum *or* eārum

D. 1. Is rēx; id rēgnum; eius rēgis; eius rēgnī. 2. Eum rēgem videō; cum eō rēge veniunt; eī rēgī pāret. 3. Mīlitēs eārum legiōnum; ad eās legiōnēs; eās legiōnēs dūcit; eae legiōnēs. 4. Ea castra; vālla eōrum castrōrum; id aedificium; mūrī eius aedificiī. 5. In eā classe; eōrum cōnsiliōrum; apud *or* inter eōs cīvēs *or* cīvīs; prō eō amīcō.

E. 1. You have often been useful to him *or* to her. 2. He hears about the danger of the Greeks from him. 3. His plan will be known to them. 4. That (The) daring soldier sailed to Troy with the fleet. 5. His kingdom was near the island. 6. We are brave but we are not a match for (*lit.* equal to) them. 7. In the meantime we had surrendered the prisoners to him. 8. Their province extends from the mountains to the sea. 9. Listen to him; he desires *or* wishes *or* wants to tell you about the citizens' safety. 10. Our allies *or* comrades *or* friends have endured *or* suffered many wounds.

F. 1. Cum fīliā (suā) ambulat. 2. Cum amīcīs eius ambulant. 3. Māter eius cōnsilium audāx cēpit. 4. Achillēs cum eō rēge potentī manēre nōn poterit. 5. Scīsne nōmina omnium sociōrum nostrōrum? 6. Ea classis nōn erat similis *or* erat dissimilis classī Rōmānōrum. 7. Cōpiae rēgis in eam urbem conveniēbant. 8. Dum ignem facimus, hostēs arcī *or* ad arcem appropinquāvērunt. 9. Audīvistīne dē morte mīlitis fortis? 10. Ea tēla gravia nōn sunt ūtilia.

LESSON 22

Motto

Explain to the students that Ovid, a famous Roman poet (43 B.C.-c. A.D. 17), wrote *Tristia* from exile on the Black Sea where he had been banished by Augustus for reasons not quite clear. The bitterness of the excerpt probably reveals his resentment at banishment to a wild and uncivilized region, far from the sophisticated society of Rome.

As soon as Lars Porsena began to march toward the city, the Romans had taken up arms. After the Romans destroyed the bridge, Porsena pitched camp near the Tiber River and began to besiege Rome with his allies. The Romans, however, did not lay down their arms. Soon there was a great scarcity of grain in the city, and the Romans were in very great danger.

Then Gaius Mucius, a daring young man, came to the senators. "Senators," he said in a loud voice, "I wish to enter the enemy camp. I have a great plan in mind, if the gods give me help. I have never seen King Porsena but I shall find him and I shall kill him. I am ready to try this (*lit.* for this attempt)."

When the senators had given their permission, Mucius hastened at once to the enemy camp. The king was sitting in the middle of the camp and near him sat his secretary. Because the secretary's robe was like the robe of the king, Mucius thought that the secretary was the king; with his sword he killed the secretary, although he had wanted to kill the·king.

NOTES: In line 10, observe the future tense after **sī** and contrast the English use of the present in an *if*-clause to denote future action.

In the last sentence of the last paragraph, the students, with the help of the footnote, will change the literal translation, *thought the secretary to be the king,* into *thought that the secretary was the king,* the normal English idiom. The terms *indirect discourse* or *indirect statement* need not be introduced at this point.

Mention the custom of regularly addressing the senators in session as **patrēs,** because their age and dignity commanded this term of respect.

Respondē Latīnē:

1. Simul atque Lars Porsena iter ad urbem facere coepit, Rōmānī arma cēperant.   2. Porsena cum sociīs Rōmam obsidēre coepit.   3. In urbe erat magna inopia frūmentī.   4. Gāius Mūcius ad patrēs vēnit.   5. "Cupiō, patrēs," magnā vōce inquit, "castra hostium inīre."   6. "Porsenam inveniam," inquit, "et eum interficiam."   7. Rēx in mediīs castrīs sedēbat. Prope eum scrība sedēbat.   8. Vestis scrībae erat similis vestī rēgis.   9. Mūcius scrībam necāvit.

168   Although it is possible to teach beginners the formation of the future tense by stem sign (or vowel change) + ending, this causes some difficulties in the third and fourth conjugations. The teacher will probably find that the easiest way to present the material is to have the students learn tense sign and ending as a unit (**-bō, -bis,** etc.; **-am, -ēs,** etc.), because they will more readily memorize these syllables. The students should then write out at the board several verbs and should place them in parallel columns so that similarities and differences in the conjugations can be seen at a glance.

A student may ask why the forms **-bō, -bis,** etc., are not used in the third and fourth conjugations. He should be told that **-ībō** was a common form in early Latin for fourth conjugation verbs, but that it had disappeared by classical times.

169 EXERCISES

A. 1. They are ordering; they were ordering; they will order. 2. He (she, it) seeks; he will ask; he (has) demanded. 3. He was; he will be; he will be able. 4. You say; you will speak; you have told. 5. He (she, it) will break; he is breaking down; he broke. 6. I shall defend; I had protected; I used to defend. 7. We are driving out; we drove out; we shall drive out. 8. They are finding; they will find; they (have) found. 9. They abandoned; they are leaving behind; they will leave. 10. You used to hesitate; you do hesitate; you will hesitate.

B. 1. Petam; petēs; petēmus. 2. Dubitābit; dubitābitis; dubitābunt. 3. Dēfendēmus; dēfendent; dēfendet. 4. Mittit; mittēbat; mittet. 5. Ascendunt; ascendēbant; ascendent. 6. Clāmant; clāmābant; clāmābunt. 7. Fugiunt; fugiēbant; fugient. 8. Sum; possum, rumpō. 9. Erat; poterat; inveniēbat. 10. Erimus; poterimus; sciēmus.

C. 1. Mittit; mittēbat; mittet. 2. Agunt; agēbant; agent. 3. Cūrat; cūrābat; cūrābit. 4. Sciō; sciēbam; sciam. 5. Dēbet; dēbēbat; dēbēbit. 6. Dēspērāmus; dēspērābāmus; dēspērābimus. 7. Rapiunt; rapiēbant; rapient. 8. Cōnstituis; cōnstituēbās; cōnstituēs. 9. Iubent; iubēbant; iubēbunt. 10. Dīcitis; dīcēbātis; dīcētis.

D. 1. They saw the enemy in the middle of the woods; therefore they began to take up arms. 2. Do not besiege their city; they will bravely defend their city. 3. I think that you are beautiful; sit with me, Julia, not with him. 4. I'll take a large part of the forces (troops) with me into the middle of the province. 5. The Romans will be ready for this attempt and will not lay down their arms. 6. Soldiers, put those arms in the middle of the camp; leave them there. 7. I think that his (her) plan is good; he (she) will not put aside his (her) plan. 8. We are seizing their town; they will seize our town. 9. He is the foremost (*lit.* first) of the Greeks; he will be able to lead them to victory. 10. The enemy are approaching the camp; they are shouting in a loud voice.

E. 1. Cum eīs (iīs) pācem faciēmus. 2. Est parātus ad id perīculum. 3. Capite arma, cīvēs; nōlīte ea dēpōnere. 4. Erimus amīcī neque inimīcī eīs (iīs). 5. Mediīs in castrīs arma relinquent. 6. Nāvēs prōvinciam obsidēre coepērunt. 7. Obsidiōne urbem capere poterimus; nōn dubitābimus. 8. Est īnsula in mediō flūmine; nōn magna est. 9. Magnā vōce clāmat; ad eum accēdere nōn audeō. 10. Simul atque (ac) Porsena ad castra accessit, Rōmānī arma cēpērunt.

ascension, act of rising; *audition,* a (critical) hearing; *completion,* act of filling up or finishing; *desperation,* loss of hope; *diction,* manner of speaking, vocal expression; *expulsion,* driving out; *habitation,* act of dwelling, residence; *petition,* (formal, written) request; *retention,* act of holding back; *vision,* act or power of seeing, something seen, unusual discernment

LESSON 23

Motto

This poem by Catullus is in the form of a dinner invitation, a frequent type of occasional verse among the Alexandrine poets who were his models.

Calling attention to **mī Fabulle** will afford a quick review of vocative formation; **cēnābis** and **favent** are examples of future tense formation learned in the last lesson.

172 Mucius (Part 2)

After the death of the secretary, the Etruscan soldiers dragged Mucius to the king. "Who are you?" asked Porsena. "Why did you kill my secretary?"

"I am a Roman citizen named Gaius Mucius," said Mucius. "I wanted to kill the enemy of my fatherland. Listen to me. I am not alone. Many young Romans will try to kill you, unless you remove your troops, both cavalry and infantry, from the city and free my country from siege. If you leave our country, you will be safe."

"My soldiers will burn you alive," said the king, "unless you tell me the names of the young men."

"It is not easy to frighten a Roman," replied Mucius. "I will not tell you their names. Romans have no regard for their bodies (*lit.* do not love their bodies). Look!"

There was a fire on the altar near the king. At once, Mucius thrust his right hand into the fire. The king was thunderstruck at the courage of the Roman. He said, "You are a brave man; I shall let you go home unharmed."

After Mucius had left, Porsena sent envoys to Rome to treat for peace. The Romans gave the king a large number of hostages and the king made peace with the Romans.

Afterward, the Romans called Mucius "Scaevola" or "Lefty" because he had lost his right hand.

Reference: Livy, II, 12 and 13.

Respondē Latīnē:

1. Eum necāvit quod vestis scrībae erat similis vestī rēgis. 2. Nōn est sōlus.
3. Sī ex fīnibus Rōmānīs discesserit, incolumis erit. 4. Mīlitēs Mūcium vīvum incendent. 5. Nōn est facile Rōmānum terrēre. 6. Ignis erat prope

rēgem in ārā. 7. Mūcius dextram manum ignī iniēcit. 8. "Tū es," inquit rēx, "vir fortis." 9. Rōmānī rēgī magnum numerum obsidum dedērunt. 10. Mūcium Scaevolam appellābant quod manum dextram āmīserat.

173 Stress the fact that the perfect system of all verbs, even irregular verbs, is formed in the same way.

Attention will need to be centered on the fact that the third person plural of the future perfect does not suffer the vowel weakening that occurs in the future of **sum (erunt)** but remains **-erint.** If it is pointed out to the pupils that less frequently used forms are less subject to change and that the future perfect is one of the forms used less often, it may help to fix this difference in their minds.

175 Since this use of future and future perfect represents a perfectly logical time relationship, it will be easy for the pupil to understand. This does not, however, imply the ability to use the forms correctly, and until the pupil has had considerable practice, the teacher will need to keep him constantly aware of the difference between English and Latin tense usage in conditional and temporal sentences relating to future time.

176   EXERCISES

A. 1. *Fut. Perf.,* he will have carried. 2. *Perf.,* he (has) carried. 3. *Fut.,* he will move. 4. *Imperf.,* he was moving. 5. *Pres.,* he is moving. 6. *Pluperf.,* we had led. 7. *Perf.,* we (have) led. 8. *Fut.,* we shall take. 9. *Pres.,* we are taking.

B. 1. Dabunt. 2. Dabant. 3. Habuerāmus. 4. Habēmus. 5. Mittēs. 6. Mīseris. 7. Faciam. 8. Fēcī. 9. Venit. 10. Veniet.

C. 1. eris. 2. poteris. 3. sēderimus *or* sedēbimus. 4. fēcerint. 5. dēposuerint. 6. erimus. 7. dīxerit. 8. vīderit. 9. vēnerit. 10. rūperō.

D. 1. Set fire to the enemy's camp. 2. Will there be a fire on the altar? 3. It is not easy to frighten (the) Romans. 4. He won't tell the young men's names, will he? No. 5. I shall let you go away in safety if you obey me. 6. Don't leave Rome unless we order you to. 7. If you are happy, we'll be happy, too. 8. Unless the citizens give hostages, Porsena will attack the walls of the city. 9. If the king sends envoys to treat for *or* to make peace, the Romans will make peace. 10. The (foot) soldiers who are hurrying to Rome will free the city from danger of (*lit.* and) siege.

E. 1. Līberā (-te) urbem nostram obsidiōne. 2. Eōs omnēs dīmittēmus. 3. Sī ex fīnibus nostrīs discesseris (discesseritis), incolumis eris (incolumēs eritis). 4. Nōlīte relinquere nōs; nōlīte incendere oppida nostra. 5. Sī nōbīscum eris (eritis), erimus laetī. 6. Cum Porsena Rōmam lēgātōs mīserit, pācem faciēmus. 7. Nārrābisne (Dīcēsne) mihi nōmina adulēscentium?

8. Castra movēbit cum eum discēdere iusserimus. 9. Ignem in ārā pōnam nisi mē vetueris (vetueritis). 10. Is rēx magnum numerum obsidum līberābat.

SUPPLEMENTARY EXERCISE

1.
capiō capere cēpī captum

Pres.	capiō	I take, am taking
Imperf.	capiēbam	I was taking
Fut.	capiam	I shall take
Perf.	cēpī	I have taken, I took
Pluperf.	cēperam	I had taken
Fut. Perf.	cēperō	I shall have taken

2.
expellō expellere expulī expulsum

Pres.	expellit	he drives out, he is driving out
Imperf.	expellēbat	he was driving out
Fut.	expellet	he will drive out
Perf.	expulit	he has driven out, he drove out
Pluperf.	expulerat	he had driven out
Fut. Perf.	expulerit	he will have driven out

178   THE DRESS OF A ROMAN WOMAN

References: Becker, pp. 431-450; Evans, pp. 24-28; Houston, pp. 108-119; Johnston, pp. 202-209; Lester, pp. 70-77; Showerman, *Rome and the Romans,* pp. 56-64; Wilcox, pp. 28-39.

LESSON 24

Motto

These lines, another illustration of the Martial epigram, reveal the writer's witty, mocking tone. Reread the Diaulus motto of Lesson 12 and compare the two for mood and style.

179   A Traveler and a Roman Citizen (Conversation)

Traveler. Who lives in this house?

Citizen. Pompey, a great general, lives in this big house in the winter and Caesar lives in that house.

Traveler. Where are these men, Pompey and Caesar?

Citizen. The latter is in Gaul; the former, in Rome.

Traveler. Does Caesar have sons and daughters?

Citizen. Caesar does not have a son but he has a daughter named Julia. She is Pompey's wife.

Traveler. Look at those two little boys. They are crying.

Citizen. Come with me and we shall help them. Why are you crying, boys?

Big Boy. We don't know the way, sir (*lit.* kind sir).

Citizen. Don't cry, boys. I will show you the way. Where do you live?

Big Boy. We live with our grandfather. Our grandfather is a merchant and lives near the Forum.

Citizen. Will you go with us, traveler? I shall lead this boy but carry that one, because he is little and tired.

Traveler. I shall gladly go with you, because I too do not know the streets in Rome. My home is in Sicily.

Citizen. When did you come to the city?

Traveler. I came by ship from Sicily in the fall; I was in the famous Greek cities for a large part of the winter; in the early spring I crossed the sea to Italy. Before summer I shall leave Rome and hurry along the Appian Way to my father's country estate. There I shall remain all summer. Before autumn I shall quickly return to Sicily.

Citizen. This is my house. I shall give the two boys to my slave. The slave will take them to their grandfather. Come into my house, traveler.

NOTE: Refer to the maps on pp. 156, 172 of the text.

Respondē Latīnē:

1. Pompeius in hāc domō magnā habitat; Caesar in illā habitat. 2. Rōmae est. 3. Uxor Pompeiī est fīlia Caesaris. 4. Lacrimant quod viam nōn sciunt. 5. Puerī cum avō suō habitant. 6. Hunc puerum dūcet. 7. Illum portābit quod puer est parvus et dēfessus. 8. Domus viātōris in Siciliā est. 9. Prīmō vēre mare ad Italiam trānsiit. 10. Ante aestātem Rōmā discēdet. Ante autumnum ad Siciliam nāvigābit.

180 It will help the students to distinguish between **hic** and **ille** if the teacher will point to tangible objects and identify them simultaneously. Objects close at hand: **hic liber, hic puer, haec puella, hae puellae.** Objects more remote, **ille liber, ille puer, illa puella, illae puellae.** Mention may be made of the inelegant "this here" and "that there" identification.

Following this graphic illustration, proceed to the "former . . . latter" concept.

It is easy to illustrate this use of **hic** and **ille** graphically for the students. When two people or things are mentioned, the second is the one nearer the speaker or writer in point of time and is therefore **hic** (*the latter*); the more remote is **ille** (*the former*).

182 EXERCISES

A. 1. hunc; huic; hōs. 2. illīus; illī; illīs. 3. hōc; hoc; huius. 4. eōrum; eīs (iīs); eam. 5. ille illud; illōs. 6. huius; huius; hunc. 7. eae; ea; eī. 8. illī; illōrum; illō. 9. hic; hanc; huic. 10. haec; huic; hanc.

B. 1. Haec oppida vidēbitis. 2. Hīs puerīs librōs dedimus. 3. Rīpae hō-rum flūminum sunt altae. 4. Hās classēs (classīs) coēgērunt. 5. Hōs peditēs mīserāmus.

C. 1. Viātor viam scit. 2. Mitte ad mē illum lēgātum. 3. Illum puerum portāre nōn possum. 4. Fīlia illīus mulieris est pulchra. 5. Illud perīculum nōn timēbit.

D. 1. This traveler is unhappy; that one is happy. 2. That battle was fierce. 3. He gave money to this soldier. 4. These were the reasons for (*lit.* of) that serious war. 5. Early in the spring (at the beginning of spring) we'll sail to that island. 6. His grandfather ordered the soldiers to approach the town; they did not hesitate. 7. These soldiers began to lay down (their) arms. 8. These troops did not wage war in winter. 9. In summer we'll collect a large number of ships. 10. We'll keep those travelers from reaching the mountain.

E. 1. Illae nāvēs frūmentum ad sociōs nostrōs portābunt. 2. Haec aedificia sunt similia aedificiīs Gallōrum. 3. In hāc parte flūminis sunt multī pontēs. 4. Mīlitēs fortēs illum pontem dēfendent. 5. Prīmō vēre avum meum vidēbō. 6. Nōn prohibēbis (prohibēbitis) mē eum vidēre. 7. Lēgātus illī imperātōrī (ducī) victōriam nūntiābit. 8. Parvī puerī ā cīve bonō auxilium petīvērunt; ille eīs auxilium dedit. 9. Hunc puerum parvum, sī erit miser, ad mātrem eius dūcam. 10. Equitem peditemque (et peditem) vīdimus; hic erat Rōmānus, ille Gallus.

REVIEW LESSON FOUR

II. A.

is puer

	Singular	Plural
Nom.	is puer	eī (iī) puerī
Gen.	eius puerī	eōrum puerōrum
Dat.	eī puerō	eīs (iīs) puerīs
Acc.	eum puerum	eōs puerōs
Abl.	eō puerō	eīs (iīs) puerīs

haec nox

	Singular	Plural
Nom.	haec nox	hae noctēs
Gen.	huius noctis	hārum noctium
Dat.	huic noctī	hīs noctibus
Acc.	hanc noctem	hās noctēs
Abl.	hāc nocte	hīs noctibus

illud animal

	Singular	Plural
Nom.	illud animal	illa animālia
Gen.	illīus animālis	illōrum animālium
Dat.	illī animālī	illīs animālibus
Acc.	illud animal	illa animālia
Abl.	illō animālī	illīs animālibus

B. nārrō nārrāre nārrāvī nārrātum   sedeō sedēre sēdī sessum

Singular	Plural	Singular	Plural
nārrābō	nārrābimus	sedēbō	sedēbimus
nārrābis	nārrābitis	sedēbis	sedēbitis
nārrābit	nārrābunt	sedēbit	sedēbunt

iaciō iacere iēcī iactum

Singular	Plural
iaciam	iaciēmus
iaciēs	iaciētis
iaciet	iacient

C.   dēfendō dēfendere dēfendī dēfēnsum

Singular	Plural
dēfenderō	dēfenderimus
dēfenderis	dēfenderitis
dēfenderit	dēfenderint

līberō līberāre līberāvī liberātum   sum esse fuī futūrum

Singular	Plural	Singular	Plural
līberāverō	līberāverimus	fuerō	fuerimus
līberāveris	līberāveritis	fueris	fueritis
līberāverit	līberāverint	fuerit	fuerint

D.   rumpō rumpere rūpī ruptum

Pres.	rumpit	he breaks, he is breaking
Imperf.	rumpēbat	he was breaking
Fut.	rumpet	he will break
Perf.	rūpit	he has broken, he broke
Pluperf.	rūperat	he had broken
Fut. Perf.	rūperit	he will have broken

obsideō obsidēre obsēdī obsessum

Pres.	obsidētis	you besiege
Imperf.	obsidēbātis	you were besieging
Fut.	obsidēbitis	you will besiege
Perf.	obsēdistis	you (have) besieged
Pluperf.	obsēderātis	you had besieged
Fut. Perf.	obsēderitis	you will have besieged

possum   posse   potuī

Pres.	**possunt**	they are able, can
Imperf.	**poterant**	they were able, could
Fut.	**poterunt**	they will be able, can
Perf.	**potuērunt**	they have been able, could
Pluperf.	**potuerant**	they had been able
Fut. Perf.	**potuerint**	they will have been able

E. 1. huic lēgātō, fortī mīlitī, audācī nautae 2. inimīcā sorōre, parvō animālī, classe nostrā 3. illī montēs altī, ea gravia tēla, hī magnī pontēs 4. ācrium proeliōrum, equitum potentium, hārum urbium pulchrārum 5. sociōs incolumēs (-īs), cīvēs (-īs) nōtōs (-ās), viātōrēs dēfessōs 6. putāmus, iubēmus, trādimus 7. fuistis, dīmīsistis, dēposuistis 8. cupīveritis, cēperitis, convēneritis

F. 1. dative. 2. **-e, -al, -ar.** 3. **-ium.** 4. **-ēs; -īs.** 5. **-ī; -ia.** 6. **ego; tū; is, ea, id.** 7. **suus, sua, suum; eius; eōrum; eārum.** 8. **-re,** present infinitive; present, imperfect; future. 9. **-ī,** perfect indicative; perfect, pluperfect; future perfect. 10. future perfect.

III. A. 1. There was a fire in the middle of the altar; the citizens had ordered (the) slaves to put a small animal on (in) the fire. 2. At the beginning of spring (In early spring) (the) farmers will plow and in autumn they will send (the) grain to the city. 3. Warships are unlike the small ships which are on our river. 4. Horatius ordered the soldiers to break (tear) down the bridge and alone he threw (hurled) heavy weapons against the enemy. 5. "I am a Roman citizen," Mucius said to the king in a loud voice, "and I am not afraid of death!" 6. Stay (Remain) with me this summer; don't leave the city with him. 7. That infantryman told us this (these things); we were angry and did not answer him. 8. The Romans were (well-) known to their neighbors; their neighbors feared (them) because of their great courage. 9. If you free our hostages, we will make peace with you. You don't desire a fierce battle, do you? 10. The general and the officer were speaking to their men. The latter warned about the danger of (a) war and the former praised the courage of (his) brave men.

B. 1. hostium 2. Proeliō ācrī 3. magnā (cum) celeritāte 4. frātrī suō 5. eī 6. nāvī (nāve) longā 7. eam 8. eōrum 9. Ille (is) viātor dēfessus 10. mīserint 11. illīus adulēscentis 12. ignī (igne) ferrōque (gladiōque) 13. omnibus mulieribus puellīsque 14. Victōriam facilem 15. mediō agrō

IV. A. 1. pungent, irritating 2. hostile, unfriendly 3. makes easy (less difficult) 4. all-powerful; everlasting (undying) 5. nearness 6. one who advocates and supports peace (one who opposes war) 7. assemble, come together 8. greed, avarice, covetousness 9. city 10. inactive, requiring much sitting

B.

Prefix	Root	Suffix	Meaning
1. convocation			
con-, together	**vocāt(um)** from **vocō**	**-iō**, act of, result of	the result of being called together, meeting, assembly, convention
2. invisible			
in-, not	**vīs(um)**, supine from **videō**	**-(i)bilis,** able to be, able to	not able to be seen
3. remission			
re-, back	**miss(um)**, supine from **mittō**	**-iō**, act of, result of	act of being let go back, releasing, relinquishment, pardon
4. inaccessible			
in-, not	**access(um)**, supine from **accēdō**	**-(i)bilis,** able to be, able to	not able to be approached

V. A. "The Romans—the race that wears the toga," the expression of national feeling by the poet Vergil in his "Aeneid." The toga was the distinctive dress of the Roman citizen worn on the street, in the Forum, at public functions, forbidden to slaves and strangers. Roman boys at the age of 17 put aside the **toga praetexta** to put on the **toga virīlis** when they enrolled as citizens. Senators, consuls, other high officers wore togas with a purple border. Emperors wore a purple toga embroidered with gold.

B. 1. **tunica**—a loose woolen shirt reaching the knees worn by both men and women under the toga and stola respectively. 2. **palla**—a square piece of cloth worn by women "over the left shoulder, drawn across the back, then brought over or under the right shoulder and round the body"; it was used over the **stola** out of doors. It could be worn drawn over the head like the toga. 3. **stola**—a shawl-like wrap, the woman's formal garment, corresponding to the man's toga, fuller and more elaborate than the **tunica** with a belt at the waist; from the top to the belt the stola was open at the sides; the front and back pieces were fastened at the shoulders with clasps. It was bloused at the waist and made to overhang enough to allow the bottom of the dress just to clear the ground. It might have sleeves and borders at top and bottom.

C. 1. Neither men nor women normally wore hats. Men drew their cloaks or togas over the head in bad weather as the women did the **palla.** Travelers wore broad-brimmed hats as did theater-goers in the windy open theater. Sometimes women wore a veil. 2. Men and women at home wore sandals but stronger shoes outside the house. At dinner guests reclined bare-footed.

D. 1. Very elaborate with high styles, false hair and knots. Pins, nets, ribbons were used as well as flowers and coronets. 2. She used pots of rouge, vermilion and white lead for her complexion and root to rub under the eyes with blue on her temples. She might wear a mask of meal at night washing it off in the morning with asses' milk. False eyebrows were kept in "a little box."

E. 7; 4; 10; 2; 3; 6; 5; 9; 1; 8

VI. 1. Both animals wanted water. 2. The wolf had the higher position; the lamb, the lower. 3. He accused the lamb of making the water muddy and of having insulted him two years before. 4. He argued that the water ran downstream from the wolf toward him. 5. When the lamb answered that he had not yet been born two years ago, the wolf replied that the lamb's father had insulted him.

LESSON 25

Motto

Explain to the students that Marcus Cato (234-149 B.C.) was an early Roman who deplored the extravagance, lax moral standards, interest in foreign habits and customs which characterized the Roman life of his day. Sensing an urgent need for reform, he constantly pleaded in his speeches and other works for a return to the virtues of the "good old days." The motto quoted here furnishes an example of his practical philosophy.

184   Cloelia (Clelia)

After Porsena had fought many battles with the Romans, he pitched camp near the Tiber. From their citadel, the Romans could see the camp of cavalry and infantry which the king had pitched. Porsena was holding as hostages in the camp many girls, the daughters of Roman citizens. For a long time the girls waited for help in vain; after many days, they began to despair of their safety. "What can we do?" they asked. "Shall we be able to escape from this camp and reach Rome?" Finally, one of the girls named Clelia thought of this scheme; she decided to escape from the camp and take the other girls with her. With the rest of the girls, she swam through enemy missiles (across) to the other bank of the Tiber. Thus, all the girls were able to reach the city safely.

When a guard reported the girls' escape, Porsena angrily sent a messenger to Rome and told the Romans to send Clelia back to the Etruscans alone. Nevertheless, he afterward praised Clelia. "No one is braver than that girl," he said. "I shall return the girl unharmed, if the Romans send her back."

And so the Romans sent Clelia to Porsena. Because of her great courage, Porsena had high regard for the girl (*lit.* held the girl in great honor) and quickly returned her safely to the Romans.

After the Romans and Etruscans had made peace, the Roman people set up a statue of Clelia on the Sacred Way near the temples of the gods.

NOTES: Call attention to the translation of Latin adjectives by English adverbs in lines 12, 14, 21 of the reading.

Find the Sacred Way on the map on page 157 and tell the class that it was the street on which processions passed to the temple of Jupiter on the Capitoline and for this reason was called "sacred."　　　·

References: See Livy II, 13; according to this account, ten youths and ten maidens were held as hostages. The girls escaped but the Romans sent them all back, whereupon Porsena freed them and five of the young men as well.

For Sacra Via and the Forum, see Robathan, Chap. III; Showerman, *Eternal Rome,* pp. 123-126; Shumway, pp. 5-53; Treble and King, pp. 19-30.

Respondē Latīnē:

1. Castra equitum peditumque (quae rēx posuerat) vidēre poterant.   2. Multās puellās, fīliās cīvium Rōmānōrum, tenēbat.   3. Dē salūte dēspērāre coepērunt.   4. Cloelia ex castrīs effugere et reliquās puellās sēcum dūcere cōnstituit.   5. Porsena erat īrātus. Rōmānōs Cloeliam ūnam ad Etrūscōs remittere iussit.   6. Rōmānī Cloeliam ūnam ad Porsenam remīsērunt.   7. Rēx Rōmānīs Cloeliam reddidit.   8. Puella erat incolumis.   9. Posteā in Forō statuam Cloeliae posuērunt.   10. Cloelia ad alteram rīpam trānāverat.

185 One way to remember these adjectives is to group together those which have similar meanings (**alius, alter; ūnus, sōlus**) and those which are opposites (**ūllus, nūllus; uter, neuter**).

186 Along with **reliquus, cēterī,** and **tōtus,** review in phrases other adjectives that are translated in English with *of:* for example, **medius.** Although they have not yet been studied, **summus,** *top of;* **īmus,** *bottom of;* **extrēmus,** *end of;* **ultimus,** *last of* may also be considered.

187 If the pupils are studying a Romance language, they will be interested in seeing the similarities between the numbers in the parent and in the derived language. The numbers from 1-10 might he written on the board in parallel columns, by one pupil in Latin, by another in French, by another in Spanish, and so on. The numbers should then be read aloud by the pupils, taking each number in order in the various languages (for example, L. **ūnus,** Fr. *un,* Sp. *uno,* It. *uno*) to show the differences in pronunciation. (See p. 1 in the text for numbers 1-5.)

188 A short rapid drill using these three numbers with nouns will help to fix them in the pupils' minds. This drill could be done first with open, then with closed, books. It is wise to keep the drill as simple as possible, for example: *of one boy, of two boys, of three boys;* (he knows) *one boy, two boys, three boys; to one girl, to two girls, to three girls,* (I see) *one girl,* etc.

If the teacher wishes to save class time and if the pupils can spend some time in the language laboratory, this is an exercise that could easily be prepared as a tape for individual pupil drill.

190   EXERCISES

A.   1. ūnō, duābus, quattuor.   2. ūnīus, ūnīus, trium.   3. Ūnī, duōbus, tribus.   4. Quīnque, trēs, tria.   5. Duo, decem, trēs.

B.   1. ūllō; nēmō; nūllī.   2. aliōs; aliōs.   3. Utrī; neutrī.   4. Aliī; aliī. 5. tōtam; tōtam.   6. alterīus; alterīus.   7. sōla; cēterās.   8. Ūna; cēterae; reliquīs.   9. Alterī; alterī; sōlum.

C.   1. There are many animals in the rest of this forest.   2. We have no other route (way).   3. The Romans had ordered the other messenger to approach the camp with speed (swiftly).   4. He had reported to no one the flight of the other (rest of the) girls.   5. Which one will be able to command the whole (all) of Gaul?   6. The Etruscans are friendly to some, hostile to others.   7. Neither leader (general) reached the city safely (*lit.* unharmed).   8. They were able to reach Rome later without any danger. 9. I could wage war with the first legion only.   10. I'll give one part of the loot (booty) to the cavalry, the other (part) to the infantry.

D.   1. Sunt nūlla templa in reliquō colle.   2. Horātius sōlus cum hostibus proelium fēcit.   3. Cōnsilium est ūtile neutrī cīvitātī.   4. Porsena est similis nūllī aliī rēgī.   5. Haec (Ea) cīvitās nōbīs est amīca; cēterae cīvitātēs (sunt) inimīcae.   6. Gallī tōtam Italiam superāre nōn potuerant.   7. Cōnsulī sōlī fugam equitum nūntiābimus.   8. Utram fīliam vocat māter? Neutram vocat.   9. Rēx reliquōs (cēterōs) obsidēs Rōmānīs reddidit.   10. Aliī captīvī effugere potuērunt, aliī ad portās castrōrum accēdere nōn audent.

LESSON 26

Motto

Identify Sextus Propertius (c.47-c.16 B.C.) as a poet of love who wrote the history of his passion for "Cynthia" in his first book of elegies.

The poem affords examples for a teacher who would like to review personal pronouns, future tense formation and the adjective **sōlus** learned in the last lesson.

Marcus. Today we shall see the beautiful temple of Castor and Pollux which is in the Forum.

Lucius. Who are Castor and Pollux?

Marcus. Once upon a time, there were in Greece two brothers, Castor and Pollux; the mother of the two brothers was Leda and their father was the god Jupiter.

Lucius. Why did the Romans build a large temple to two Greeks?

Marcus. Because the brothers fought for Rome. Haven't you heard about the brothers?

Lucius. No, I haven't.

Marcus. Do you want to?

Lucius. Oh, yes.

Marcus. Listen to me. After Porsena had made peace with the senate and the Roman people, he abandoned the Tarquins and with his cavalry and infantry left Roman territory.

Lucius. What did the Tarquins do?

Marcus. After the withdrawal of the Etruscans, the Tarquins went quickly to Mamilius, a Latin king, and asked for help. Soon Mamilius with the kings of thirty Latin cities was ready for war; he marched to Lake Regillus with his own troops and those of his allies. The Romans too prepared for war. Aulus Postumius, dictator, and Titus Aebutius, master of the horse, hastened to Lake Regillus with large forces of cavalry and infantry. They stationed all their cavalry on the right and left wings (*lit.* on the right wing and on the left).

Lucius. Did the two armies fight a battle?

Marcus. There was a fierce battle. The Romans were very angry (*lit.* the anger of the Romans was great) because the Tarquins were in the Latins' army. The Romans frequently made fierce attacks (*lit.* a fierce attack) on the enemy's ranks, and the enemy on the Romans. Finally, two cavalrymen, riding white horses, were seen.

Lucius. Were the cavalrymen Pollux and Castor?

Marcus. That's right. They appeared suddenly and along with the Romans made an attack on the Latin cavalry. The Latins could not keep ranks and fled.

Lucius. And so the Romans won. What did the two horsemen do after the battle?

Marcus. In the city of Rome meanwhile, the old men and the women were waiting for the arrival of the troops. But before the Roman army could reach the city, the two brothers hurried to Rome; they bathed their horses and washed their weapons in the spring of Vesta and reported the victory. They were never seen afterward (*lit.* Afterward no one could see them).

Lucius. The Romans must love the two brothers (*lit.* The Romans love the two brothers, don't they?).

Marcus. They do. And, because the brothers freed the city from the greatest danger, they built the large temple of Castor and Pollux in the Forum near the temple of Vesta.

References: Livy, II, 19; Ovid, *Fasti,* 100; Bulfinch, *Bulfinch's Mythology,* pp. 129-130; Gayley, pp. 242-245; Hamilton, *Mythology,* pp. 46-47; Hertzberg, p. 353; Larousse, p. 228; Macaulay, "Battle of Lake Regillus" (*Lays of Ancient Rome*).

Respondē Latīnē:

1. Templum Castoris et Pollūcis in Forō est. 2. Māter duōrum frātrum erat Lēda et pater erat deus Iuppiter. 3. Rōmānī duōbus Graecīs magnum templum fēcērunt quod frātrēs prō Rōmā pugnāvērunt. 4. Porsena, postquam pācem cum senātū populōque Rōmānō fēcit, Tarquiniōs relīquit. 5. Mamilius iter ad Lacum Rēgillum fēcit. 6. Atrōx erat proelium. 7. Duo equitēs (albīs equīs vectī) appāruērunt. 8. Duo equitēs erant Castor et Pollūx. 9. Rōmam properāvērunt; equōs armaque in fonte Vestae lāvērunt; victōriam nūntiāvērunt. 10. Castorem Pollūcemque amant.

NOTE: Identify Castor and Pollux as the brothers of Helen of Troy.

196 To keep the place constructions clear in the students' minds, some oral or board drill is needed. Make a list of phrases employing all possibilities, for example: they went *to Rome* (**Rōmam**); they are *at Rome* (**Rōmae**); they came *from the city* (**ab urbe**); they went *to the city* (**ad urbem**); they are *home* (**domī**); they went *home* (**domum**); they left *home* (**domō**); they are *in the country* (**rūrī**). Repeat these ideas using other names of cities: **Corinthus, -ī,** *f.;* **Karthāgō, Karthāginis,** *f.;* **Athēnae, -ārum,** *f.;* **Delphī, -ōrum,** *m.,* and other common place nouns, such as **oppidum, castra, patria, flūmen.** When it seems that the students have control of the construction, inject some proper nouns which do not omit the preposition or have a locative case (for example, **Gallia, Āfrica, Sicilia, Germānia**) and include these as the drill is continued.

Since the names of the small islands of the Aegean will not occur in the readings of this text, it is not necessary for the student to learn that they, too, have a locative form. The teacher could, however, mention the fact.

197 EXERCISES

A. 1. Ad Forum, ad Britanniam, ad urbem, Rōmam, domum. 2. Rōmā, ab (ex) oppidō, domō, ā (ē) Siciliā, ab (ex) agrīs. 3. In camerā, in oppidō, Rōmae, in marī, domī. 4. In silvā, in urbe, in īnsulā, Rōmam, Rōmā.

B. 1. Impetūs sustinēre poteritis. 2. Domōs (domūs) hōrum ducum incenderant. 3: Exercitibus imperāvimus; exercitūs nōbīs pāruērunt. 4. Cupitisne audīre dē impetibus exercituum? 5. Nōnne sunt nāvēs in illīs lacibus?

C. 1. Custōs domum servāvit. 2. Dux exercitūs audāx est. 3. Est magnus lacus in hāc terrā. 4. In manū meā tēlum habeō. 5. Exercitus rēgis exercituī Rōmānō nōn est pār.

D. 1. -ō, -ū. 2. -ōs, -ūs. 3. -ua. 4. -ō, -ū. 5. -ās, -ūs. 6. -ū, -um. 7. -um, -uum, -ōrum. 8. -ū. 9. -um. 10. -um, -am.

E. 1. We shall order the (staff) officers to assemble from all the armies. 2. The dictator stationed all his cavalry on the left wing. 3. They hurried from the lake to the mountain. 4. I arrived in (at) Rome with all my infantry and cavalry troops. 5. They think that the two brothers are gods (*lit.* the two brothers to be gods). 6. He sent a message (messenger) to the senate after the departure (withdrawal) of the army. 7. Why did you make an attack on us? 8. Aebutius will lead the right wing. 9. Why are the citizens standing near the temple of Vesta? They are waiting for the arrival of the legions. 10. What are you holding in your hand?

F. 1. Cum duābus fīliābus (suīs) domum properāvit. 2. Postquam templum vīdimus, domum properāvimus. 3. Aestāte domō ad lacum veniēmus. 4. Duae sorōrēs meae nunc sunt domī et adventum trium frātrum nostrōrum exspectant. 5. Cum reliquīs (cēterīs) peditibus (reliquō peditātū), dictātor ad dextrum cornū pervēnerat. 6. Quīnque lēgātōs ad senātum mittere cōnstituerāmus. 7. Dē discessū trium exercituum Latīnōrum audīvit. 8. Ūnam legiōnem in hostēs (hostīs) impetum facere iubēbit. 9. Neutrum cornū ad nōs pervenīre poterit. 10. Alter frāter domī est; alter domum venit.

SUPPLEMENTARY EXERCISES

A.   Singular

Nom.	adventus noster	cornū dextrum
Gen.	adventūs nostrī	cornūs dextrī
Dat.	adventuī nostrō	cornū dextrō
Acc.	adventum nostrum	cornū dextrum
Abl.	adventū nostrō	cornū dextrō

B.   Plural

Nom.	lacūs lātī	manūs meae	omnēs mercātōrēs
Gen.	lacuum lātōrum	manuum meārum	omnium mercātōrum
Dat.	lacibus lātīs	manibus meīs	omnibus mercātōribus
Acc.	lacūs lātōs	manūs meās	omnes(-īs) mercātōrēs
Abl.	lacibus lātīs	manibus meīs	omnibus mercātōribus

198 From the fourth declension nouns we get many English derivatives. Ask for two English derivatives with meanings from **domus** and **cornū.** Possible derivatives are:

dome—It. **duomo** fr. **domus;** domestic—**domesticus** fr. **domus;** domicile—**domicilium** fr. **domus**

cornea—**corneus** (adjective) fr. **cornū;** cornucopia—**cornū** + **cōpia** Check a dictionary for other possibilities.

Manuscript and *manufacture* both come from **manus.** Show how the meaning of these words has changed from the original meaning.

Dexter and **sinister** are interesting Latin adjectives. Ask for the meaning of *dexterous, dexterity, ambidextrous.* Ask for a sentence containing the adjective *sinister* so as to show its meaning. Point out that the first meaning of *sinister* in English is merely *on the left* or *left hand.* This is the meaning attaching to the word in medicine and in heraldry.

The students will be interested to know that among the Romans themselves the left was the fortunate side because in taking auspices the Romans faced south with the east, the lucky side, on the left. Thunder on the left was a most favorable omen, indicating Jupiter's pleasure. The idea of the left as the unfortunate side came to the Romans from the Greeks, to whom the left was inauspicious.

199 WORD STUDY

accessus, accessūs, *m.,* approach (to), access, entrance; **āctus, āctūs,** *m.,* driving, movement, action; **ascēnsus, ascēnsūs,** *m.,* going (climbing) up, ascent; **conventus, conventūs,** *m.,* coming together, assembly; **respōnsus, respōnsūs,** *m.,* answer, response

LESSON 27

Motto

This is the motto of the United States Coast Guard.

Compare it with **Semper Fidēlis** of the Marine Corps. Cite the principal parts of **parō** and show how a verbal adjective **parātus, -a, -um** can be formed from the supine **parātum.** Point out that this adjective, *prepared,* is passive. Proceed at once into the material of this lesson.

200 The Golden Apple

Once upon a time on Mount Ida near Troy, lived a handsome young man named Paris. Paris was the second son of Priam, king of Troy, and of his wife Hecuba. Because of an oracle, Priam was afraid of Paris and he had abandoned the boy, ignorant of his parentage (*lit.* parents), on Mount Ida.

Shepherds had taken care of the little boy they found. Paris lived among the shepherds and guarded the sheep. On the mountain lived Oenone, a beautiful nymph. When Paris saw her he fell in love with her and married her. After many years, Paris learned the names of his parents, but he remained on the mountain with his beloved wife.

The gods and goddesses lived on Mount Olympus in Greece. They were all under the command of Jupiter. They called Jupiter the king of gods and father of men.

While Paris was living on Mount Ida, there was a wedding on Mount Olympus. Peleus married the nymph Thetis and he invited to the feast all the gods and goddesses, except one, the goddess Discord. Nevertheless, even though she had not been invited, Discord came to the feast and with her hand she threw a golden apple into the midst of the gods and goddesses. On the apple was the inscription (*lit.* word) "For the fairest."

NOTE: Tell the students of the oracle: Cassandra, daughter of Priam, had prophesied that the child Paris would be the ruin of the state. Ask the students to keep this in mind so that they may see how it eventually came true.

Respondē Latīnē:

1. In monte Īdā prope Trōiam habitābat pulcher adulēscēns, Paris appellātus. 2. Paris erat fīlius Priamī et uxōris Hecubae. 3. Propter ōrāculum Priamus Paridem timēbat. 4. Puerum, īnscium parentium, in monte Īdā relīquerat. 5. Pāstōrēs parvum puerum inventum cūrāverant. 6. Post multōs annōs Paris nōmina parentium cognōvit. 7. Deī et deae in monte Olympō in Graeciā habitābant. 8. Omnēs sub imperiō Iovis erant. 9. Pēleus nympham Thetidem in mātrimōnium dūxit. 10. Discordia aureum mālum mediōs in deōs et deās iēcit.

203   EXERCISES

A. 1. a broken bridge. 2. bodies of the soldiers who have (had) been killed 3. (well-)known names (names that are [were] known) 4. the besieged town 5. the abandoned boy (child) 6. inhabitants of the captured city 7. to the wounded soldier 8. across the fields which had been destroyed (across the devastated fields) 9. with his beloved wife 10. in behalf of (for) the king expelled from Rome.

B. 1. puer āmissus 2. in urbem superātam 3. post castra capta 4. nautīs vulnerātīs 5. corpora virōrum interfectōrum 6. prope (ad) pontem ruptum 7. cum obsidibus relictīs 8. in agrīs arātīs 9. ex oppidō vāstātō 10. mātris amātae

C. 1. āmissī 2. captae 3. coāctum (comportātum) 4. relictārum 5. vulnerātus 6. vulnerātus 7. redditōs 8. expulsōs 9. vīsus 10. captum 11. captam 12. conditae 13. missus 14. vāstātōs 15. Līberātī

D. 1. The farmers were plowing the fields after they (which) had been laid waste. 2. I have the money (which was) given to me. 3. The Greeks attacked and captured the citadel of Troy. 4. The queen has a golden crown.

73

5. He learned (knows) about the teacher's death from the slaves. 6. We'll return the boy (child) who was found (that we found) to his parents. 7. The Gauls, wounded by arrows, cannot walk to the camp. 8. The enemy killed the garrison stationed on the island. 9. Those states fought bravely against the power of the Roman people. 10. These wicked men will pay the penalty for wrongs which have been learned (are known).

E. 1. (Is) vulnerātus fortiter pugnāvit. 2. Servus captus poenās dabit. 3. Graecī territī arma dēposuērunt. 4. Audīvistīne verba ducis exercitūs superātī? Dūc nōs ad eum. 5. Propter (Ob) inopiam aquae, servī territī ad flūmen properāvērunt. 6. Ad exercitum cōpiam hastārum ad nōs missam remittēmus. 7. Pōns, tempestāte ruptus, nōbīs nōn ūtilis erit. 8. Sī Priamus in mātrimōnium Hecubam dūxerit, rēgīna nova Trōiae habitābit. 9. Cēterī deī (dī) Iovī imperium dederant. 10. Dē proeliō prō mūrīs (ante mūrōs) urbis factō nōn cognōverāmus.

NOTES: Errors on the first verb of sentence 8 would indicate need for review of Section 175; errors concerning the omission of the preposition with **Trōiae** in sentence 8, for review of Section 196.

Dī in sentence 9 (sometimes written dī) is a common form for the nominative plural, **deī**.

SUPPLEMENTARY EXERCISES

A. exspectātus, remissus, redditus, līberātus, incēnsus, obsessus, dēpositus, ruptus

B. **arātus,** *nom. sing. masculine,* plowed
  comportāta, *nom. sing. feminine; nom. or acc. pl. neuter,* collected
  monitae, *gen. or dat. sing. feminine; nom. pl. feminine,* warned, advised
  vocātī, *gen. sing. masculine or neuter; nom. pl. masculine,* called, summoned
  nūntiātum, *acc. sing. masculine; nom. or acc. sing. neuter,* announced, reported
  iussus, *nom. sing. masculine,* ordered
  datae, *gen. or dat. sing. feminine; nom. pl. feminine,* given
  vīsum, *acc. sing. masculine; nom. or acc. sing. neuter,* seen
  mōnstrātā, *abl. sing. feminine,* shown
  complētus, *nom. sing. masculine,* filled
  mōtae, *gen. or dat. sing. feminine; nom. pl. feminine,* moved
  retentōs, *acc. pl. masculine,* held back, retained

204 Call the students' attention to the special meaning of **cognoscō** in the perfect tense. **Cognōvī** means *I have learned;* hence, *I know.* **Cognōveram** means *I had learned;* hence, *I knew.*

TEACHER'S NOTES

LESSON 28

Motto

The source of the lesson motto is Suetonius: *Divus Titus,* 8. Compare the line with a famous quotation from Horace: *Odes,* I, 11, 8, **Carpe diem,** "Seize the opportunity (*lit.* Pluck the day)."

205 The Golden Apple (Part 2)

Before the feast all the goddesses had been friends; but now, after Discord had thrown the golden apple, there was a quarrel on Mount Olympus, for three goddesses demanded the apple. Great was the hope of Juno, the first goddess, who was the wife of Jupiter and queen of the gods. The second goddess was Minerva, goddess of wisdom, who alone of all the gods and goddesses was able to hurl the thunderbolts of Jupiter. The third was Venus, goddess of beauty; she was the wife of Vulcan, the god of fire; all the gods loved her for her beauty, but Jupiter had given her to Vulcan as his wife because Vulcan forged (*lit.* made) the thunderbolts.

For many days Jupiter was sad, for the three goddesses kept demanding the apple and he could not settle the controversy (*lit.* decide the matter). And so on the tenth day, he sent the three goddesses with Mercury, the messenger of the gods, to Paris on Mount Ida. Paris was sitting on a huge rock, when suddenly Juno and Minerva and Venus stood before him with Mercury.

NOTES: Point out the difference beween Latin and English idioms in lines 14-15: **ad montem Īdam ad Paridem,** *to Paris on Mount Ida.*

The use of **cum,** *when,* with the indicative in the last sentence of the reading is an example of the **cum inversum** construction. In this construction, the natural dependence of the clauses is reversed, the main idea of the sentence being expressed in the **cum**-clause and the subordinate idea in the main clause. This reversal of the natural dependence of the clauses, which has been purposely retained in the English version, has the effect of intensifying the drama of the situation.

Respondē Latīnē:

1. Postquam Discordia aureum mālum iēcit erat in monte Olympō iūrgium. 2. Trēs deae mālum postulāvērunt. 3. Prīma dea erat Iūnō. 4. Secunda dea erat Minerva. 5. Tertia dea erat Venus. 6. Vulcānō eam dederat, quod Vulcānus fulmina faciēbat. 7. Iuppiter erat trīstis, quod trēs deae mālum postulābant neque rem dēcernere poterat. 8. Trēs deās ad montem Īdam ad Paridem mīsit.

77

207 Point out that just as the first declension may be considered the **a**-stem declension and the second the **o**-stem declension, the fifth is the **e**-stem declension. (The third and fourth declensions actually form one group, a consonant declension, because **i** and **u** are semi-consonants. Nevertheless, the student who thinks of the fourth declension as **u**-stem and thinks of the third as consonant or **i**-stem has a usable frame of reference.)

208 The ordinal numbers in Latin provide many related English words. *Primitive, primer, quart(er), quintet, sextet, octave, octagon, decade, decimal* are only a few of those which the students will be able to mention. To spend some time in word study here will facilitate memorization of the Latin numbers.

209 Pupils will often confuse *time within which* and *duration of time*, for they will think that the word *during* or such expressions of time as *six weeks* or *five days* automatically imply length or extent. If they are told that the accusative is used only to answer the question *how long* and that the ablative is used whenever the time phrase answers the question *when*, they will understand more clearly the *time within which* construction. For example, in the sentence, *He will arrive within six days,* we have the answer to the question, *When will he arrive?*

212   WORD STUDY

1. **A.M.**, ante merīdiem; **P.M.**, post merīdiem; **M.**, merīdiē.   2. **per diem,** *by the day;* **sine diē,** *without setting a day* (a form for adjournment of a meeting without setting a day for reconvening); **rē** (abl. of **rēs**), *in the matter of* (in legal and business use); *about, concerning;* **dē diē in diem,** *from day to day* (**dē d.i.d.** is an abbreviation occasionally used in medicine to indicate that a remedy is to be continued until further notice); **per annum,** *by the year;* **annō Domini,** *in the year of Our Lord;* **verb sap.,** *a word to the wise (is sufficient).*   3. An *annual* report is one given *each year,* covering the year's activities; a *biennial* plant is a plant whole life is *two years;* a *triennial* conference is one which occurs *every three years;* a *perennial* joke is one which comes up all the time (*lit.* lasting through the year); a *decimal* fraction has as its denominator *ten* or some power of *ten;* a *secondary* school is a high school (the one which the pupil attends *second*); a *vigilant* guard is *watchful; diurnal* motion is that which occurs *daily* or which lasts *for a day,* as the *diurnal* motion or revolution of the earth; a *diary* is a record *day by day.*

213   EXERCISES

A. 1. Aciem. We see the battle line. 2. Omnem spem. You have placed your entire hope of safety in flight. 3. Tertiō diē . . . Siciliam. The sailors reached Sicily on the third day. 4. Quārtā hōrā diēī. He will come at the fourth hour of the day. 5. Merīdiē. We shall dismiss the troops at noon. 6. Ūnum diem. He waited one day for the arrival of the staff-officer (ambassador). 7. Magna . . . spēs. Great was the hope of Juno. 8. Prīmā aciē. He stationed the cavalry in the first battle line. 9. Magnam spem. They have high hope of victory. 10. Secundā vigiliā. The army withdrew during the second watch.

B. 1. Omnēs (-īs) rēs. We are getting everything ready. 2. Multōs annōs. He lived in Rome many years. 3. magnīs rēbus . . . audācēs. Be daring in important matters. 4. Duōs diēs. He remained in the temple two days. 5. Multae rēs . . . nōtae. Many things (matters) are well-known to you. 6. Trēs horās. The boy kept throwing stones into the river for three hours. 7. Tribus diēbus. He will arrive within three days. 8. Multās hōrās. We couldn't find the children for many hours. 9. Paucōs diēs. After a few days we reached a large (huge) lake. 10. magnīs rēbus. He had told me about the important matters.

C. 1. avī, virtūtis, corporis, adventūs. 2. caedēs(-īs), diēs, mīlitēs, peditēs. 3. manuum, rērum, vōcum, noctium. 4. pāstōrī, magistrō, puerō, patrī. 5. saxīs, diēbus, impetibus, sociīs. 6. populum, tempus, exercitum, salūtem. 7. vēre, itinere, agrō, mātre. 8. virginem, merīdiem, proelium, pontem. 9. rēgēs, obsidēs, capita, annī. 10. vigiliīs, equitibus, equīs, cīvibus.

D. 1. Did you see the enemy's battle line before the fighting? 2. Before the enemy made their first attack on us, we had great expectations of victory. 3. For many hours we were able to keep the enemy from seizing the hill, for we fought bravely. 4. They kept fighting (fought) bravely from the second hour of the day until noon. 5. Within two hours the sad (gloomy) goddess flew from Olympus across the sea to Sicily. 6. After a few days the rest of the sailors sailed to Spain. 7. During the third watch they came to us and demanded a large amount of grain. 8. Surely you hadn't left the other (rest of the) things in the building the whole winter? 9. In early summer we took up arms because it was dangerous for us to be without arms. 10. We'll tell you the things we know (what we have learned) in a few days.

E. 1. In magnīs rēbus fortis et sapiēns esse dēbēs. 2. Dē arce saxa ingentia iaciēbant. 3. Num hī hominēs trīstēs magnam spem victōriae habēbant? 4. Erat Rōmae ingēns templum Minervae, deae sapientiae. 5. Multōs annōs amīcīs (suīs) pecūniam et multās aliās rēs ūtilēs (multa alia ūtilia) dabant. 6. Quārtō diē exercitum (suum) merīdiē redūcere cōnstituit. 7. Ē fīnibus suīs expulsī, Germānī ā nōbīs agrōs(fīnēs) postulāvērunt. 8. Aequum est,

Gallī, nūntium haec verba ducī sapientī vestrō dīcere. 9. Quamquam sunt in hāc silvā ingentī multa genera animālium, pauca (eōrum) vidēmus. 10. Decimā hōrā ad portam castrōrum aciem dūxit, nam erant dēfessī.

SUPPLEMENTARY EXERCISES

A.

Singular

Nom.	omnis spēs	magna rēs	prīma aciēs
Gen.	omnis speī	magnae reī	prīmae aciēī
Dat.	omnī speī	magnae reī	prīmae aciēī
Acc.	omnem spem	magnam rem	prīmam aciem
Abl.	omnī spē	magnā rē	prīmā aciē

Plural

Nom.	rēs malae	trēs diēs
Gen.	rērum malārum	trium diērum
Dat.	rēbus malīs	tribus diēbus
Acc.	rēs malās	trēs diēs
Abl.	rēbus malīs	tribus diēbus

B. pulsus reductus coāctus raptus revocātus

LESSON 29

Motto

Marcus Tullius Cicero (106-43 B.C.) was the greatest of Roman orators and a statesman dedicated to saving the Roman Republic. Explain that *De Amicitia,* an essay on the nature and principles of friendship, was one of about thirty philosophical works written by Cicero which were based on Greek thought.

215   The Golden Apple (Part 3)

"Hail, Paris," said Mercury, "we have been sent to you by Jupiter, father of men and king of gods. Look at the golden apple that was thrown among the goddesses by the goddess Discord. On the apple is written the phrase ' For the Fairest ' (*lit.* ' For the most beautiful '). Because three goddesses desire the apple, we have come to you, for you will be the judge. Do not hesitate to obey the command of Jupiter. Give the apple to the fairest, Paris."

When the apple had been given to Paris by Mercury, the three goddesses spoke.

Juno's words were: "If you give me the apple, Paris, I will give you the kingdom of Asia. You will be powerful and will rule a long time."

Minerva's words (were): "I will give you glory in war, if you give me the apple. You will overcome all your enemies."

Venus's words (were): "I will give you as your wife the most beautiful woman in the world, Helen, a Greek girl. Now she is the wife of Menelaus, king of Sparta, but I will give her to you, if you give me the apple."

Because Paris wanted the most beautiful woman to be his wife, he gave the apple to Venus. After a ship was built with the help of Venus, Paris came to the homeland of Menelaus with a few companions. There Paris and his comrades were welcomed by Menelaus; they remained in the palace of Menelaus for many days. Because Venus was friendly to Paris, Helen soon fell in love with the Trojan. By night they fled to the ship and sailed to the city of Troy. Paris and Helen lived happily in Priam's palace.

NOTE: Point out that the English *glory in war* is in Latin **glōriam bellī** since the genitive **bellī** is a modifier of the noun.

Respondē Latīnē:

1. In mālō scrīptum est verbum "Pulcherrimae." 2. Mercūrius et trēs deae ad Paridem vēnērunt quod deae mālum cupiunt et Paris iūdex erit. 3. Rēgnum Asiae Iūnō dabit. 4. Glōriam bellī Minerva dabit. 5. Paris Venerī mālum dedit quod pulcherrimam fēminam esse uxōrem suam volēbat. 6. Ad patriam Menelāī vēnit. 7. Paris et sociī ā Menelāō acceptī sunt. 8. Quod Venus erat Paridī amīca, Helena Trōiānum amāvit. 9. Ad urbem Trōiam nāvigāvērunt. 10. In rēgiā Priamī habitābant.

216 Emphasize the agreement of the participle with the subject. Point out that the participle ending is variable with the first and second person subjects as well as with third person pronoun or noun subjects, depending on the gender and number of *I, you, we.* To illustrate, give the example *I have been seen* and ask first a boy and then a girl to translate it. Continue with the verb *you were seen* pointing first to a boy, then to a girl. Follow the same pattern with the plural *we were seen* and *you were seen.* Explain that a compound subject consisting of both masculine and feminine genders requires a masculine participle: **Mārcus et soror ex urbe ductī sunt.**

217 It may help the students to distinguish the ablative of agent to tell them that 3 *p's* are associated with this ablative use: a *passive* verb, action done by a *person* or *persons,* and the *preposition* **ā** or **ab** always expressed.

218   EXERCISES

A. 1. *Perf. Pass.,* he was sent. 2. *Perf. Act.,* he (has) sent. 3. *Perf. Pass.,* they have been sent. 4. *Pres. Act.,* they are sending. 5. *Fut. Act.,* they will send. 6. *Perf. Pass.,* you have been carried. 7. *Perf. Act.,* you (have) carried. 8. *Fut. Act.,* you will carry. 9. *Perf. Pass.,* you have been carried. 10. *Imp. Act.,* he was moving. 11. *Perf. Pass.,* they have been moved. 12. *Perf. Pass.,* I was ordered.

B.   1. *Perf. Pass.*, amāta est.   2. *Perf. Act.*, amāvit.   3. *Imperf. Act.*, monē-
bat.   4. *Fut. Act.*, monēbit.   5. *Perf. Pass.*, monitus est.   6. *Pluperf. Act.*,
monuerat.   7. *Pres. Act.*, capiunt.   8. *Perf. Pass.*, captī sunt.   9. *Perf. Act.*,
cēpērunt.   10. *Fut. Act.*, capient.

C.   1. laudātus est   2. acceptī sunt   3. vulnerātae sunt   4. prohibitī estis
5. victī sumus   6. amātus es   7. amāta es   8. datum est   9. captum est
10. relictī (-ae) sumus

D.   1. ā mīlite   2. ā magistrō   3. sagittā   4. gladiō   5. ā vōbīs   6. ab hostibus   7. ā nōbīs   8. ab adulēscente fortī   9. tēlīs   10. ab exercitū

E.   1. Many words have been written (were written) in this (that) book.
2. Don't hesitate to obey this general's command.   3. The rest of the troops
were collected by the kings of Asia.   4. Great fame in war will be given to
Paris by Minerva.   5. Many (men *or* soldiers), both Trojan(s) and Greek(s),
were killed near the river.   6. The enemy's battle line has been seen by our
soldiers; it is next to the palace.   7. Many cities were destroyed with fire by
the Roman army.   8. The Roman citizens, (after being) freed from danger
by the infantry, formed a plan.   9. After Paris reached Troy, he was welcomed by his father.   10. The citizens, frightened by the arrival of the
wicked young men, fled to that citadel.

F.   1. Ūnum verbum in mālō aureō scrīptum est.   2. Multōs annōs Priamus
Trōiae rēgnābat.   3. Prīmā lūce ā Trōiānīs captī sunt.   4. Prīmā lūce adventum peditum (peditātūs) exspectābimus.   5. Reliquum praesidium in
castrīs ā merīdiē ad mediam noctem manēbat.   6. Līberī (Puerī) ā pāstōre
servātī domum portātī sunt.   7. Ab amīcīs nostrīs revocātī, noctū ad īnsulam properābimus.   8. Mediā nocte magnus numerus cōpiārum (magnae
cōpiae) mūrō appropinquāvit (appropinquāvērunt) neque urbem capere
potuit (potuērunt).   9. Puerī, ā mātre vocātī, in cameram venīre dubitant.
10. Postquam nāvis auxiliō deae aedificāta est, Paris cum paucīs sociīs ad
Graeciam nāvigāvit.

SUPPLEMENTARY EXERCISES

A.

	Active	Passive
1.	accēpērunt	acceptī-ae-a sunt
2.	laudāvērunt	laudātī-ae-a sunt
3.	remōvērunt	remōtī-ae-a sunt
4.	coēgērunt	coāctī-ae-a sunt
5.	mīsērunt	missī-ae-a sunt
6.	audīvērunt	audītī-ae-a sunt

B.   1. ambulābant   2. victī-ae sumus   3. discēdet   4. nūntiāveram   5. con-
vēnērunt   6. postulās   7. Nōlī scrībere   8. accepta est   9. incēnsum est
10. rēgnābat

82

219 The vocabulary will suggest related English words: *scribe, scripture, scribble, transcription, invincible, lucid(ity), translucent.*

Some of the students may be familiar with the lines:

> I thank whatever gods may be
> For my unconquerable soul.
>
> from *Invictus* by William E. Henley

LESSON 30

Motto

Identify Publilius Syrus (*c.* 85-43 B.C.) as a celebrated mime of Syrian origin who was brought to Rome as a slave and later manumitted. The motto may be from a collection of his sayings probably taken from his plays.

Note that the pronoun **quī** is often found equivalent to **is quī** (he who). This use of the coordinating relative is discussed in Lesson 38.

220 The Golden Apple (Part 4)

In a short time, however, Paris and his new wife were wretched rather than happy (*lit.* not happy but wretched), because Menelaus had come across the sea to Troy with the Greek princes. For nine years Greek leaders fought with Trojan leaders. Many brave men were killed on the plain of Troy. Hector, the bravest of Priam's sons, was slain in battle. Achilles, a famous Greek leader, killed Hector and dragged his body in the dust behind his chariot.

Afterward Paris killed Achilles. Paris, wounded by a poisoned arrow, fled to the nymph Oenone and sought help from her. Nevertheless, angry because Paris had forgotten their friendship and love, Oenone did not give him her help. And so Paris died.

Finally the Greeks captured Troy through a trick. A large horse had been built by the Greeks. Some soldiers had been hidden in the horse; others sailed to the island of Tenedos. The Trojans found the big horse and speedily took it into the city of Troy. At night, while the Trojans were sleeping, the Greeks jumped down from the horse and set fire to the city. The other Greeks came from the island of Tenedos. The Greeks killed many Trojans and took many men and women to Greece. Menelaus took Helen back with him. He forgot the wrongdoing of his wife and reigned with her in Greece for many years.

NOTES: Remind the students of the oracle concerning Paris. Read Tennyson's "Oenone" to the class.

References: For the story of Troy, see: Bulfinch, *Bulfinch's Mythology,* pp. 171-190; Gayley, pp. 269-317; Hamilton, *Mythology,* pp. 256-290; Hertzberg, pp. 267-294.

Respondē Latīnē:

1. Miserī erant quod trāns mare Menelāus cum prīncipibus Graecīs Trōiam vēnerat. 2. Novem annōs pugnābant. 3. Hector erat fortissimus fīliōrum Priamī. In proeliō interfectus est. 4. Paris Achillem necāvit. 5. Īrāta erat quod memoriam amīcitiae et amōris Paris dēposuerat. 6. Per īnsidiās Trōiam cēpērunt. 7. Trōiānī equum magnum invēnērunt et eum in urbem cum celeritāte dūxērunt. 8. Noctū Graecī ex equō dēsiluērunt et urbem incendērunt. 9. Multōs virōs fēmināsque ad Graeciam portāvērunt. 10. Helenam sēcum reportāvit.

221 The formation of the pluperfect and future perfect passive follows so closely the pattern of the perfect passive that the students will encounter no difficulty. Emphasize again the agreement of the participle, pointing out that there are six possible endings for the participle: **-us, -a, -um, -ī, -ae, -a,** depending on the gender and number of the subject.

224   **EXERCISES**

A. *Pluperf. Pass.*, it had been sent. *Imperf. Act.*, I was sending. *Fut. Perf. Pass.*, I shall have been sent. *Fut. Perf. Act.*, we shall have sent. *Pres. Act.*, he is sending. *Perf. Act.*, you (have) sent. *Pluperf. Act.*, we had sent. *Fut. Perf. Pass.*, we shall have been sent.

B. 1. *Imperf. Act.*, dūcēbant. 2. *Fut. Act.*, (ea) dūcet. 3. *Perf. Act.*, dūxī. 4. *Pluperf. Act.*, dūxerat. 5. *Fut. Perf. Pass.*, ductī erunt. 6. *Pluperf. Pass.*, ductus erās. 7. *Perf. Pass.*, ductae sunt. 8. *Fut. Perf. Act.*, dūxerit. 9. *Pres. Act.*, dūcimus. 10. *Fut. Act.*, dūcēmus.

C. 1. Trōia ā Graecīs capta est. 2. Cōpiae ā prīncipibus coāctae erant. 3. Multī virī in equum abditī erunt. 4. Altum templum ā nōbīs aedificātum est. 5. Magna pecūnia ā vōbīs reportāta erat. 6. Equus magnus ā Trōiānīs inventus erit. 7. (Nōs) ab eō monitī erimus. 8. Quō (eī) ā tē missī sunt? 9. Quandō urbs ab eīs (iīs) incēnsa est? 10. (Tū) ā mē vīsus erās.

D. 1. Command will have been given to this famous general alone. 2. All (of) Gaul had been conquered by these (those) chieftains. 3. War will have been prepared (for) by your enemies. 4. Some had been left behind (abandoned) in the city, others had been taken to the fields. 5. We shall not forget the war. 6. Because the forest extends far, they will fear an ambush. 7. At that time a bold (daring) plan had been formed by the Greeks. 8. What will the other army do when we have left the field? 9. In a short time all the holy temples of the captured city had been burned. 10. If the troops are hidden among the hills, we'll be able to withstand the enemy (enemy's) attack.

E. 1. Oppida ab magnō exercitū incēnsa sunt. 2. Castra ab (ex) eō campō mōta erant. 3. Dux noster sagittā et hastā longā vulnerātus erat. 4. Cīvēs perīculō ab hōc (eō) rēge clārō līberātī erant. 5. Sī īnsidiās timet (timēbit), ante merīdiem in campum currūs mittet. 6. Sī cornū dextrum ante quīntam hōram ibi collocātum erit, hostēs ab collibus discēdent. 7. Graecī cum hīs (eīs) prīncipibus multa proelia fēcerant sed numquam victī erant. 8. Sī prīncipēs in equum abditī erunt, brevī tempore Trōiam capere poterimus.

SUPPLEMENTARY EXERCISES

A. 1. **dīmittō   dīmittere   dīmīsī   dīmissum**

	Active	Passive
Perf.	dīmīsit	dīmissus est
	he sent away	he has been let go
Pluperf.	dīmīserat	dīmissus erat
	he had sent away	he had been let go
Fut. Perf.	dīmīserit	dīmissus erit
	he will have sent away	he will have been let go

2. **rapiō   rapere   rapuī   raptum**

Perf.	rapuit	raptus est
	he seized	he has been seized
Pluperf.	rapuerat	raptus erat
	he had seized	he had been seized
Fut. Perf.	rapuerit	raptus erit
	he will have seized	he will have been seized

3. **terreō   terrēre   terruī   territum**

Perf.	terruit	territa est
	she frightened	she has been frightened
Pluperf.	terruerat	territa erat
	she had frightened	she had been frightened
Fut. Perf.	terruerit	territa erit
	she will have frightened	she will have been frightened

4. **vocō   vocāre   vocāvī   vocātum**

Perf.	vocāvit	vocātus est
	he has called	he has been called
Pluperf.	vocāverat	vocātus erat
	he had called	he had been called
Fut. Perf.	vocāverit	vocātus erit
	he will have called	he will have been called

B. 1. Memoriam uxōris suae dēposuerat. 2. Memoriam adventūs eius retinuerant. 3. Rōmam ductī erāmus. 4. Nisi mox vēneris, līberī tuī memoriam tuī dēpōnent. 5. Sī nūntius captus erit, in cōpiās rēgis impetum faciēmus.

Many English words are connected with **tempus.** These sentences will suggest some of them.

The teacher has only a _____ certificate and therefore he will be able to hold the position only _____. A _____ of his at college was here yesterday. He delivered an _____ speech to the students in which he advised them not to _____. He also advised them to think not only of things _____ but of spiritual things as well.

Ask the students to explain the meaning of the italicized words:

1. The gift was most *acceptable.* 2. *Brevity* is the soul of wit. 3. What is a *translucent* screen? 4. He cannot pay the interest, let alone the *principal.* 5. An *insidious* plot is being hatched. 6. Take down the lesson in shorthand and then *transcribe* it. 7. The *edifice* was the architect's memorial. 8. The paper has a strong *reportorial* staff.

226 WORD STUDY

1. portable, navigable, laudable, arable 2. credible, reducible 3. The Latin prefix **in-** sometimes has the meaning of the English *in:* inhabitable. It sometimes gives the adjective a negative meaning: indubitable, invincible, invulnerable.

LESSON 31

Motto

Call attention to the word **quid** and explain that it means *why* when used as an interrogative adverb.

Translate the second part of the motto with the ablative handled in a literal fashion, *With the name changed, the story is told about you.* Show how the English version in the text is merely a better wording of the meaning gained from the literal version.

227 The Sabine Maidens

The city of Rome was founded by Romulus, the first king of the Romans. In the town which had recently been built on one of the seven hills, there were many men but few women. Moreover (However) the inhabitants of the nearby cities did not want to marry their daughters to Romans for many reasons. And so, because he wanted the Romans to have wives, Romulus formed the following plan.

All the neighbors, especially the women, wished to see the buildings which had been built on the Palatine Hill. And so, when everything was ready, Romulus invited his neighbors to a great show, for which he had very carefully prepared. At dawn many people from the nearby towns were on hand:

the Sabines too, who were the nearest, had gathered with their women and children. Finally the time for (*lit.* of) the show came.While the Sabines were watching the show, at a given signal the Roman youths rushed in and grabbed the girls. After the kidnapping of the maidens, their parents fled sadly. They said, "The gods will punish you Romans for these grave wrongs." Then they hurried home and decided to prepare for war.

Afterward the girls forgave the Romans and lived happily at Rome with their husbands. On hearing this news (*lit.* these things), the parents called a halt to the war. After peace was established, the number of inhabitants gradually increased and after a few years there were many thousand people in Rome.

NOTES: Point out **tempus spectāculī** in line 14 as another example of how frequently the Latin genitive is best translated by an English phrase which begins with a preposition other than *of* (for example **aurī cupidus,** *eager for gold:* **flūmina Galliae,** *the rivers in Gaul*).

Reference: Livy, I, 4.

Respondē Latīnē:

1. Rōma ā Rōmulō condita est. 2. Erant paucae fēminae in oppidō nūper aedificātō. 3. Incolae urbium fīnitimārum Rōmānīs fīliās in mātrimōnium dare nōlēbant. 4. Multīs dē causīs eās dare nōlēbant. 5. Rōmānōs uxōrēs habēre volēbat. 6. Omnibus rēbus parātīs, Rōmulus fīnitimōs convocāvit. 7. Sabīnī cum mulieribus līberīsque convēnerant. 8. Signō datō, adulēscentēs incurrērunt virginēsque rapuērunt. 9. Virginibus raptīs, maestī fūgērunt.

228 Refer again to the motto with the literal and free translations of **nōmine mūtātō.** Carry this idea into the ablatives absolute of this section: **Cōpiīs coāctīs,** *with troops collected;* **Oppidō incēnsō,** *with the town burned;* **Ponte ruptō,** *with the bridge destroyed;* **Armīs dēpositīs,** *with arms laid aside;* **Rēge vulnerātō,** *with the king wounded.* Beginning with such a literal version of the circumstances, the student can plunge at once into the main idea of the sentence, which, from its context, will at once suggest a more suitable English phrase or clause for the ablative absolute; for example, the translation, *With the bridge destroyed, they will build a new bridge,* at once suggests, *Because (since, as) the bridge is destroyed (has been destroyed),* as good English versions of the ablative absolute in this sentence.

If this same procedure is carried through in Section 231, Exercises A and C, the student will quickly develop facility in translating the ablative absolute from Latin into English; for example: In sentence 1 of Exercise A, *With the enemy conquered, the Romans withdrew. After the enemy was conquered, the Romans withdrew* or *After conquering the enemy, the Romans withdrew;* in sentence 1 of Exercise C, *With Rome founded, Romulus collected many citizens. When Rome had been founded, Romulus . . .* or *After founding Rome, Romulus . . .* or *Having founded Rome, Romulus . . .*

230 At first, students will have a tendency to try to put all participial phrases into the ablative. It will be necessary for the teacher to have them check frequently with this section and to review Section 202.

231   EXERCISES

A. 1. After (On) the defeat of the enemy, the Romans withdrew. 2. After (Since) peace has been made, we shall lay down (our) arms. 3. With all the buildings burned, the traders fled. 4. Although the soldier had lost his sword, he fought bravely without a weapon. 5. When the hostages are returned, we shall make peace. 6. Because Hector had been killed (After the murder of Hector), Paris slew Achilles. 7. With the bridge destroyed (broken down), Horatius jumped (down) into the river. 8. After Romulus had founded the city, he was never seen again. 9. Because the boys had returned the money, they were not punished. 10. After the golden apple had been given to Venus, Paris married Helen.

B. 1. Fīliā (suā) āmissā 2. Rēgibus expulsīs 3. Urbe obsessā 4. Urbe multōs diēs obsessā 5. Puerō līberātō 6. Equitātū dīmissō (Equitibus dīmissīs) 7. Duce (Imperātōre) vulnerātō 8. Hōc (Eō) librō lēctō

C. 1. After founding the city of Rome, Romulus gathered many citizens. 2. When the buildings had been built on the Palatine Hill, many of the neighbors came to Rome. 3. On learning of these circumstances, he caught and punished the slaves (See Sec. 230). 4. After peace had been made (established), the soldiers were sent home. 5. On learning these circumstances (this), he pardoned the prisoners. 6. We made an attack and drove the enemy out of the camp. 7. After war had been waged, our neighbors made peace with us. 8. After the battle was over, the enemy laid aside their arms. 9. After laying down their arms, the Sabines had stopped the war. 10. Because the boy had lost the money, he was forbidden to leave the house.

D. 1. Pecūniā acceptā, rem nostram auximus. 2. Exercitū victō (superātō), bellō dēstiterant. 3. Superātī (Victī), pācem petīvērunt. 4. Signō datō, impetum fēcērunt. 5. Obsidēs acceptī Rōmae relictī sunt. 6. Obsidibus acceptīs, bellum nōn timuērunt (timēbant). 7. Oppidō multōs diēs obsessō, cīvēs arma dēposuērunt. 8. Urbs ā nostrīs (cōpiīs) capta incēnsa est. 9. Urbe incēnsā, omnēs incolae Rōmam ductī sunt. 10. Aestāte, agrīs arātīs, rem nostram augēre poterimus (possumus).

SUPPLEMENTARY EXERCISE

1. On learning these facts (circumstances), the chiefs began to stop fighting (cease from war). 2. Although he had lost twelve ships, he was able to sail

in (with) the rest. 3. Even though a few were wounded, our men came safely to camp. 4. Gradually the number of our enemies had increased. 5. When a signal was given (At a given signal), our soldiers made an attack. 6. Although their forces have been conquered (overcome), the Sabines will not lay down their arms. 7. After sending all his cavalry, the general ordered us to punish our neighbors. 8. Even though the general had taken the mountain, he did not engage in battle but was waiting for reinforcements.

233 WORD STUDY

absistō *intransitive,* go away, desist from; **cōnsistō,** *intransitive,* take one's stand, halt; **exsistō,** *intransitive,* come forth, appear, arise; **īnsistō,** *intransitive,* set foot on, pause, hesitate; **resistō,** *intransitive,* stand again, halt, resist

REVIEW LESSON FIVE

II. A.   hic lacus   domus

	Singular	Plural	Singular	Plural
Nom.	hic lacus	hī lacūs	domus	domūs
Gen.	huius lacūs	hōrum lacuum	domus	domuum
Dat.	huic lacuī	hīs lacibus	domuī, domō	domibus
Acc.	hunc lacum	hōs lacūs	domum	domōs, domūs
Abl.	hōc lacū	hīs lacibus	domō (domū, *rare*)	domibus

	aciēs		spēs āmissa	
Nom.	aciēs	aciēs	spēs āmissa	spēs āmissae
Gen.	acieī	_____	speī āmissae	_____
Dat.	acieī	_____	speī āmissae	_____
Acc.	aciem	aciēs	spem āmissam	spēs āmissās
Abl.	aciē	_____	spē āmissā	_____

NOTE: **Diēs** and **rēs** are the only fifth declension nouns having complete plural forms.

B.   vincō vincere vīcī victum

Passive

Perfect		Pluperfect	
Singular	Plural	Singular	Plural
victus sum	victī sumus	victus eram	victī erāmus
victus es	victī estis	victus erās	victī erātis
victus est	victī sunt	victus erat	victī erant

Fut. Perf.

Singular	Plural
victus erō	victī erimus
victus eris	victī eritis
victus erit	victī erunt

III. 1. **-ī; -ūs.** 2. masculine; feminine; neuter. 3. **-ēī** or **-eī.** 4. feminine; masculine. 5. **-am, -um, -em, -um; -em; -ārum, -ōrum, -um** *or* **-ium, -uum; ērum; -ās, -ōs, -ēs, -ūs; -ēs.** 6. nominative; accusative; **-ua.** 7. **-ius, -ī; altus.** 8. accusative; without; ablative; without; locative. 9. **-ae, -ī; -ī; -e;** ablative. 10. active; passive. 11. adjective; case, number; gender; tense; voice.

IV. A. 1. No money was given to the six young men because they had not obeyed their parents that day. 2. (For many days) the father had sailed on the wide sea with the one son; now he was approaching the beautiful cities of Greece with the other son. 3. During the fourth watch the rest of the enemy's infantry was overcome and many prisoners were awaited by our leader. 4. Some (of the) girls could stay in Rome with their mothers but others were sent back to the wicked king as hostages. 5. After he had been driven out of his homeland, Tarquin did not hesitate to demand help from the enemy chieftain. Wasn't this a very great wrong? 6. After peace had been made with the senate and the Roman people, Porsena forgot Tarquin and stopped fighting. 7. The two goddesses were angry because they had asked in vain for the apple; Venus alone was happy because of the gift she had received. 8. Why is Achilles sitting in his camp after (although) the signal for battle has been given? 9. The citizens did not know about the plot and in a few hours the huge horse was brought into the city.

B. 1. merīdiē 2. Custōdibus vīsīs 3. dicta 4. Utrī virō 5. domī 6. quīnque diēs 7. neutrīus prīncipis 8. Decimā legiōne missā 9. Tribus annīs 10. collocātum erit

C. 1. Fuga captīvōrum ā servō nūntiāta est. 2. Magister sapiēns ab adulēscentibus amātus erat. 3. Currus noster ā nōbīs inventus est. 4. Suntne datae ā tē poenae?

V. A. revokable (revocable) audible vulnerable legible defensible
   The effect of adding the prefix **in-** is to give the adjective a negative connotation.

B. **adventus,** arrival; **ascēnsus,** climbing, ascent; **discessus,** departure, withdrawal; **status,** standing, position, condition

C. 1. watchfulness 2. wordiness 3. treacherous and harmful but enticing 4. state of being on neither side 5. allowing light to pass through 6. horn of plenty 7. relating to guardianship 8. opportunity to decide between two propositions 9. relating to earthly life and to time as contrasted with the eternal 10. having to do with punishment 11. without a designated day or indefinitely 12. in the year of Our Lord

D. January from **Iānus,** the god of beginnings; February from **februa,** a purification ceremony; March from **Mārtius** (Mars), the god of war; April from **aperīre,** to open; May from **maior,** greater; June from **Iūnō,** the queen of the gods; July from **Iūlius,** Julius Caesar; August from **Augustus,** the first Roman emperor; September from **septem,** seven; October from **octō,** eight; November from **novem,** nine; December from **decem,** ten.

VI. 1. Cloelia 2. Castor and Pollux 3. Vulcan 4. Priam 5. Paris 6. Oenone 7. Discord 8. Titus 9. Juno 10. Venus 11. Minerva 12. Mercury 13. Olympus 14. Hector 15. Achilles

VII. 1. The dog was carrying meat in his mouth as he swam. 2. He saw his reflection in the water. 3. He thought he was seeing another dog and tried to snatch the meat. 4. He lost his own food.

LESSON 32

Motto

These lines provide a commentary on the economic conditions of Martial's day, a period in which great wealth was being concentrated in the hands of a few wealthy men. Martial is probably speaking from bitter experience since, after the fall of his patrons, the Senecas, his own situation became difficult and uncertain.

Call attention to the alliteration in the second line: **nūllīs nunc nisi.**

Ask the students to find the translation for **Dantur opēs;** point out the **-ntur** ending of the verb and thus lead into the grammar of the lesson, the present passive.

234   Liscus (Part 1)

Liscus, a Gallic leader, was a brave and daring soldier. Summoning his soldiers to the town which was the capital of his kingdom, he delivered the following speech:

"Gauls, you are being warned by me. The Romans are hurrying into Gaul on forced marches. Our towns are being attacked by their army, our fields (are being) destroyed; many of our soldiers are being killed; our women and children are (being) frightened by the approach of the enemy.

"We are citizens of a free state. No one has ever called us cowards. We shall never forget the wrongs done by (*lit.* wrongdoing of) the Romans. Remember your courage. For many reasons we ought to defend ourselves with arms. We shall soon engage in battle with the enemy. When the battle with the enemy begins (*lit.* has begun), do not hesitate to fight for your country even to the death."

While this was taking place, a Roman army was approaching the capital of Liscus' realm. They set fire to the Gallic villages and the inhabitants of the nearby towns could see the smoke from (*lit.* of) the fires. When the Romans had reached the gate of the town, a Roman staff-officer shouted in a loud voice:

"Listen to me, Gauls. Your villages are being burned; some Gauls are being killed, others captured. Many old men and women are being taken for slaves (*lit.* led into slavery). You have no hope of safety. If you hand over ten of your leaders as hostages and if the rest of the soldiers lay down their arms, we will spare the children, the old men, and the women."

NOTE: Point out the use of the dative with **parcō** in the last sentence and ask the pupils to name some other verbs which require the dative (for example, **imperō, appropinquō,** and **ignōscō**).

Respondē Latīnē:

1. Gallī ā Liscō monentur.   2. Oppida Gallōrum áb exercitū Rōmānō vāstantur.   3. Nēmō umquam Gallōs ignāvōs appellāvit.   4. Gallī memoriam iniūriārum Rōmānōrum numquam dēpōnent.   5. Mox proelium cum Rōmānīs committent.   6. Exercitus Rōmānus ad caput rēgnī Liscī accēdēbat.   7. Fūmum ignium vidēre poterant.   8. "Audīte mē, Gallī," magnā vōce clāmāvit.   9. Vīcī incenduntur; aliī Gallī interficiuntur; aliī capiuntur. Multī senēs et fēminae in servitūtem dūcuntur.   10. Gallīs parcent sī decem ex prīncipibus obsidēs trādiderint.

235   Tell the students that in early Latin **-re** was the more common ending for the second person singular passive, that it was rarely used in the present tense in classical times (except in the imperative), but that it was frequently used in other tenses, especially by Cicero. After Cicero's time, **-ris** became the more usual ending in all tenses of the present system; Livy and Tacitus prefer **-ris.**

Point out that the second person singular passive ending in **-re** is practically never found in the present tense of third and fourth conjugation verbs (except in the imperative).

Emphasize the difference between the **iō** verbs of the third and fourth conjugations in the spelling of the second person singular passive.

236   Point out that, in most instances, the present progressive is the better English version of the Latin present passive, since in English the verb *to be* plus a perfect passive participle is often the statement of a completed, not a present, action. For example, *you are moved* frequently means *you have been moved; he is lost* means *he has been lost,* and *they are seized* means *they have been seized; the bridge is broken* means *the bridge has been broken.*

EXERCISES

A. 1. You are being moved; you are being led; you are being called. 2. They are being summoned; they are being taken; they are let go. 3. You are being sent; you are being besieged; you are being praised. 4. He is being frightened; he is being seized; it is being lost. 5. We are being ordered; we are seen (seem); we are being welcomed. 6. You are being prevented; you are found; you are being left behind. 7. I am being ordered; I am being compelled; I have been heard. 8. The field is being destroyed. The rock is being thrown. The rock has been thrown.

B. 1. Movet; movētur. 2. Līberāmus; līberāmur. 3. Pūniunt; pūniuntur. 4. Mittō; mittor. 5. Petis; peteris. 6. Vetat; vetātur. 7. Interficiunt; interficiuntur. 8. Vocāmus; vocāmur. 9. Retinētis; retinēminī. 10. Agunt; aguntur.

C. 1. Exercitūs ad oppida accēdunt. 2. Equitēs ad lēgātōs mittuntur. 3. Labōrāre iubēminī. 4. Obsidēs ā nōbīs accipiuntur. 5. Ea oppida oppugnantur.

D. 1. Paucī peditēs ā nōbīs capiuntur. 2. Oppidum nostrum ā Rōmānīs oppugnātur. 3. Servus ā cīve bonō līberātur. 4. Agrī nostrī ā sociīs vestrīs vāstantur. 5. Saxa ā mē iaciuntur.

E. 1. You are being ordered to work, I am not. 2. A great victory is being reported to our neighbors by this messenger. 3. The bridge is being broken down by the storm. 4. Large forces are being hidden in the woods. 5. Have the Sabines ever besieged the city of Rome? 6. While the Sabines are watching the show, the girls are being kidnapped. 7. Now that a new city has been founded by the shepherds, many inhabitants are being gathered. 8. The enemy seem(s) to be afraid of our army. 9. Don't punish those unhappy slaves; pardon them. 10. We are being led or taken by forced marches into the nearby province.

F. 1. Ōrātiō ā duce in Forō habētur. 2. Urbs in colle conditur. 3. Agricolae, quamquam sunt senēs, in servitūtem dūcuntur. 4. Quis ex urbe ā cīvibus īrātīs expellitur? 5. Nōlī(-te) dēpōnere memoriam amīcōrum tuōrum (vestrōrum) quī in proeliō interfectī sunt (in proeliō interfectōrum). 6. Sine (ūllā) causā nostrī agrī (fīnēs) ā Gāllīs paulātim vāstantur.

SUPPLEMENTARY EXERCISES

A. 1. Vōs ā patre monēminī. 2. Ego saepe laudor. 3. Pecūnia tibi datur. 4. Ego in servitūtem dūcor. 5. Arma ā vōbīs trāduntur.

B. 1. Fortēs mīlitēs laudantur. 2. Ōrātiōnēs ā ducibus habentur. 3. Hae rēs ā vōbīs sciuntur. 4. Parcite nōbīs. 5. Prōvinciae Rōmānae vāstantur.

C. 1. Arma ā vōbīs nōn capiuntur. 2. Hostēs ab incolīs videntur. 3. Num obsidēs Rōmānīs ā vōbīs dantur? 4. Vulnus grave ab eō accipitur. 5. Hostēs ab eīs in urbe inveniuntur.

237 Ask the students to suggest meanings for the italicized words in phrases such as these, basing their answers on the Latin vocabulary: a *senile* ruler, a *parsimonious* employer, involuntary *servitude, contention* between friends, *commission* to buy a painting.

LESSON 33

Motto

Identify Vergil (70-19 B.C.) as an epic poet and the *Aeneid* as a narrative poem of nearly 10,000 lines which was his greatest contribution to the body of Latin literature.

Ask the students to notice **dabitur,** the verb in the quotation, to give its translation and to suggest the tense and voice.

238 Liscus (Part 2)

On hearing the words of the officer, the Gauls were very much disturbed. All of Gaul was being attacked by the Romans, towns were being stormed and destroyed, farms devastated, and the inhabitants driven out. And so, after calling a council of war, Liscus answered the Roman officer:

"It is wrong for the Romans to come into Gaul. We are not hostile to you. We seek peace and friendship with (*lit.* the peace and friendship of) the Roman people. I am warning you; if you attack our city, we will fight for our beloved children and wives. We will remember the wrong you commit (*lit.* your wrongdoing). Some day we will conquer you; we will spare no one."

Meanwhile, not far from the city, camp was being set up and (was being) fortified by a rampart and trench, grain was being gathered, a garrison was being stationed, and a battle formation (was being) drawn up. No hope for peace was left.

For many days the Romans besieged Liscus' town. But, as they were not able to capture the town by blockade, they decided to storm it. And so the Roman officer called the soldiers together before he made the attack.

"Today," he said, "we shall attack this town. If you are brave, you will take it. Nothing will be able to stop us. Many gifts and great rewards will be given to you. You will be considered brave soldiers. The friendship of the Roman people will be sought by the chieftains of all of Gaul."

Then he drew up his battle line and gave the signal to begin battle (*lit.* of battle). They drew close to the walls of the town. Suddenly the Gauls made a sortie from all the gates. The battle continued for six hours.

Finally, after many had been killed and many wounded, the Gauls were driven back and were forced to lay down their arms. The freedom of the brave Gauls was lost.

NOTE: Explain that a *sortie* or *sally* is a sudden outbreak and attack of a beleaguered force.

Respondē Latīnē:

1. Omnis Gallia occupābātur, oppida expugnābantur et dēlēbantur, agrī vāstābantur, incolae expellēbantur. 2. Inīquum est Rōmānōs in Galliam venīre. 3. Gallī Rōmānīs nōn sunt inimīcī. 4. Castra pōnēbantur et vāllō fossāque mūniēbantur, frūmentum comportābātur, praesidium collocābātur, aciēs īnstruēbātur. 5. Quod oppidum obsidiōne capere nōn poterant, expugnāre cōnstituērunt. 6. Priusquam impetum fēcit, mīlites convocāvit. 7. Oppidum capient, sī erunt fortēs. 8. Aciē īnstrūctā, signum proeliī dedit. 9. Gallī repulsī arma dēpōnere coāctī sunt. 10. Lībertātem āmīserant.

240 The vowel change in the second person singular from **-bis,** active, to **-beris,** passive, needs to be emphasized, since this is not the usual kind of vowel change. The normal vowel weakening is from **a** or **e** to **i,** rather than the reverse. Compare compounds of **capere** and **tenēre,** such as **accipere** and **retinēre.**

241   EXERCISES

A. 1. We shall be brought back (in)to Germany. 2. The Gauls were being conquered. 3. A temple will be built. 4. You will be sent with the staff-officer (envoy). 5. The attack was being withstood. 6. (The) camp was being pitched. 7. The troops will be placed in ambush. 8. The battle line was being drawn up. 9. I shall be called a brave soldier. 10. You will be sent to Greece.

B. 1. Bellum gerēbātur. 2. Oppida dēfendēbantur. 3. Fossae complēbantur. 4. Discēdere vetābimur. 5. Multa (Multae rēs) ad tē (vōs) mittentur. 6. Prohibēbāmur. 7. Lībertās nostra āmittētur. 8. Multa dōna dabuntur. 9. Sapientēs (esse) vidēbantur. 10. Magnum praemium accipiētur.

C. 1. I shall be praised; I was being praised; I am being praised. 2. They are being received; they will be received; they used to be received. 3. It will be sent back; it is being given back; it was being returned. 4. We are moved; we were being moved; we shall be moved. 5. You will be left behind; you are being abandoned; you were being left. 6. It will be set up (drawn up); it is being destroyed; it is being surrendered. 7. They will be withstood; they were being fortified; they are being reported. 8. They are being found; they are being hidden; they will be built. 9. You are being seen (you seem); you will be led; you are being taken. 10. You used to be called; you will be blockaded; you are being prevented.

D. 1. Impetus ā mīlitibus sustinēbitur. 2. Castra ā duce pōnēbantur. 3. Asia ā nōbīs vincētur. 4. Captīvī ā custōde removēbuntur. 5. Fīliae eius ā mē vocātae sunt.

E. 1. If an attack is made, they will be driven back. 2. If the city is captured, great rewards will be given us. 3. A messenger was sent right up to
the wall. 4. The children were standing under the bridge. 5. If they are
conquered, freedom will be lost. 6. If hostages are given, our garrison will
be taken out of your city. 7. During the second hour a battle line was being
drawn up by the general. 8. Germany was being conquered by very large
armies.

F. 1. Lībertās nostra āmittētur, nisi hostēs reppulerimus. 2. Quod fuerat
rēx malus, ā cīvibus miserīs Rōmā expellēbātur. 3. Tertiō annō bellī multa
oppida et Italiae et Siciliae expugnābantur et dēlēbantur. 4. Signō proeliī
datō, impetum in aciēs hostium faciēmus. 5. Lēgātīs ad nōs ab hostibus
missīs, pāx et amīcitia petēbantur.

SUPPLEMENTARY EXERCISES

A. **accipiō accipere accēpī acceptum**   **dēleō dēlēre dēlēvī dēlētum**

	Active	Passive	Active	Passive
Pres.	accipiunt	accipiuntur	dēlēmus	dēlēmur
Imperf.	accipiēbant	accipiēbantur	dēlēbāmus	dēlēbāmur
Fut.	accipient	accipientur	dēlēbimus	dēlēbimur
Perf.	accēpērunt	acceptī sunt	dēlēvimus	dēlētī sumus
Pluperf.	accēperant	acceptī erant	dēlēverāmus	dēlētī erāmus
Fut. Perf.	accēperint	acceptī erunt	dēlēverimus	dēlētī erimus

vincō vincere vīcī victum

	Active	Passive
Pres.	vincit	vincitur
Imperf.	vincēbat	vincēbātur
Fut.	vincet	vincētur
Perf.	vīcit	victus est
Pluperf.	vīcerat	victus erat
Fut. Perf	vīcerit	victus erit

B. 1. Saxa ā puerīs iaciuntur. 2. Legiō ab imperātōre remittētur. 3. Cōpia
aquae ā puellā portābātur. 4. Id oppidum ā nōbīs oppugnābitur. 5. Gallī
ā Rōmānīs repulsī sunt.

C. 1. Mox praemia vōbīs omnibus dabuntur. 2. Propter fugam exercitūs
suī Etrūscī magnopere territī sunt (terrēbantur). 3. Prīmā lūce sinistrum
cornū trāns flūmen mittēbātur. 4. Castra ā legiōne in mediā silvā pōnentur.

242 Ask the students to explain the meaning of the italicized words: a
blood *donor, annihilation* of the human race, *delete* the punctuation, *indel-
ible* ink, an *instructor,* an insect *repellent,* a *repulsive* manner. Then ask them
to give other derivatives for some of the words found in this vocabulary and
to use them in sentences.

Ask for the English proverb suggested by **Post proelium, praemium.**

References: For the Roman house, see Becker, pp. 231-280 (household utensils), pp. 283-314; Johnston, pp. 72-103; Showerman, *Rome and the Romans,* pp. 76-88; Treble and King, pp. 30-43; for Pompeii, see Maiuri; Pliny, *Letters,* VI, 16 and 20.

LESSON 34

Motto

The quotation is part of a poem in which Juvenal attacks the wickedness of women with biting sarcasm. The writer paid the penalty for his sarcasm when he was banished for ridiculing an actor, the favorite of the Emperor Domitian.

Note **ipsōs** used to intensify **custōdēs;** also note **quis,** the subject of the question.

244 The Exploits of Leonidas

Father. Have you heard of the deeds of brave Leonidas?

Son. No, I haven't. Who was Leonidas?

Father. King of the Spartans.

Son. Who were the Spartans?

Father. A brave people of ancient Greece.

Son. What were Leonidas' exploits?

Father. Once, Xerxes, king of the Persians . . . you've heard about the Persians, haven't you?

Son. Yes.

Father. When Xerxes led a huge army against (*lit.* into) Greece, he conquered a large part of the country and was marching toward the center of Greece. At that time the Spartans had two kings. Which king did they send against the Persians?

Son. Leonidas?

Father. Yes. They sent Leonidas.

Son. How large an army did Leonidas have, how many soldiers?

Father. He had a small army and few troops. With the small army he marched to a narrow pass, where he stationed his troops very carefully (*lit.* with great care).

Son. Did the Persians come to the pass too?

Father. First, Xerxes sent a messenger.

Son. What did he say?

Father. In a loud voice he said, "Lay down your arms and be friends with (*lit.* friendly to) the Persians."

Son. What did Leonidas reply?

Father. "Come and get them." Then the messenger said, "You won't be able to see a thing (*lit.* you will see nothing), because of the number of spears and arrows with which we shall bombard you (*lit.* of our spears and arrows)." "(Then) we will fight in the shade," he answered. Xerxes, angered (at this), decided to lead picked fighting men against the Greeks. But he kept the soldiers back for four days; on the fifth, he made his attack.

Son. Whose troops were braver?

Father. Those (*lit.* the troops) of Leonidas. That day the Persians did not defeat the Greeks. They did not defeat them the following day. Then the Persian troops made an attack on the Greeks from the rear.

Son. How could they attack from behind? How (*lit.* by what path) did they cross the mountain?

Father. A Greek traitor showed them the way. At daybreak the Greeks were surrounded both in the front and in the rear. They stood off the enemy's attacks bravely, but Leonidas, their brave leader, was killed. All the Greeks too were killed, to the last man.

References: Herodotus, VII, 207-228; Pausanias, IV, 35, 9; X, 19-22.

Respondē Latīnē:

1. Leōnidās erat rēx Lacedaemoniōrum. 2. Erant (*They were*) fortis populus Graeciae antīquae. 3. Eō tempore duōs rēgēs habuērunt. 4. Leōnidam contrā Persās mīsērunt. 5. "Dēpōnite arma," inquit, "et este amīcī Persīs." 6. "Venī," respondit Leōnidās, "et ea cape." 7. Mīlitēs dēlēctōs contrā Graecōs dūcere cōnstituit. 8. Quattuor diēs mīlitēs retinēbat. Quīntō diē impetum fēcit. 9. Cōpiae Leōnidae erant fortiōrēs. 10. Prōditor Graecus eīs viam mōnstrāvit.

245 It would be worthwhile to invent short drill sentences which will emphasize the difference in the use of the interrogative pronoun and the interrogative adjective. These sentences should include the word *what* in both its English uses, as (1) a pronoun and as (2) an adjective: (1) *What* did you see? (2) *What girl* did you see? (1) *What* did she give you? (2) *What book* did she give you?

247 If the students have not already learned the interrogative adjectives, adverbs, and adverbial phrases given here, it would be well for them to do so now.

248 EXERCISES

A. 1. Whom do you obey? 2. To whom are the footsoldiers being sent? 3. By what road did you come to Rome? 4. Which sister do you love? 5. What sister were you calling? 6. For what reasons (Why) were they unfriendly to us? 7. How many sailors are in the Roman fleet? 8. Where had the camp been pitched? 9. When will the Persians come to Greece?

B. 1. Quō 2. Unde 3. Quae 4. Quibuscum 5. Quōmodo 6. Quanta
7. Cui 8. Ad quōs 9. Cuius 10. Quō in oppidō

C. 1. Quam in prōvinciam senātus equitēs (equitātum) mīsit? 2. Quōmodo viātor dēfessus ad sinistram rīpam (flūminis) pervēnit? 3. Quantam fāmam habet imperātor cōpiārum vestrārum? 4. Quot nāvēs sunt in illō magnō lacū? 5. Quibuscum pugnābant frātrēs? 6. Quae oppida ā vōbīs capta erant? 7. Cuius currus illīs adulēscentibus audācibus trāditur? 8. Quibus ignōvit? Quōs pūnīvit?

SUPPLEMENTARY EXERCISES

A. 1. Quantus. How large an army is making an attack upon us from the rear? 2. Ad quōs. To whom are reinforcements being sent? 3. Ā quibus. By whom has our citadel been surrounded? 4. Nōnne est. Isn't this officer's wound serious? 5. Cui. For whom is this plan dangerous?

B. 1. Utra legiō posterō diē ad angustiās pervēnit? 2. Quam in prōvinciam mīsit senātus equitātum (equitēs)? 3. Cūr es trīstis (maestus) hōc diē pulchrō? 4. Quā dē causā dēstitērunt bellō (pugnā) ā dextrā? 5. Quot equī nigrī ā campō dūcuntur? 6. Num sunt multae nāvēs in hōc lacū? 7. Ubi errābātis prīmā lūce? 8. Cuius frāter erat tēcum in fīnibus hostium?

LESSON 35

Motto

The author of these lines, Horace (65-8 B.C.), is the Roman poet probably most frequently quoted in English.

Explain that **comae** means *hair*. Call attention to the poet's use of personification to highlight the description of the scene.

251 THE LEGENDARY HISTORY OF ROME

References: Livy, I; Vergil, *Aeneid;* Bulfinch, *Bulfinch's Mythology,* pp. 207-230; Gayley, pp. 346-372; Guerber, pp. 360-377; Hamilton, *Mythology,* pp. 319-342; Herzberg, pp. 320-335.

Aeneas and Iulus (Part 1)

The city of Troy was under constant siege (*lit.* was being besieged) by the Greeks for ten years; but in the tenth year of the siege, the city was captured and set afire. A noble and brave Trojan hero named Aeneas, son of the goddess Venus, built ships and prepared to leave his fatherland. He had saved his father and his son and also his household gods from the flames; but his wife, Creusa, who had strayed from the path as she fled, perished.

For as they were leaving the city, Aeneas said (these words) to her: "Do not follow me closely (*lit.* except at a distance); the enemy are everywhere and they will see us (if we are) all together. But if we go one by one, we shall all, I hope, escape." Creusa, however, lost the way and was never again seen by poor Aeneas, even though he returned to the city at great risk.

And so he boarded ship with many Trojans, as his mother Venus had advised him. He crossed over many seas to many lands; always he kept searching for the new fatherland that the Fates had promised. But his ships were wrecked in a great storm on the African coast; nevertheless, with the help of the queen of Carthage, Aeneas began to rebuild them. The queen named Dido fell in love with the handsome Trojan; she wanted to keep him with her. But Aeneas, commanded by the gods, left Carthage. The Trojans (once) again boarded ship and after many days, although they were heading for Italy, they arrived at the island of Sicily.

Respondē Latīnē:

1. Decem annōs urbs Trōia obsidēbātur. 2. Annō obsidiōnis decimō urbs capta incēnsa est. 3. Aenēās erat vir Trōiānus, nōbilis et fortis. 4. Patrem fīliumque Aenēās servāverat. 5. Creüsa tamen viam āmīsit. 6. "Nōlī mē sequī nisi longō spatiō"; inquit Aenēās, "hostēs ubīque sunt et nōs omnēs simul cōnspicient." 7. Aenēās in urbem magnō cum perīculō rediit. 8. Per multa maria in multās terrās trānsiit. 9. Novam patriam quam fāta prōmīserant quaerēbat. 10. Nāvēs in lītus Āfricae frāctae sunt.

252 Notice that the passive of the simple verb **eō** is found only in the impersonal form **ītur, ībātur, itum est.** Compounds with transitive force are conjugated regularly; for example, **praetereor,** *I am passed over.*

The teacher will also recall that the passive infinitive **irī** combines with the supine of a verb to form the future infinitive passive; for example, **cōnspectum irī, frāctum irī.**

253   EXERCISES

A. 1. They will go. 2. They are going. 3. They went across. 4. We had gone away. 5. He was going forth. 6. Will you go? 7. He crosses over. 8. We shall return. 9. Don't go.

B. 1. Ībam, 2. Inībis. 3. Rediistis. 4. Abierāmus. 5. Adībant. 6. Nōlīte trānsīre. 7. Ī. 8. Perībit. 9. Exeunt. 10. Redierit.

C. 1. adīmus 2. exierant 3. trānsībunt 4. inībat 5. periērunt 6. Abīre 7. inīre 8. exeunt 9. abībant 10. rediit

D. 1. They could not go by that road (route) because they were afraid of an ambush. 2. Since the Greeks are ready for war, they are crossing over the sea in (their) ships. 3. For what reasons (Why) did the noble and brave hero cross the dangerous sea? 4. When (After) peace has been made (established), our leader will go from Gaul into the province with his cavalry. 5. He left the village in early summer and was never seen again. 6. Although the Trojans were seeking (heading for) Italy, they reached the island of Sicily. 7. The ships were wrecked in (by) a violent storm on the coast of Africa; many (of them) were lost, few were saved. 8. Catching sight of many buildings from shore, the sailors decided to head for the city. 9. Have you heard about the exploits of this famous young man? 10. While the Trojans were rebuilding their ships, Dido fell in love with Aeneas.

E. 1. Creüsa, dum ab urbe abit, viā āmissā, periit. 2. Trōiānī, simul atque ex urbe exiērunt, nāvēs (-īs) aedificāvērunt, nam ibi manēre nōn poterant. 3. Postquam ex patriā exiit (Patriā relictā), nāvigāvit ad Siciliam ubi multōs diēs mānsit. 4. Dum Trōiānī mare trānseunt, magna tempestās nāvēs (-īs) in lītus Āfricae frēgit. 5. Cum Aenēās ad lītus redierit, reficiet nāvēs (-īs) tempestāte frāctās. 6. Mox inībimus (in) terram nōbīs ā deīs datam. 7. Flammīs circumventī, ex aedificiō exīre nōn potuērunt. 8. Inter duās aciēs parvum spatium relictum erat. 9. Sī flammās cōnspēxeris (-tis), ascende (ascendite) statim nāvem; nōlī (-te) in urbem rūrsus inīre (in urbem redīre). 10. Perībuntne, urbe expugnātā (sī urbs expugnāta erit), mulierēs līberīque?

SUPPLEMENTARY EXERCISE

	trānseō, trānsīre, trānsiī, trānsitum	redeō, redīre, rediī, reditum
Pres.	trānseunt	redit
Imperf.	trānsībant	redībat
Fut.	trānsībunt	redībit
Perf.	trānsiērunt	rediit
Pluperf.	trānsierant	redierat
Fut. Perf.	trānsierint	redierit

254 Note that **nāvem cōnscendere** is often used in place of **nāvem ascendere**.

Ask the class to explain the meaning of the italicized words in these sentences by relating them to words in the vocabularies of Lessons 34 and 35:

1. He delivered an *inflammatory* speech. 2. In a heavy scrimmage he suffered a bad *fracture*. 3. Both brothers were decorated for *conspicuous* gallantry. 4. Do not *infringe* upon the rights of others. 5. Some people are enthusiastic about collecting *antiques*. 6. The name of Churchill will be gratefully remembered by *posterity*. 7. The china was *fragile* and I was not surprised to find a *fragment* on the floor. 8. You will never make the team if you spend so much time in the college *refectory*. 9. The stage direction at this point should be *exeunt omnes*.

LESSON 36

Motto

Show how the English word *equanimity* (**aequanimitās**) develops from the phrase **aequō animō.**

255   Aeneas and Iulus (Part 2)

When the Sicilian king heard of the arrival of the Trojans, he received Aeneas and his comrades kindly. Aeneas remained in Sicily for a long time because many of his people were sick and bodily tired. Finally, when the time was ripe, he sailed to Italy with the strong and brave; and because they had arrived safely at the pleasant shore of the promised land, they were all cheered (*lit.* happy in spirit) and gave thanks to the gods. They had completed all of their long journey and wished to board ship never again.

As soon as the Trojans reached shore, Aeneas said, "For seven years we have all wandered all over the seas (*lit.* over all seas). We have often been in great danger (but) finally we have found Italy. Here is our home; this is our native land; we shall pitch camp near the river bank."

The following day, Aeneas sent ten envoys to the king of Latium, named Latinus, who had learned of the arrival of the Trojans through a messenger. Aeneas said, "Give these gifts to the king and endeavor to obtain peace from him."

When they reached Latinus, once of the envoys said, "O king, we are Trojans. Our chieftain Aeneas has sent us to you. We shall be your friends. Do not drive us out. We hope for peace. Establish peace and friendship with us."

Respondē Latīnē:

1. Aenēān et sociōs eius benignē recēpit.   2. Quod multī suōrum aegrī et dēfessī corpore erant, Aenēās diū manēbat.   3. Quod ad grātum lītus terrae prōmissae incolumēs pervēnerant, omnēs laetī erant.   4. Deīs grātiās Trōiānī ēgērunt.   5. Septem annōs Trōiānī errāvērunt.   6. "Hīc est domus", inquit Aenēās; "haec patria est."   7. Aenēās decem lēgātōs ad rēgem Latiī mīsit. 8. Per nūntium Latīnus dē adventū Trōiānōrum cognōverat.   9. "Date," inquit Aenēās, "haec dōna rēgī et pācem ab eō petite."   10. Ūnus ex lēgātīs pācem et amīcitiam petīvit.

256 Students frequently have difficulty in distinguishing between ablative of *means, manner,* and *respect.* It is comforting for the teacher to realize that even grammarians do not agree about these categories, and to remember that the Romans themselves made no such distinctions.

It may be helpful to consider the *ablative of respect* as giving the point of view from which a thing is treated and therefore akin to the *ablative of source.* Such expressions as **ex lēge,** *according to law,* and **ex pactō,** *according to agreement,* seem to bear this out. (See Gildersleeve and Lodge, Section 397.) However, both the *ablative of respect* and the *ablative of manner* may be considered as extensions of the *ablative of instrument.*

259   EXERCISES

A. 1. Everyone loves peace. 2. Many hope for peace. 3. Few desire war.
4. He increased his property (He added to his possessions). 5. Aeneas loved his people and the queen loved her subjects. 6. He sees everyone; he sees everything. 7. We can't all do everything. 8. Fortune aids the brave.
9. The whole apple is rotten. 10. All (of) these apples are bad.

B. 1. The girls will leave with the boys; they will depart quickly. 2. There was a sword with the arrows; you will be injured by arrows. 3. He fights very courageously (with great courage); he surpasses his brother in courage. 4. This man has a lame foot (*lit.* is lame in his foot); that one walks fast (*lit.* with swift foot). 5. They are not equal to us in hope; we shall begin battle with high hope.

C. 1. in summō colle 2. ad īmum collem 3. mediō in agrō 4. per mediās silvās (per mediam silvam) 5. nōs omnēs (-īs) 6. vōbīs omnibus 7. reliquās cōpiās 8. Reliquae cōpiae 9. tōtam Galliam 10. In tōtā Galliā

D. 1. Our state excels in population (*lit.* in large number of men). 2. They were equal to us neither in number nor in speed. 3. He was captured by my men on the river bank. 4. Although our men were sick, they did not remain there. 5. We will not hand over our belongings. 6. When they finish all the long trip, they will remain in the middle of the island. 7. Establish friendship with us and stay here. 8. Because of a scarcity (lack) of all things (everything), we cannot remain here. 9. Both the good and the bad asked for the rewards (that were) due (them).

E. 1. Malī bonōs nōn amant. 2. In summō colle sunt validae mūnītiōnēs.
3. Aegrī dēfessīque in castrīs relinquentur. 4. Post longum iter omnēs Trōiānī erant dēfessī et animō et corpore. 5. Postquam proelium fēcērunt (Proeliō factō), nostrī deīs grātiās ēgērunt quod erant incolumēs. 6. Tempore idoneō omnēs ad oppidum venient; omnia vidēbunt. 7. In īmō marī sunt multae nāvēs frāctae. 8. Dux fortis cum suīs in perīculō manet. 9. Sī nōbīscum amīcitiam cōnfīrmāverint, omnibus parcēmus. 10. Prīmus nōbīscum amīcitiam cōnfīrmāvit.

SUPPLEMENTARY EXERCISE

1. in īmō lacū. 2. reliquī nūntiī (reliquōs nūntiōs) 3. prīmō vēre 4. dē summō monte 5. per tōtam Italiam 6. trāns medium campum 7. ā nōbīs omnibus 8. prō omnibus

rapidus, -a, -um, *tearing, seizing, swift*   Eng. word, rapid
timidus, -a, -um *fearful, timid*   Eng. word, timid

LESSON 37

Motto

Comment on the poetical effect of the repetition of **mīlle . . . . centum** in each line of the poem.

262   Aeneas and Iulus (Part 3)

Latinus received the ten Trojans kindly and wished to give his daughter Lavinia in marriage to Aeneas; but Turnus, an Italian hero to whom he had previously promised her, in a rage (*lit.* greatly angered) waged war against Latinus and Aeneas with three hundred soldiers. And so two hundred Latins and a hundred Trojans were killed. Aeneas himself was wounded by an arrow. Soon, however, healed by his mother Venus, he kissed his small son Iulus and said, "Learn courage from me, child, good luck from others. Today I shall defend you; but when you are a man, remember your own people and your father Aeneas!" Then Aeneas fought in single combat with Turnus for a long time and killed him.

Afterward, he married Lavinia, and, after the death of Latinus, became king of Latium. He built a town (which was) three miles from the sea, which he called Lavinium from (after) the name of his wife. After Aeneas' death, his son Iulus ruled. He founded a city, which he called Alba Longa because it was a long town and had white walls. After him eleven kings ruled in succession over a period of 300 years.

Rhea Silvia, descended from this royal house, is said to have been the mother of Romulus and Remus, the founders of the city of Rome.

NOTE: See the map p. 172 of the text and locate the places mentioned in this story.

Respondē Latīnē:

1. Latīnus fīliam Lāvīniam in mātrimōnium Aenēae dare volēbat. 2. Turnus bellum contrā Latīnum et Aenēān gessit. 3. Ducentī Latīnī et centum Trōiānī interfectī sunt. 4. Aenēās ipse sagittā vulnerātus est. 5. "Disce, puer," inquit, "virtūtem ex mē, fortūnam ex aliīs." 6. Aenēās cum Turnō, sōlus cum sōlō, diū pugnāvit. 7. Post mortem Latīnī Aenēās rēx factus est. 8. Oppidum Lāvīnium appellāvit. 9. Tria mīlia passuum ā marī aberat. 10. Urbem Albam Longam appellāvit quod et oppidum erat longum et mūrōs habēbat albōs. 11. Rēgēs per trecentōs annōs rēgnāvērunt.

263 Emphasize the spelling changes which occur in compounding numbers; **septem** + **decem** = **septendecim,** with e weakening to i which is a common change and **m** changing to **n** before **d** (*cf.* **eundem, eōrundem**).

268   EXERCISES

A. 1. 11 missiles; 15 teachers 2. with 18 sailors; with 22 sailors 3. of 300 horses; of 3 horses; of 33 horses 4. in 102 cities; in 22 cities 5. with 3 young men; with 300 young men 6. to 2 soldiers; to 2,000 soldiers; to 200 soldiers 7. a wall 7 feet high; a rampart 16 feet long 8. a river 200 feet wide; a mountain 2,000 feet high 9. The city is a mile away; the city is 3 miles away. 10. The enemy is 2 miles away; the enemy was 12 miles distant.

B. 1. sagitta quattuor pedēs longa 2. mūrus trēs pedēs altus 3. flūmen decem passūs lātum 4. fossa octō pedēs alta 5. Duodecim passūs ambulāvit. 6. Mīlle passūs ambulābat.

C. 1. mīlle ōscula 2. decem mīlia captīvōrum 3. tria mīlia animālium 4. mīlle passūs 5. duo mīlia passuum

D. 1. duōbus mīlibus mīlitum 2. Tria mīlia cīvium 3. septem mīlia passuum 4. sex mīlia passuum longus 5. novem mīlia passuum 6. multa mīlia mīlitum fortium 7. mīlle equitēs 8. mīlle passūs 9. tria mīlia passuum 10. centum mīlia passuum

NOTE: A verb in the perfect system passive (sentence 2) may agree in gender either with **mīlia** or with the word dependent on **mīlia;** for example, **tria mīlia mīlitum capta** *or* **captī sunt.**

E. 1. Yesterday our leader, warned about the new battle, drew up his battle line. 2. Today the citadel is being surrounded by the enemy; tomorrow it will be besieged. 3. An army has 2 wings, a right and a left. 4. The army had been in Gaul; it had fought with the Gauls very courageously. 5. After many fierce battles the soldiers were exhausted and were taken back 20 miles to camp. 6. In the fierce battles 300 soldiers had been killed; 200, wounded. 7. Good children are mindful of their parents. 8. One thousand soldiers, weary and sick, were left there.

F. 1. Exercitus Rōmānus duo còrnua habēbat, sinistrum et dextrum. 2. In exercitū saepe erant decem legiōnēs. 3. In legiōnibus erant multa mīlia mīlitum. 4. Exercitus in Galliā multa et ācria proelia fēcerat et tria mīlia Gallōrum interfēcerat. 5. Ducentī mīlitēs Rōmānī interfectī, trecentī vulnerātī erant. 6. Ante proelium equitēs quattuor mīlia passuum per mediam silvam contenderant. 7. Ibi, signō datō, Rōmānī cum Gallīs proelium commīsērunt. 8. Omnēs peditēs fortiter (magnā virtūte) pugnāvērunt sed mox victī sunt. 9. Trecentī Gallī captī interfectī sunt. 10. Post proelium Rōmānī rediērunt ad castra sua quae octō mīlia passuum ab oppidō aberant.

Ask the students to think of as many English words as possible related to these Latin words: **grātia, animus, validus, pēs, albus, centum, mīlle.** Compile a list of the words suggested.

Ask for an explanation of the phrase *in absentia.*

REVIEW LESSON SIX

II. A. Cardinal numbers:

1—ūnus, -a, -um	6—sex	11—ūndecim	16—sēdecim
2—duo, -ae, -o	7—septem	12—duodecim	17—septendecim
3—trēs, tria	8—octō	13—tredecim	18—duodēvīgintī
4—quattuor	9—novem	14—quattuordecim	19—ūndēvīgintī
5—quīnque	10—decem	15—quīndecim	20—vīgintī

Ordinal numbers:

prīmus, -a, -um	sextus, -a, -um
secundus, -a, -um	septimus, -a, -um
tertius, -a, -um	octāvus, -a, -um
quārtus, -a, -um	nōnus, -a, -um
quīntus, -a, -um	decimus, -a, -um

B.   **quis, quid**

	Singular		Plural		
	M. and F.	N.	M.	F.	N.
Nom.	quis	quid	quī	quae	quae
Gen.	cuius	cuius	quōrum	quārum	quōrum
Dat.	cui	cui	quibus	quibus	quibus
Acc.	quem	quid	quōs	quās	quae
Abl.	quō	quō	quibus	quibus	quibus

quī, quae, quod

	M.	F.	N.	M.	F.	N.
Nom.	quī	quae	quod	quī	quae	quae
Gen.	cuius	cuius	cuius	quōrum	quārum	quōrum
Dat.	cui	cui	cui	quibus	quibus	quibus
Acc.	quem	quam	quod	quōs	quās	quae
Abl.	quō	quā	quō	quibus	quibus	quibus

C.   dēleō, dēlēre, dēlēvī, dēlētum   repellō, repellere, reppulī, repulsum
Pres. A.   dēlet   repellimus
Pres. P.   dēlētur   repellimur

Imp. A.	dēlēbat		repellēbāmus
Imp. P.	dēlēbātur		repellēbāmur
Fut. A.	dēlēbit		repellēmus
Fut. P.	dēlēbitur		repellēmur
Perf. A.	dēlēvit		reppulimus
Perf. P.	dēlētus est		repulsī sumus
Pluperf. A.	dēlēverat		reppulerāmus
Pluperf. P.	dēlētus erat		repulsī erāmus
Fut. Perf. A.	dēlēverit		reppulerimus
Fut. Perf. P.	dēlētus erit		repulsī erimus

D. eō, īre, iī, itum

Pres.	eō	*Fut.*	ībō	*Pluperf.*	ieram
Imperf.	ībam	*Perf.*	iī	*Fut. Perf.*	ierō

E. 1. Quae proelia 2. ūnī magistrō sapientī 3. omnibus nōbīs 4. summum montem 5. trium lēgātōrum potentium 6. duābus rēgīnīs nōbilibus 7. aberunt

III. A. 1. (On) that day the infantry marched 15 miles; their camp was pitched halfway up the mountain. 2. While this was going on (happening) in the village, many soldiers were (being) wounded close to shore and a few were (being) killed. 3. Do not entrust everything to that chieftain alone; tomorrow he will be many miles away and you will be able to return home. 4. The general delivered a speech to his men: "Our towns will be surrounded and our children (will be) made slaves unless you defend our country." 5. How large was the enemy's army? How many officers were leaving with the soldiers? What weapons were they carrying? Why were they withdrawing? 6. The camp is protected by a wall (rampart) eight feet high and a trench twelve feet wide; still we shall storm it tomorrow. 7. Aeneas' father was an old man, weary and sick. Although he wanted to remain in his homeland, he boarded ship with his son and crossed (the sea) to many lands. Weren't the Trojans courageous men? 8. As soon as the fires were seen by the inhabitants of the villages, frightened they all hurried ashore. Few escaped; many perished.

B. 1. Quōrum 2. sapientiā 3. multās rēs (multa) 4. servōrum; ducentī 5. duodēvīgintī mīlia passuum 6. summum montem 7. Ad quōs 8. īnstrūcta erit 9. it 10. Quī

IV. 1. while away or not in residence 2. tendency to put off 3. remove 4. white 5. generations to follow or descendants 6. those who give 7. soundness or forcefulness 8. relating to amount 9. constantly asking or curious 10. old age

V. A. 1. Iulus 2. Lavinia 3. Xerxes 4. Livy 5. Pompeii

B. According to tradition, Romulus and Remus, the founders of Rome, were descended through their mother from Aeneas, a hero who escaped from the burning city of Troy and eventually reached Italy; there he married a native princess.

VI. 1. The she-goats wanted the privilege of wearing beards. 2. Jupiter granted their request. 3. The males were then unhappy because the she-goats were their equals in appearance and dignity. 4. Jupiter advised them to be unconcerned until the females should match them in strength and bravery.

LESSON 38

Motto

Now that the students have met a few quotations from Vergil, the teacher might tell them something about this poet and his work.

References: Duff, pp. 455-482; Glover; Hadas, *A History of Latin Literature,* pp. 140-164; Hamilton, *The Roman Way,* pp. 192-242; Mackail; Prescott; Sellar, pp. 247-411.

270   The Roman State

Seven kings in succession ruled the Roman people; the last of them was called Tarquin the Proud. After he was driven out because of a wrong committed by his son Sextus against Lucretia, a married woman of Rome, the Romans for many reasons refused to obey kings (were unwilling to submit to the rule of kings). Therefore they elected two consuls, who held rule for just a year. The Roman consuls led the armies of citizens (*lit.* armed citizens) to war and also gave laws in the city to all.

But the citizens always preferred to have consuls who were descended from those families whose fathers as senators had previously given advice to the kings and who now (*lit.* then) were advising the consuls. These were called patricians; as a rule they had a great deal of land and many slaves; they had no concern for the rest of the citizens.

They called the rest the common people; among these were the sailors, the merchants, and many others. Among this group, the common people, were some who had been slaves of the patricians and owed them services. The latter were the clients; the former, patrons. However, for very many of the common people who had no patrons, life was miserable. Finally the common people decided to leave Rome and to establish their own state a few miles from the city.

After the common people left the city, two tribunes were elected; they gave help to the commoners and defended them from injustices at the hands of the patricians.

NOTE: **Iam,** *now, already,* may be used in reference to any time; **nunc** means definitely *now, in the immediate present;* **tum,** *then,* may be used of any time. **Tunc** is a stronger form of **tum.**

Respondē Latīnē:

1. Post mortem Rōmulī populum Rōmānum sex rēgēs deinceps rēxērunt.
2. Ob iniūriam ā fīliō Sextō in Lucrētiam factam expulsus est. 3. Duōs cōnsulēs creāvērunt quī imperium annum sōlum habēbant. 4. Cōnsulēs quī ex familiīs nātī erant quōrum patrēs senātōrēs cōnsilium dederant habēre mālēbant. 5. Hī patriciī appellābantur. 6. Cēterōs plēbem appellābant.
7. Ex hāc plēbe nōnnūllī quī servī patriciōrum fuerant officiaque eīs dēbēbant clientēs erant. 8. Quod vīta misera erat, plēbs Rōmā exīre cōnstituit.
9. Pauca mīlia passuum ab urbe cīvitātem suam condere cōnstituit. 10. Plēbī auxilium dabant eamque ab iniūriīs patriciōrum dēfendēbant.

271 Note that **is, eī** are often omitted as in the motto, where **Fēlīx quī** stands for **Fēlīx est is quī.**

272   EXERCISES

A. 1. The legion that is in the camp is the tenth. 2. The legion, part of which is in the city, is the seventh. 3. The legion to which new arms have been given is the fifth. 4. The legion which he will take into Britain is the sixth. 5. The legion with which he came to Germany is the third. 6. The camp that is being set up will be very large. 7. The camp of which the wall is high has a wide trench. 8. The camp which the enemy is approaching will be taken. 9. The camp which they pitched is near the Tiber. 10. The camp in which we are staying soon will be moved. 11. The village that was set on fire was small. 12. The village, part of which they burned, was large. 13. The village that we shall burn is small. 14. The Gauls who have been captured will be led into slavery. 15. The Gauls whose boys have been captured are sad. 16. The Gauls to whom he gave rewards are happy. 17. The Gauls whom he had ordered to leave left. 18. The Gauls without whom we cannot capture these towns are fierce soldiers. 19. The Gauls with whom we have established friendship once were hostile to us.
20. The Gauls to whom reinforcements have been sent are fighting bravely.

B. 1. quae 2. quae 3. quās 4. quam 5. cuius 6. quōrum 7. cui
8. quibus 9. quō 10. quibus 11. quōcum 12. quibuscum 13. quācum
14. quod 15. quae 16. ā quō 17. ā quibus 18. quī 19. quī 20. quem

C. 1. Aid is being sought from the two tribunes by all the clients who live in Rome. 2. Patricians have many slaves over whom they rule. 3. The father of this family is Lucius, whom the Roman people (have) elected consul.

4. Clients owed services to the Roman patricians. 5. Cornelius is the patron of these clients whose farms are near the city. 6. Give me those things that (what) you have in your hand. 7. The life of armed men by whom our country is defended is often short. 8. Give everything that you have to Marcus, who recently was elected consul. 9. Those who are elected consuls will lead an army of citizens (*lit.* armed citizens) to war. 10. In this state, which is ruled by patricians, the plebeians are wretched.

D. 1. Urbēs nostrae vāstantur ab hīs Rōmānīs, quī in fīnēs (-īs) nostrōs vēnērunt. 2. Clientēs, quōrum multī nūllam pecūniam habent, ā cēterīs cīvibus auxilium petent. 3. Lacus ad quem eunt est altus. 4. Paucī patriciī in eā parte urbis quae est proxima Forō habitant. 5. Plēbs auxilium petet ā tribūnīs quī nūper creātī sunt. 6. Patriciī quibus clientēs officia dēbēbant erant nōbilēs. 7. Nāvis quā ad Siciliam nāvigāvimus est pars classis Rōmānae. 8. Ex hīs virīs quōs vidēs aliī sunt mercātōrēs, aliī nautae. 9. (Eī) quī rēgī cōnsilium dant bonum cōnsilium dare dēbent. 10. Ob iniūriam factam (quae facta erat), cīvēs rēgem Rōmā expulērunt.

NOTE: In sentence 8 of Exercise D, notice the use of **ex** and the ablative for *some of these men* (refer to line 16 of Section 270).

273   Ask the students to show the meaning of the italicized words by relating them to the Latin words with which they are associated: 1. This artist does work that is highly *creative*. 2. The lawyers had a large *clientele*. 3. I hope you will *patronize* your school activities. 4. A *tribunal* has been appointed to decide the case. 5. "*Familiarity* breeds contempt." 6. The Mayor wore his *regalia* of *office*.

LESSON 39

Motto

This motto, taken from an opening line of Ode XVI of Book I by Horace, may be used both to introduce the comparative **pulchrior** and to illustrate the *ablative of comparison*. There is no clue to the identity of **fīlia pulchrior**.

275   Xerxes Decides to Conquer Greece

Once in a large city of Persia, more beautiful than the other cities of the world, lived a king named Xerxes. He was angry with the Greeks who lived in Greece and on the islands because in many wars auxiliary forces had been sent from there to the Persians' enemies.

And so Xerxes decided to conquer Greece and the islands. After he had gathered ships and soldiers from all around, he got ready to sail across the sea. Calling the soldiers and sailors together, he said, "It will be easy to conquer the Greeks. Although they are brave and daring, the Greeks are not braver or more daring than you. For, of all soldiers, you are the bravest and boldest; you have won many victories. Where have you seen a more powerful king, a more famous people, or a fiercer army? In a short time you will be able to gain victory again."

The Persians decided first to conquer the islands which are near Greece. It was easy to approach some islands because the shore was level and the hills overlooking the sea were rather low(lying); it was difficult to approach others because the islands were high and had very high mountains. But on the islands were a few fortified cities.

Nevertheless, because the inhabitants of the islands were always free men of free states (free men and [citizens] of free states), they did not wish to submit to (*lit.* obey) Persian rule.

Reference: Herodotus, VII, 8

Respondē Latīnē:

1. Xerxēs in magnā urbe Persidis habitābat. 2. Is erat īrātus Graecīs quī in Graeciā īnsulīsque habitābant. 3. Multīs bellīs auxilia ad hostēs Persārum ab īnsulīs missa erant. 4. Xerxēs Graeciam īnsulāsque vincere cōnstituit. 5. "Graecōs superāre," inquit, "erit facile." 6. Persae omnium mīlitum fortissimī et audācissimī sunt. 7. Aliīs īnsulīs appropinquāre facile erat quod lītus erat aequum; aliīs appropinquāre difficile erat quod īnsulae erant altae et montēs altissimōs habēbant. 8. Quod semper līberī erant līberārumque cīvitātum imperiō Persicō pārēre nōlēbant.

282 EXERCISES

A. 1. A brave leader; a braver, rather brave, too brave, somewhat brave leader; a very brave leader, the bravest leader. 2. Brave boys; more courageous, somewhat, too, rather brave boys; very, most courageous boys. 3. A short time; a shorter, rather, somewhat, too short time; the shortest, very short time. 4. In the deep sea; in the too, rather, somewhat deep, deeper sea; in the deepest, very deep sea. 5. Of this happy girl; of this rather, too, somewhat happy, happier girl; of this happiest, very happy girl. 6. To a longer, rather, too, somewhat, fairly long river; to a very long, extremely long, the longest river; to longer, rather, too, somewhat long rivers. 7. With very bold, the boldest soldiers; with a bolder, somewhat, rather, too bold soldier; with a very bold, the boldest soldier. 8. Within the wider, rather, too, somewhat wide rampart; within very wide, the widest ramparts; within wider, rather, too, somewhat wide ramparts.

B. 1. clārior; clārissima. That famous city; that rather famous city; that very famous city. 2. ūtilius; ūtilissimum. A useful plan; more useful advice; very useful advice. 3. amīciōrēs; amīcissimī. These friendly shepherds; these rather friendly shepherds; these very friendly shepherds. 4. graviōra; gravissima. Three serious wounds; three fairly serious wounds; three extremely severe wounds. 5. potentiōrem; potentissimum. In the presence of a powerful king; with a more powerful king; near the most powerful king. 6. audāciōrēs; audācissimōs. To daring boys; to bolder children; to very daring boys. 7. altiōre; altissimō. In the deep sea; in the rather deep sea; on the exceptionally deep sea. 8. nōbiliōribus; nōbilissimīs. With noble women; with rather noble women; with very noble women.

C. 1. I am happier than my grandfather. 2. That soldier has many very serious wounds. 3. We had traveled from this very famous state. 4. In a short time they will inform the king about the Persians' new stratagem (*lit.* plan). 5. These hills are lower than those mountains. 6. The spear was very useful for many years. 7. In early spring he led the army to the province by a rather long route. 8. Informed about the flight of these cavalrymen, the infantry again returned to their fortified camp.

D. 1. Haec turris est altior quam vāllum *or* vāllō (**without** quam). 2. Nostrī ā prīncipibus audāciōribus semper dūcentur. 3. Aestāte noctēs brevissimae, hieme longiōrēs sunt. 4. Fortissimae legiōnēs in illīs oppidīs collocābantur. 5. Vīdistisne umquam rēgem potentiōrem? 6. Ille mīles multa et gravissima vulnera habet. 7. Hoc cōnsilium nōbīs est ūtilissimum. 8. Lacūs flūminibus lātiōrēs, sed flūmina saepe longiōra quam lacūs sunt. 9. Quod tempus est brevissimum, lēgātum certiōrem statim facere dēbēmus.

SUPPLEMENTARY EXERCISES

A. 1. This braver legion; this very daring soldier; this rather useful plan. 2. These very high gates; these too powerful kings; these extremely wide rivers. 3. Into a fairly deep river; into the rather broad forest; into a very famous city. 4. In a very wide trench; on a wider rampart; on the highest citadel. 5. With braver boys; with the most noble soldiers; with happier women.

B. 1. Aqua altior; urbs clārissima; vir clārior. 2. Mīlitis fortissimī; maris lātiōris; flūminis longiōris. 3. Trāns pontem longissimum; trāns campum lātiōrem; trāns fossam altissimam. 4. Ā multīs et clārissimīs urbibus; ā portīs altiōribus; ab itinere longiōre. 5. Fortissimō adulēscentī; rēgīnae clāriōrī; nautae audācissimō.

C. 1. Who is preparing for a rather long war? 2. On the third day the travelers arrived at a fairly wide river. 3. If the consul is informed of the victory, he will send the troops back to the city. 4. As soon as the consul was informed of the more serious danger, he drew up his battle line. 5. We have no other route shorter than that one.

283 Call attention to the words **difficilis** and **humilis** and tell the students that these two adjectives do not form the superlative in the same way as **altus** and **fortis**. This statement will introduce the material of Lesson 40, Section 285.

LESSON 40

Motto

The motto may be used to introduce the work of Section 285. Attention should also be drawn to the words **difficilis** and **humilis** in the vocabulary of Lesson 39, Section 283 and to **humiliōres** in Section 282, exercise C, sentence 5. Ask for the meanings of the words *dulcet* and *placid* and for the Italian *dolce,* a direction in music.

284   Amphissus

On one of the islands was a Greek citizen, named Amphissus, who was more daring than the rest of the citizens. He gathered many young men, the fiercest soldiers, whom he had drafted (*lit.* collected) the previous year. He led his forces down from the heights to the shore by the most direct (*lit.* shortest) route. While this was happening, a large number of (*lit.* very many) enemy ships were seen. On seeing these ships, the Greeks raised a (very) loud shout.

When they had sailed up close to the shore, it was very difficult for the Persians to land, especially because the young Greeks, who were much more daring, made a very fierce attack. Soon the Persians were driven back to the ships. Then something worse happened to the Persians, for the next day several of their ships were set on fire. The rest of the ships at once left shore and did not dare attack the other islands. All the islands were free because of the very great courage of the inhabitants of one island.

The upper class (*lit.* best) citizens wanted to give Amphissus a very large sum of money. Amphissus said, "I refuse to accept money. All good men ought to defend their country. I am no braver than the other soldiers. We are all free men. We will always remain free."

Respondē Latīnē:

1. Audācior cēterīs cīvibus erat Amphissus.   2. Ā locīs superiōribus ad lītus cōpiās dūxit.   3. Superiōre annō cōpiās coēgerat.   4. Nāvibus vīsīs, Graecī clāmōrem maximum fēcērunt.   5. Quod adulēscentēs Graecī impetum ācerrimum fēcērunt, difficillimum nāvibus ēgredī erat.   6. Persae ad nāvēs repulsī sunt.   7. Complūrēs nāvēs incēnsae sunt.   8. Propter virtūtem

incolārum ūnīus īnsulae līberae erant omnēs īnsulae. 9. Optimī cīvēs Amphissō plūrimam pecūniam dare volēbant. 10. "Pecūniam accipere nōlō," inquit Amphissus. "Omnēs bonī patriam dēfendere dēbent."

285-287 It might be advantageous to take an extra day on this lesson and to have the students memorize the words and phrases of these sections. If the teacher has access to an overhead projector, the words or phrases can be flashed on a screen a few at a time. This is a convenient method of oral drill or testing.

289   **EXERCISES**

A. 1. A fierce soldier; a rather fierce soldier; the fiercest soldier. 2. An easy route; an easier journey; a very easy journey. 3. These fast horses; these swifter steeds; these very swift horses. 4. Many friends; more friends; most friends. 5. A good son; a better son; the best son. 6. Of this pretty girl; of this rather beautiful girl; of this very beautiful girl. 7. In a small camp; in a smaller camp; in a very small camp. 8. Because of a wicked master; on account of a somewhat bad master; because of a very poor teacher. 9. On the vast sea; on a larger sea; on a very vast sea. 10. Over a low hill; over a rather low hill; over the lowest hill.

B. 1. celerior; celerrima. A rather swift ship; the swiftest ship. 2. ācrius; ācerrimum. A sharper battle; a very sharp battle. 3. melior; optimus. A better boy; a very good boy. 4. minor; minimus. A smaller village; the smallest village. 5. difficilius; difficillimum. A rather hard journey; a most difficult route. 6. humiliōre; humillimō. On the lower shore; on the lowest shore. 7. maiōribus; maximīs. About more important matters; about very great things. 8. pulchriōre; pulcherrimā. With a rather beautiful woman; with a very pretty woman. 9. plūrēs; plūrimōs. To more soldiers; to very many soldiers.

C. 1. To a larger camp; into the largest camp; very many animals; more citizens. 2. With very pretty girls; more courage; the most useful books (of a very useful book); in a smaller camp. 3. On a better ship; a very illustrious city; the lowest ships; to several citizens. 4. A much better son; a woman a little more graceful (slender); across most rivers; in (on) a larger sea. 5. Last year; to higher ground; with exceptional courage; more hope.

D. 1. Multō meliōrēs puerī; optimī puerī; optimae puellae; hae domūs pulcherrimae. 2. In paulō minōrem urbem; ad complūrēs urbēs (-īs) pulcherrimās; ex (ā) maximō oppidō; ad arcem altam. 3. Per illum maximum campum; multō clāriōrī ducī; cum virīs nōbilissimīs; ad maiōra castra. 4. Cum hīs quattuor equitibus; ā mīlitibus ācriōribus; plūs aquae; plūra animālia. 5. Ad loca superiōra; proximō (posterō) diē; prīmā lūce; plūs virtūtis.

114

E. 1. My wife is pretty; she is much prettier than your wife; she is the prettiest of all wives. 2. What is better (more admirable) than courage? 3. What is better in a man than a good mind? 4. On learning of this, the king of the Persians had collected very many warships. 5. In winter the days are much shorter. 6. Our men had stood on the top of the mountain for several hours. 7. The next day he collected more grain and very many cavalry(men). 8. Britain is many miles wider than Ireland. 9. At dawn they made a very fierce attack on the largest number (force) of the enemy. 10. It is very easy to reach the bottom of the mountain.

F. 1. Mīlitēs sunt miserrimī quod pessimum imperātōrem habent. 2. Equitēs sunt celeriōrēs peditibus (quam peditēs); equī nigrī Gallōrum sunt celerrimī. 3. Erit difficilius ad īnsulam posterō (proximō) diē pervenīre. 4. Hoc cōnsilium erit ūtilius nōbīs quam vōbīs (tibi). 5. Est melius cōpiās in proximā silvā prīmā lūce collocāre. 6. Quod fīliī erant pessimī, Tarquinius Rōmā expulsus est. 7. Plūs frūmentī nōbīscum portāre nōn possumus. 8. In hōc lātissimō flūmine sunt complūrēs pontēs. 9. Germānia est lātior multīs mīlibus passuum Galliā (quam Gallia). 10. Quid est melius virtūte (quam virtūs)?

SUPPLEMENTARY EXERCISE

Positive	Comparative	Superlative
brevis, breve short	**brevior, brevius** shorter, rather short, too short	**brevissimus, -a, -um** shortest, very short
similis, simile like	**similior, similius** more like	**simillimus, -a, -um** most like
bonus, -a, -um good	**melior, melius** better	**optimus, -a, -um** best
audāx, audāx, audāx bold	**audācior, audācius** bolder	**audācissimus, -a, -um** boldest
celer, celeris, celere swift	**celerior, celerius** swifter	**celerrimus, -a, -um** swiftest

VOCABULARIES OF LESSONS 39-40

Ask the students to explain the meaning of the italicized words in sentences such as these and to suggest other related English words: 1. Do not *abbreviate* the names of cities in the composition. 2. Small class size will *accelerate* progress. 3. "*Brevity*" is the soul of wit." 4. The *clamorous* throng frightened the children. 5. Cultivate the grace of *humility*. 6. Is the infection *localized*? 7. Your order will be given *priority*. 8. The teacher will not *reiterate* the warning.

maior	major(ity)	**optimus**	optimist(ic), optimism
minor	minor(ity), minus	**pessimus**	pessimist(ic), pessimism
plūs	plus, plural(ity)	**prīmus**	prime, primer, primary, primitive
superior	superior(ity)	**proximus**	approximate(ly), proximity

LESSON 41

Motto

Note the alliteration in this phrase which can be identified as the motto of the Olympic Games.

292 Very Famous Orators

Quintus and Sextus are brothers. The latter is a small boy and the former, a foot taller than his brother. The boys' father fought fiercely and bravely in Gaul. There he was twice wounded in the feet and now limps (*lit.* walks badly). Every day the boys come to school. Quintus reads well but writes poorly. When the boys read, Quintus easily outshines Sextus. The teacher of the boys, named Crassus, is not only a great orator but also was the teacher of Cicero, a very great speaker.

Tomorrow the boys will not be in school but will visit the Forum together with their father. There they will listen to the speeches which Cicero and Hortensius, very famous Roman orators, will deliver to the people concerning the Manilian Law. Manilius has proposed a law concerning Pompey to the Roman people.

Pompey, a great leader, is especially popular with (*lit.* loved by) the Roman people because he has saved them from danger. Very often grain is carried to Rome by boat (*lit.* boats) from Sardinia, Sicily and Africa. Many pirates, very bold men who live in Cilicia, a province in (of) Asia, wander far and wide over the entire sea. They have sailed on the Mediterranean and have captured many ships. When Pompey was made general, he got ships ready as quickly as possible and fought very bravely and fiercely against the pirates. Pompey easily conquered the pirates on the sea and soon drove them to Cilicia. So, Pompey's reputation is great and all the enemies of Rome fear him.

Now Mithridates, king of Pontus, who formerly waged war with the Roman armies, is fighting again in Asia. Pompey wants to fight as soon as possible with this king who has cruelly slaughtered many Roman citizens. Tomorrow Cicero will deliver a speech to the Romans concerning the danger of war with Mithridates. He wishes Pompey to be the leader of the war with Mithridates and will speak in behalf of the Manilian Law. Manilius also wants

Pompey as leader. Hortensius will speak against the law. The boys, Quintus and Sextus, want to hear the speeches of the famous orators.

References: Cicero, *Pro Lege Manilia;* Haskell, p. 77 and pp. 143-147; Strachan-Davidson, pp. 62-63 and pp. 81-89; Wilkin, pp. 53-66. See also the map on p. 64 of the text.

294 The irregular adverbs of this section should be memorized in all three degrees.

296   EXERCISES

A. 1. To return quickly; to go back more quickly; to return very quickly. 2. To be far away; to be farther away; to be very far away. 3. To fight for a long time; to fight longer; to fight for a very long time.. 4. To conquer easily; to conquer rather easily; to conquer very easily. 5. We are walking as fast as possible; I shall leave as soon as possible; the boys are fighting as well as possible. 6. Today he can speak more freely; yesterday he could not speak freely; tomorrow, I hope, he will be able to speak very freely. 7. This girl writes well but reads very badly; her sister reads better (rather well) but writes worse (quite poorly). 8. Children ought not answer boldly (impudently); young men often answer too boldly; surely old(er) people don't answer very boldly? 9. The farmer is less brave than the sailor; the trader is the least brave (not at all brave). 10. Their wives were very much afraid; when the fields (farms) are destroyed, they will be even more afraid.

B. 1. peius; pessimē. To write rather poorly; to write very badly. 2. crūdēlius; crūdēlissimē. To kill too cruelly; to kill most ruthlessly. 3. facilius; facillimē. To conquer more easily; to conquer very easily. 4. diūtius; diūtissimē. To fight longer; to fight for a very long time. 5. sapientius; sapientissimē. To speak more wisely; to speak very wisely. 6. melius; optimē. The old man cannot see better; the old man can't see very well. 7. potentius; potentissimē. That king governs more powerfully; that king governs with very great authority. 8. Clārius; clārissimē. My brother cried out (shouted) more loudly; my brother cried out very loudly. 9. celerius; celerrimē. The troops will cross the mountains more quickly; the troops will cross the mountains very quickly. 10. lātius; lātissimē. The enemy destroyed the farms more widely; the enemy destroyed the fields far and wide.

C. 1. In lātiōre campō ācriter pugnāverant. 2. Cōpiās ad summum collem celerrimē dūxit. 3. Hodiē domī diūtius manēbimus. 4. Nostrī sociī auxilia quam saepissimē mīsērunt. 5. Haec puella pulcherrima peius scrībit. 6. Meum cōnsilium, Lūcī, est multō melius quam tuum. 7. Hic liber est nōbīs ūtilissimus, nam bene legimus. 8. Bis altissimum collem facilius ascendimus. 9. Hic ōrātor est longē optimus. 10. (Ea) est minimē laeta omnium līberōrum.

117

D. 1. At first the pirates are greatly frightened because of the reputation of Pompey. 2. So the officers had gathered as many ships as possible. 3. The slave could carry the water more easily and faster than the little boy. 4. The next day they had withstood the attack very easily. 5. This attack will be less easily held off by the pirates. 6. Meantime, while this was going on, that extremely cruel king again killed very many Roman citizens. 7. As quickly as possible they began to move the camp nearer. 8. The horsemen often leap down from their horses and fight among the footsoldiers. 9. We shall gather the largest possible number of sailors and set sail tomorrow. 10. When the pirates learn of Pompey's arrival, they will be more frightened.

E. 1. Incolae oppidī mulierēs līberōsque audācter dēfendent. 2. Puellae legunt (lēgērunt) nōn sōlum melius sed etiam celerius quam puerī. 3. In minōre oppidō diūtius manēbant. 4. Rōmānī hostēs (-īs) nōn facile superāvērunt quod illī erant audācissimī. 5. Noster imperātor prō virīs (suīs) quam prīmum pugnāre dēbet. 6. Gallī cum Rōmānīs ācerrimē et audācissimē pugnāvērunt. 7. Facillimē omnēs (-īs) impetūs equitum (equitātūs) diūtissimē sustinēbimus. 8. Ūnā cum nōbilissimō prīncipe tōtīus Galliae ierat. 9. Quam amīcissimum praesidium in maiōre arce collocābō. 10. Gallī ā Rōmānīs victī sunt quod Rōmānī ducēs fortiōrēs quam Gallī (Gallīs) habēbant.

SUPPLEMENTARY EXERCISES

A.

Positive	Comparative	Superlative
lātus, -a, -um	**lātior, lātius**	**lātissimus, -a, -um**
wide	wider, rather wide, too wide, somewhat wide	very wide, widest
gravis, grave	**gravior, gravius**	**gravissimus, -a, -um**
serious	more serious	very, most serious
bonus, -a, -um	**melior, melius**	**optimus, -a, -um**
good	better	very good, best

B.

lātē	**lātius**	**lātissimē**
widely	more widely	very widely
graviter	**gravius**	**gravissimē**
heavily	more heavily	very heavily
bene	**melius**	**optimē**
well	better	very well, best

LESSON 42

Motto

Refer again to Catullus as a great Latin lyric poet whose favorite subject was his love for his mistress.

Ask the students to translate **Iuppiter ipse** in line 2 and to notice the effect of the intensive pronoun.

References: Livy I, 57-60 and II, 23, 28 and 32-33; Allen, pp. 10-22 and pp. 29-51; Frank, pp. 21-56; Herzberg, pp. 335-345; Mommsen, pp. 15-75.

The Commission of Ten: Verginia (Virginia) (Part 1)

Because there was disagreement for many years between patricians and plebeians concerning the laws, a commission of ten men was finally elected in place of the two consuls; this board was ordered by the people to formulate new and just laws. For the consuls were consulting their own interests and those of their friends and relatives (their own class) and were not looking out for the plebeians. And so the commissioners wrote ten tables of laws. One of the commissioners, named Appius Claudius, seemed to be friendly to the commoners; therefore, he was re-elected by the people. Then he became haughty and cruel, although he had formerly been friendly to the plebeians. Because of his cruelty, they could no longer support his rule.

Finally a crime committed in the city put an end to the control of the board of ten men. For a young girl, Verginia, daughter of Lucius Verginius, had been engaged to Lucius Icilius, an ex-tribune. Appius Claudius wanted to have her for himself and, while Verginia's father was away in camp, having tried other methods in vain, he ordered his client, Marcus Claudius, to take the girl in slavery. As she was coming into the Forum, Marcus Claudis laid his hand on her. He said she was not Verginius' daughter; he addressed her as a slave and the daughter of his slave; he ordered Verginia to follow him. Then Claudius brought the girl to the judgment seat of Appius.

Lucius Icilius and Publius Numitorius, the girl's uncle, intervened. Icilius turned to Appius. "Do not act contrary to the law, Appius," he said. "The maiden is the freeborn daughter of a freeborn citizen."

Appius answered, "I shall postpone the case (*lit.* thing) till the following day. Claudius will waive his right for one day only. Moreover, unless the man who is called the girl's father is here tomorrow, the maiden will be Claudius' slave."

NOTE: The person denoted by *his* in the phrase *his client* in line 16 and by *his* in the phrase *his slave* in line 19 is clearly indicated by the word **suum** and **suae** in the Latin passage.

300 The students should learn the verbs new to them which are used with reflexive pronouns.

301 EXERCISES

A. 1. The boy will hurt himself. 2. The consul issued laws for his own (people). 3. The consul is never mindful of himself. 4. The general took many soldiers with him. 5. The inhabitants surrendered to us at once. 6. The defeated king took his own life. 7. The enemy hid in the woods.

8. He talks about himself; he talks about him. 9. He forced the Sabines to give him hostages. 10. Some hid; others surrendered.

B. 1. Sē; mē; eam. 2. Nōs; sē; sē. 3. Eōrum; suī; tuī. 4. eī; sibi; tibi (vōbīs). 5. sēcum; sēcum; nōbīscum.

C. 1. Though many have (had) been wounded, we are defending (defended) ourselves as bravely as possible. 2. After friendship was established, the inhabitants of the town joined (with) the Romans. 3. He took his family with him to Italy. 4. They killed these men (them) without reason and against the law. 5. Terrified by these events, this maidservant hid in that room. 6. If they put a stop to their wrongdoing, they will be able to join (with) us. 7. We never see ourselves as our neighbors see us. 8. The next day they moved themselves and their arms from that place. 9. We are seeking more extensive (larger) and better farms for ourselves and the common people. 10. Whom are you consulting? Whose interests were you looking out for?

D. 1. Sē armaque sua trādere coāctī sunt. 2. Cēterae cīvitātēs propter crūdēlitātem decemvirī nōbīscum sē coniungere dubitābunt. 3. Sī oppida incēnsa erunt (Oppidīs incēnsīs), in silvās sē abdent. 4. Ille rēx superbus sēcum mīlle peditēs et duo mīlia equitum habēbat. 5. Crās avunculus meus (cum) amīcīs sē iunget. 6. (Eī)quī sē laudant ab aliīs numquam laudantur. 7. Nōlī tē movēre ex hōc locō. Sī tē movēbis (mōveris), eris magnō in perīculō. 8. Habēmus nōbīscum plūs frūmentī quam vōbīscum habētis. 9. Quod vidētur esse plēbī amīcus, iterum creātus est. 10. Sibi suīsque cōnsuluit.

SUPPLEMENTARY EXERCISE

1. Numquam sē laudat. 2. Numquam sē laudant. 3. Mīlitēs sēcum dūxit. 4. Rēx sē interfēcit. 5. Sabīnōs obsidēs sibi dare coēgit. 6. Nōbīs (Nōbīscum) sē iungent. 7. Mē nōn dēdam. 8. Sē in silvās abdidērunt. 9. Dē sē dīcit. 10. Dē eā dīcit.

VOCABULARIES OF LESSONS 41-42

Ask the students to suggest as many English words as possible related to these Latin words and compile a list on the board: **lēx, bis, iūs, modus, frūstrā, iniciō.**

LESSON 43

Motto

Call attention to the use of the genitive case in the phrase **bonae voluntātis.** Mention other phrases such as *a man of great character* and *a lesson of little value.* Ask the students to suggest other similar phrases and thus anticipate the grammar of the lesson, the genitive of description.

On the same day that Appius made this reply, Verginia's friends decided to send Icilius' brother and Numitorius' son, very courageous men, (from there) to Verginius in camp. When they were told to go, they were unafraid and delivered the message as fast as they could right to her father (*lit.* to the father himself). Meanwhile Appius went home. He forbade Verginius to return to Rome. Nevertheless, this evil design was too late, because Verginius, informed of the wrong done his daughter, had at once started out for the city.

But at Rome the citizens assembled in the Forum at dawn. Then Verginius very sadly escorts his daughter there with a crowd of friends. In vain, they tried to seek freedom for Verginia. Appius, a very cruel man, refused to listen (give way, yield).

Then Verginius said, "I want to say a few words to my daughter in private." When permission was granted, he led his daughter toward the shops and there, snatching a knife from a butcher, he said, "I give you your freedom, daughter, in this, the only way I can." At the same time, he pierces the girl's breast and looking back at the judge's platform, says, "With this blood, Appius, I doom you yourself and your life to destruction."

Then all the plebeians left Rome again because they feared injustice at the hands of the decemvirs; the decemvirs were forced to give up the rule (resign). Consuls and plebeian tribunes were once more elected.

Verginius himself was elected tribune and Appius, having been thrown into prison, committed suicide.

NOTE: Point out the use of the imperfect to express the idea of continued attempts, as in line 12 (**petēbant**).

Reference: Livy, III, 44-58.

305   The English adverbs *also* and *likewise* are often the best translations for **īdem: Hannibal ad Rhodanum cum P. Cornēliō Scīpiōne proelium commīsit; cum hōc eōdem Clastidiī cōnflīxit.** *Hannibal joined battle at the Rhone with Publius Cornelius Scipio; he likewise fought with him at Clastidium* or *he fought with him at Clastidium also.*

306   Although the *ablative of description* is not discussed in Book I, it might be advisable to prepare the students for future study of this construction. The teacher could explain that the first, but only the first, of these descriptive phrases might be rendered by the ablative.

307   EXERCISES

A.   1. The consul himself (with his own lips) praised me.   2. The consul again praised himself.   3. We shall joyfully welcome the chieftain in person.   4. We gave a very lovely (handsome) gift to the girl herself.   5. On that very day the enemy retreated.

B. 1. At the same time he saw cavalry of the enemy. 2. The general of the same army was fighting very bravely. 3. The infantry of their own accord retreated to the same place. 4. For the same reason (the) grain has not been gathered. 5. We shall hurry to the province by the same route as before.

C. 1. The king of the Etruscans was a man of great cruelty (a very cruel man). 2. The citizens are building a five-foot wall. 3. These soldiers, very courageous men (men of the highest courage), will dare to cross that river. 4. A garrison of three legions was sent there. 5. The infantry marched two miles.

D. 1. ipse; sē 2. Ipse; ipse 3. ipsō; Ipsō 4. Eōdem; Eādem 5. pedum; magnae virtūtis

E. 1. The orator himself, a man of (such) great wisdom, told us this. 2. He had heard this from the citizens themselves. 3. When we get the opportunity, we shall finish (put a stop to) the war which is too long. 4. Don't go there without us because it is a dangerous place. 5. Within a few days the general himself will return to the larger camp. 6. The three sons of the king himself will go to the same camp by night. 7. With my very own eyes I saw the blood of the wounded consul. 8. The infantry had marched twelve miles that very day. 9. The legion itself returned to the same camp from which it (they) had marched in early spring. 10. Because everything was ready (had been prepared), we ourselves could make a sally from the same gate.

F. 1. Imperātor ipse suōs līberābit. 2. Eādem dē causā praesidium in oppidō relictum erat. 3. Ipse eques, vir magnae virtūtis, mūrum ascendit. 4. Ipsa flūmen trānsīre nōn dubitāvit. 5. Legiō ipsa ad eadem castra rediit.

REVIEW LESSON SEVEN

A tape prepared in advance of the review lesson is a good means of presenting vocabulary or grammar review. The rapid response that a tape demands is partcularly good in a review lesson because the emphasis should be on speed and accuracy.

Use of the overhead projector is also recommended for review drill.

Review is important, but it can also become tedious to the pupil. This is one place where the teacher needs to provide a variety of approaches.

II. A. quī, quae, quod

Sing.	M.	F.	N.	Pl.	M.	F.	N.
Nom.	quī	quae	quod		quī	quae	quae
Gen.	cuius	cuius	cuius		quōrum	quārum	quōrum
Dat.	cui	cui	cui		quibus	quibus	quibus
Acc.	quem	quam	quod		quōs	quās	quae
Abl.	quō	quā	quō		quibus	quibus	quibus

B.

certus, -a, -um	**certior, certius**	**certissimus, -a, -um**
certain	more certain	most certain
brevis, breve	**brevior, brevius**	**brevissimus, -a, -um**
short	shorter	shortest
pulcher, -chra, -chrum	**pulchrior, pulchrius**	**pulcherrimus, -a, -um**
pretty	rather pretty	very pretty
celer, celeris, celere	**celerior, celerius**	**celerrimus, -a, -um**
swift	swifter	swiftest
difficilis, difficile	**difficilior, difficilius**	**difficillimus, -a, -um**
difficult	more difficult	most difficult
nōbilis, nōbile	**nōbilior, nōbilius**	**nōbilissimus, -a, -um**
noble	nobler	noblest
bonus, -a, -um	**melior, melius**	**optimus, -a, -um**
good	better	best
magnus, -a, -um	**maior, maius**	**maximus, -a, -um**
large	larger	largest

C.

	minor, minus				**plūrēs, plūra**	
Sing.	M. and F.	N.	Pl. M. and F.	N.	M. and F.	N.
Nom.	minor	minus	minōrēs	minōra	plūrēs	plūra
Gen.	minōris	minōris	minōrum	minōrum	plūrium	plūrium
Dat.	minōrī	minōrī	minōribus	minōribus	plūribus	plūribus
Acc.	minōrem	minus	minōrēs	minōra	plūrēs	plūra
Abl.	minōre	minōre	minōribus	minōribus	plūribus	plūribus

D.

Positive	Comparative	Superlative
laetē	laetius	laetissimē
graviter	gravius	gravissimē
miserē	miserius	miserrimē
ācriter	ācrius	ācerrimē

E.

male	peius	pessimē
facile	facilius	facillimē
diū	diūtius	diūtissimē
magnopere	magis	maximē

F.

	Singular			Plural		
	M.	F.	N.	M.	F.	N.
Nom.	ipse	ipsa	ipsum	eīdem	eaedem	eadem
Gen.	ipsīus	ipsīus	ipsīus	eōrundem	eārundem	eōrundem
Dat.	ipsī	ipsī	ipsī	eīsdem	eīsdem	eīsdem
Acc.	ipsum	ipsam	ipsum	eōsdem	eāsdem	eadem
Abl.	ipsō	ipsā	ipsō	eīsdem	eīsdem	eīsdem

G. eiusdem fēminae (mulieris); ipsīus mulieris; eīdem cōnsulī (ad eundem cōnsulem); cōnsulī ipsī (ad cōnsulem ipsum); eīdem virī; virī ipsī; eundem ducem (imperātōrem); ducem ipsum.

III. 1. Because of the wrongs (which had been) done by the patricians, the common people left Rome (along) with the leaders whom they had chosen (elected). 2. Because the time was short, the consul, informed of the rather serious danger, ordered the leaders to attack as soon as possible. 3. Because the enemy were nearing (our) camp with great speed, our soldiers got ready for a rather sharp battle. 4. After our father heard this, he turned to us and said, "Don't be afraid, boys. Go, hide in the woods. I shall defend you and our home and myself as bravely as possible." 5. Pirates were very cruel men who used to sail all over the sea. Once they kidnapped (the) two children of the Roman consul on the Appian Way near Rome and very boldly took them over into Asia. 6. Those who were called clients once had been slaves of patricians; those to whom they were clients (whose clients they were) were called patrons. 7. Tomorrow my sister will reach Italy by the shortest route. She will soon go to Rome where she will remain three days. On the fourth day she will sail both to Sicily and to (some) other much smaller islands. 8. The little sons of that woman were in extremely great danger. Their mother, however, was very courageous. After killing the large animal, she led the boys with her to safety.

IV. A. 1. according to law 2. curved marks indicating short vowel sounds 3. personal capacity, ability 4. relating to or resembling (that of) an uncle 5. manner 6. a person of power or distinction in a certain field

B. that is; in the same place; by the very nature of the case; the same

V. 4; 3; 6; 9; 10; 11; 5; 7; 2; 12

VI.   The Faithful Dog

Once a thief in the night tossed (some) bread to a dog. By this bait (By the food thrown) he (the thief) was trying to catch the animal. "Oh, ho," said the dog. "You are trying (wish) to prevent me (my tongue) from barking in defense of my master's property. You are greatly mistaken. For that sudden kindness of yours bids me be on my guard. You will not make a profit at my expense (by my neglect of duty)."

TEACHER'S NOTES

LESSON 44

Motto

The source of this line is *Metamorphoses* X. It is with these words that Hippomenes announces his intention to compete with Atalanta in a footrace. Ask the students to suggest an English proverb or maxim expressing the same thought: "God helps those who help themselves." To note the intensifying effect of the pronoun **ipse** will review the grammar of the preceding lesson.

310   Camillus and the Faliscan Teacher (Part 1)

A few years before Rome was captured by the Gauls, Marcus Furius Camillus, a very famous and brave man, was appointed Roman dictator, for the Romans wished to take Veii. Therefore with many men (*lit.* large forces) Camillus marched on the city as quickly as possible. The city was besieged for ten years; the inhabitants, while awaiting help from their neighbors, fought very bravely; many were killed attempting to hold off the Roman attack. Finally the city was taken.

After the capture of Veii, luck granted Camillus an early victory as he was waging war with the Faliscans, inhabitants of Falerii. It was the custom among the Faliscans to entrust several children at a time to the same man, who acted as both teacher and companion. A man who was considered (*lit.* seemed) exceptionally learned (*lit.* to be superior in knowledge) taught the children of the leaders. In time of peace, he took the children outside the city every day. Not giving up this practice during time of war, he took them sometimes on shorter and again on longer excursions (*lit.* distances) from the gate. Finally he led the boys between the outposts of the enemy and the Roman camp. When he was brought before Camillus, he added to his evil deed (these) terrible words. For he said, "I wish to hand over the city of Falerii into the hands of the Romans. And so I have given these boys, whose parents are the leaders there, into your power."

NOTE: Locate the two towns of Etruria on the map (p. 172), showing their proximity to Rome.

311   Review the definition of a participle at this point making sure that the students understand its adjectival function and noun agreement. Mention again that a participle retains some verbal characteristics since it may have adverbial modifiers and noun objects: **In senātū audācter dīcēns, populum Rōmānum monuit.** *Speaking boldly in the Senate, he warned the Roman people.* **Discessit sēcum fīliam fortiter dūcēns.** *He withdrew, bravely leading his daughter with him.*

312 Mention that the endings for the present participle declension are those of third declension adjectives already learned (**-i** stem) except for the ablative singular (**-e**).

314 Encourage the students to give the translation which makes the *best sense* from the context of the Latin.

Refer again to the lesson motto to illustrate the present participle with the value of a noun. *"God helps the daring (ones)."*

317 EXERCISES

A. 1. I saw a boy throwing a stone. 2. I see a boy throwing a stone. 3. We shall see them sitting in the room. 4. Though the soldier was fighting bravely, he was injured. 5. The soldier will be hurt though he will fight bravely. 6. The leader is capturing the fugitives. 7. The leader captured those fleeing. 8. He came to the lake with a companion who wanted water. 9. He is the son of a merchant living in Italy. 10. We gave money to the boy who was standing in the street.

B. 1. pugnāns 2. dīcentēs 3. exeuntēs (discēdentēs) 4. pōnentēs 5. exspectantēs 6. sustinentēs 7. labōrante 8. expugnantium 9. timentibus 10. properantī (contendentī)

C. 1. Our allies, while waging war, conquered the enemy in many battles. While this was going on, our allies approached the plain. 2. The enemy made a fierce attack against the soldiers as they were pitching camp. The soldiers were attacked while camp was being set up. 3. The farmer did not interrupt his work while plowing the fields. The field was destroyed by the cruel enemy while it was being plowed. 4. The soldiers are returning with a horseman who is dragging a prisoner. As the prisoner is being dragged (along) by the cavalryman, the soldiers are returning to camp. 5. Many were watching him as he tore down the bridge. While the bridge was being torn down by the young men, Horatius was holding off the enemy attack.

D. 1. Mē invītō 2. Frūmentō comportātō 3. Mārcō duce 4. Hīs rēbus dictīs (Hōc dictō) 5. Puellā aegrā 6. Camillō dīcente 7. Castrīs mūnītīs 8. Urbe captā 9. Tē cōnsule 10. Peditibus pugnantibus

E. 1. Everyone loves a lover. 2. Yesterday, before you came to Rome, I heard the orator delivering a speech. 3. While he was brought to Camillus, he was seen by all. 4. After the grain had been carried into the town, the farmer was heard calling his slaves. 5. Our companions were hurt as they were leaving the woods. 6. Meantime, as the boys were being drawn farther from the gate, the teacher was captured by the Romans. 7. We heard the shouts of the slaves as they were plowing the fields. 8. Those who seemed to know more than the rest (*lit.* to surpass the others in knowledge) became the teachers of our children. 9. They reach the Roman guard standing in the gate. 10. Although (only) a small part of the summer remained, and winters are early in these places, he still hastened to sail to Britain.

F. 1. Prīnceps lēgātōs dīcentēs (-īs) audīvit. 2. Est fīlius cōnsulis in Āfricā pugnantis. 3. Tē invītō hōs puerōs nōn docēbō. 4. Dictātōrem ante domum stantem vīdimus. 5. Ante domum stantēs, dictātōrem vīdimus. 6. Quem, Camillō duce, timēs (timētis)? 7. Eōs quī nostrōs fīliōs docent eōsdem ex oppidō ēdūcere prohibēre nōn possumus. 8. Sī ūnum modo verbum addideris, expellēris. 9. Modo erat nōbīs et amīcus et socius, modo inimīcus perīculōsus. 10. Camillō impetum faciente (Dum Camillus impetum facit), Falīscī effūgērunt.

319 WORD STUDY

abstineō	abstinentia, self-denial, temperance	abstinence
audiō	audientia, hearing, listening	audience
cōnsciō	cōnscientia, joint knowledge, consciousness	conscience
cōnstō	cōnstantia, firmness	constancy
conveniō	convenientia, harmony	convenience
efficiō	efficientia, conformity, efficiency	efficiency
repugnō	repugnantia, resistance, incompatibility	repugnance
prōvideō	prōvidentia, foresight, providence	providence

LESSON 45

Motto

Call attention to the fact that **moritūrus** is not formed on the perfect participle. Another common verb showing this irregularity is **orior, orīrī, ortus sum,** whose future participle is **oritūrus.** This motto introduces deponent verbs (Lesson 49).

320 Camillus and the Faliscan Teacher (Part 2)

Camillus, who, as we have explained before, had come with an army to besiege Falerii, was a very brave and righteous man; when he heard the teacher's words, he said: "You have come neither to a nation nor a general (who acts) like you. There are laws of war as well as laws of peace, and we have learned to observe them properly no less than bravely. It is not the custom of the Roman people to make war against children; we have taken up arms against those who have made war on us without reason and have given aid to our enemies. I am going to conquer Falerii, as I did Veii, with Roman skill, courage, work and weapons."

Then Camillus stripped him (the teacher), bound his hands behind his back, and handed him over to the children. He said, "We are going to punish

129

this traitor. You, whom he wanted to betray to us, are going to drive him to the city, beating him with switches (all the way); he will pay the penalty for his crime in full view of his own people."

Now when the people heard this and saw this sight, the senate was summoned and the whole state decided to ask the Romans for peace. The Faliscan envoys, who had been put in charge of this undertaking, were brought in to the (Roman) senate and said: "Gentlemen (of the Senate), conquered by you and your general in a victory such as this, we surrender to you; we expect to (*lit.* are going to) live better under your control than under our own laws."

References: Livy V, 27. See the map on p. 172 of the text.

323   EXERCISES

A. 1. A boy about to throw a stone; animals going to kill the gladiator. 2. A woman on the point of speaking; boys about to fall asleep. 3. The girl is about to point out the way (road); the girl was going to point out the road. 4. The enemy intends to attack us; the enemy were about to attack us. 5. The prisoner was about to pay the penalty; the prisoner had been on the point of being punished.

B. 1. I am answering; I am going to answer. 2. He was going; he was going to go. 3. They are giving; they intend to give. 4. They were departing; they were going to withdraw. 5. You are hurrying; you are going to hurry.

C. 1. Dēligō; dēlēctūrus sum. 2. Nōs dēdimus; nōs dēditūrī sumus. 3. Regēbat; rēctūrus erat. 4. Rogābant; rogātūrī erant. 5. Dīcitis; dictūrī estis.

D. 1. fugiēns; fugitūrus; fugitūrus est. 2. dēfendentēs; dēfēnsūrī; dēfēnsūrī sunt. 3. ascendentem; ascēnsūra; ascēnsūra erat. 4. capientēs (-īs); captūrī; captūrī erant.

E. 1. We are going to report the slaughter of the infantry to the general. 2. He saw the soldiers standing in front of the camp. 3. With peace made, the envoys will leave Rome quickly. 4. I heard the voices of soldiers as they were crossing the bridge. 5. Were they going to prepare for war again? 6. We'll not leave (abandon) the slave who has been punished in full view of everyone. 7. While the king was establishing friendship, the citizens formed a daring plan. 8. From whom is he going to hear about this business? He is going to hear from many (people). 9. After the enemy had besieged the town for thirty days, they retreated. 10. We intend to conquer the Germans easily by means of Roman skills.

F. 1. Cum tribus legiōnibus in Galliam iter factūrus sum. 2. Hunc servum miserum, ut suprā dēmōnstrāvimus, pūnītūrī erant. 3. Dux ipse, Gallīs victīs, Rōmam reditūrus fuerat. 4. Hic vir iūstus memoriam omnium amīcōrum suōrum retinēre cōnsuēvit. 5. Ex cōnsuētūdine cōpiam frūmentī

130

ad incolās vīcī missūrus erat. 6. Pōnitisne castra hīc (in hōc locō) urbem nostram obsessūrī? 7. Omnia cōnsilia ā plēbe capta cognōverant. 8. Nēmō, praesertim eī quī animālia timent, per hanc eandem silvam īre audēbit. 9. Flammīs vīsīs, agricola properāvit ad locum ubi aedificia incēnsa erant. 10. Mōs (cōnsuētūdō) est populī Rōmānī arma capere contrā eōs quī lēgēs pācis nōn gerunt (lēgēs pācis nōn gerentēs).

324 Although the teacher may not care to emphasize defective verbs at this point, it is helpful to remember that **meminī,** *I remember* (*lit.* I have recalled) and **ōdī,** *I hate* (*lit.* I have conceived a hatred of) are also perfect tenses denoting a present state resulting from a completed action.

325   THE DAILY LIFE OF A WELL-TO-DO ROMAN

References: Becker, pp. 366-407 and pp. 451-495; Cowell, *Everyday Life in Ancient Rome*, pp. 76-80 and pp. 142-147; Johnston, pp. 27-33 and pp. 224-239; Showerman, *Rome and the Romans*, pp 128-136 and 137-147; Treble and King, pp. 43-50.

LESSON 46

Motto

Students would find it helpful to memorize this legal term as an example of the double dative (Section 331).

326   PYRRHUS (318-272 B.C.)

References: Livy, XII, XIII, XIV, in the summaries, *Periochae* (Loeb Classical Library, IV). Books XI-XX of the *Ab Urbe Condita* are among the lost books.

King Pyrrhus (Part 1)

Almost a hundred years after the events which we have related, the people of Tarentum, who lived in a large city in the southern part of Italy, committed a very grave injustice against the Roman people, for, with no formal declaration of war, they had suddenly attacked and destroyed a Roman fleet in the harbor.

Roman envoys were sent to Tarentum by the senate because of this outrage. The Tarentines were unwilling to confer with the Romans; they insulted them harshly and drove them out of Tarentum. Therefore, the Romans did not hesitate to declare war. One army was left at Rome to guard the city; two armies marched against the enemy. Although many cities fought on the side of the Tarentines against the Romans, the Roman generals were

131

victorious and seemed likely to continue to be so (*lit.* were victors and seemed about to be victors). And so the people of Tarentum sent envoys across the sea to Pyrrhus, the king of the Epirotes, to seek help (for themselves) from him. To aid the Tarentines, Pyrrhus, who commanded a large army, brought many elephants to Italy along with his troops. The elephants proved (*lit.* were) very useful to the king, for the Romans, terrified by their strange (*lit.* never before seen) appearance, could not hold the enemy but were forced to yield in the first battle, which took place near Heraclea.

After the battle the king, who had had a great deal of experience in warfare, was looking at the bodies of the slain and he discovered that they all faced the enemy. "It will be very difficult to defeat such courageous men in battle," he said. "Perhaps I shall be able to conquer them by other means."

327 This dative, with certain verbs, as well as the dative with compound verbs discussed in Section 328, is an extension of the *dative of indirect object.* The teacher can help the student recognize this by showing how the following meaning of each of these verbs suggests a dative; for example, **appropinquō,** *draw near to;* **crēdō,** *give credence to;* **ignōscō,** *grant pardon to;* **imperō,** *issue an order to.*

The teacher should point out that a verb compounded with **ad-** may be followed by an *accusative of place to which (limit of motion)* or the *dative;* for example, **terrae appropinquāmus** *or* **ad terram appropinquāmus.**

329 The teacher will need to emphasize the difference in construction between English and Latin in these sentences. In the last example, *sword* and *hindrance* in English are regarded as being the same; therefore *hindrance* is a predicate nominative. Latin, on the other hand, considers that *sword* **(gladius)** functions or serves *for* or *as a hindrance* **(impedīmentō).** This distinction is not always made in post-Ciceronian Latin, which shows a tendency toward the predicate nominative.

330 In its widest sense, the term *dative of interest* as used in Section 330 includes the *dative of advantage,* the *dative of disadvantage,* the *ethical dative,* the *dative of reference,* and *the dative of agent.* Some grammarians use the term *dative of reference* as the general term for this group of datives.

332   EXERCISES

A. 1. A good citizen obeys the laws. 2. Camillus is in charge of two legions. 3. This is of great use (very useful) to us. 4. We are meeting (met) the returning cavalry. 5. He is eager for both money and glory. 6. He, she, *or* it is a help to some, a hindrance to others. 7. As the cavalry were returning, they met us. 8. These soldiers will be left to guard the city. 9. Don't harm that boy. 10. He is watching out for the safety of his soldiers.

B. 1. colloquiō 2. montibus (ad montēs) 3. ōrātōrī 4. Omnibus exercitibus vestrīs (tuīs). 5. praesidiō impedīmentīs 6. nōbīs 7. sibi 8. Eī
9. fīliō meō; tibi 10. huic legiōnī; praesidiō

C. 1. The staff-officer, a very courageous man, had been put in charge of
the cavalry. 2. The king in person freed the terrified inhabitants from danger. 3. The cavalry came again to reinforce the legion. 4. Our leader, after
gathering his troops from everywhere, demanded hostages from the Gauls.
5. The chiefs who are in command of all Gaul will assemble in the Forum.
6. These states are a great worry (cause of great concern) to us. 7. The
Greeks crossed the sea intending to seek aid for themselves from the Romans. 8. Pyrrhus, to aid the people of Tarentum, brought many elephants
to Italy along with his troops. 9. With one army left in Rome to guard the
city, two armies marched against the enemy. 10. He feared for the infantryman whom he had sent to the other consul.

D. 1. Nōlī (Nōlīte) bellum indīcere, nam tibi (vōbīs) nōn nocuimus.
2. Rōmānī duōs exercitūs praesidiō urbī relīquērunt. 3. Mārcus castrīs
praefectus est. 4. Imperātor castrīs Mārcum praefēcerat; ille trēs diēs eīs
praefuit. 5. Exercituī accēdentī resistere nōn poterimus. 6. Hic magister
īrātus puerīs dēfessīs nōn parcet. 7. Magnō ūsuī nōbīs erit tuum cōnsilium
audācissimum. 8. Nostrī, facultāte datā, hostibus statim occursūrī sunt.
9. Meae fīliae saepe timeō; (ea) est magnae cūrae mihi. 10. Parentēs bonī
līberīs cōnsulunt; sapientēs (-īs) cōnsulunt (cōnsilium ā sapientibus petunt).

SUPPLEMENTARY EXERCISE

1. The consul spared the prisoner. 2. We're nearing the bridge. 3. He had
given orders to his troops. 4. He is favorably inclined toward his clients.
5. You will not be able to persuade me. 6. I believe (trust) you. 7. We are
about to meet the enemy. 8. Obey your parents. 9. Don't harm us.
10. They have resisted every attack.

333 Ask the students to explain the italicized words, basing their answers
on the vocabulary study of the most recent lessons: a *credible* story, the
store's *credit* policy, a *colloquial* expression, the *mores* of a primitive tribe, a
credulous teacher, a dormitory *prefect, concomitant* circumstances, *Opus* 20,
a government *subsidy*.

LESSON 47

Motto

We have already met the sayings of Publilius Syrus in preceding lessons.
Identify him again as a slave who was taken to Rome during the first century B.C. There, he became famous for his mimes, which are represented
today only by a number of epigrammatic sayings.

Ask the students to find the meaning for the verb form **mūtārī.** Use the words *mutation* and *commutation* in sentences and ask for explanations. It is good to keep the students constantly aware of the English language debt to Latin.

334   King Pyrrhus (Part 2)

And so Pyrrhus sent Cineas, a shrewd speaker, to the senate at Rome. He told the senate that King Pyrrhus himself wished to set a day for a conference with the Romans. He wanted to come to the city to establish peace with the Romans.

Appius Claudius, however, who had refrained from (attending) public meetings for a long time because of his blindness, on hearing that the senate was treating with the envoy sent by Pyrrhus, was led into the senate house. There, after Claudius had emphatically (*lit.* with great zeal) warned the senate that the king was dangerous and that the Roman people ought not trust such an enemy, the senators said that they did not wish to establish peace with Pyrrhus.

Afterward (a certain) one of Pyrrhus' soldiers voluntarily came to the consul, Gaius Fabricius. He said, "For a large reward (*lit.* If you will give me a large reward), I shall do harm to the king; I shall give him poison." The consul sent him back to Pyrrhus, and, through a messenger (message), informed the king about this plot.

Then the king crossed into Sicily, hoping that, if things went well there, he could return with larger forces and conquer the Romans. But meanwhile they successfully waged war in Italy against the Lucanians (in Southern Italy) and other enemies. When Pyrrhus returned to Italy after five years, on being conquered by the Romans near Beneventum, he exclaimed that he was forced to withdraw from Italy.

Reference: See the map on p. 156 of the text.

NOTE: Because **possum** lacks the future infinitive, the present infinitive **posse** is used in line 18 to follow the verb **spērō (spērāns),** which regularly requires the indirect statement with the infinitive in the future.

337   EXERCISES

A. 1. Pyrrhus is in Sicily. The messenger says that Pyrrhus is in Sicily. The messenger said that Pyrrhus was in Sicily. 2. The leader is going to Gaul. We think that the leader is going to Gaul. We thought that the leader was going to Gaul. 3. The king is fighting with the Gauls. We hear that the king is fighting with the Gauls. We heard that the king was fighting with the Gauls. 4. The city is being attacked. We perceive that the city is being attacked. We perceived that the city was being attacked. 5. The king cannot conquer the Romans. I understand that the king cannot conquer the Romans. I understood that the king could not conquer the Romans.

B. 1. . . . rēgem bellum in Italiā gerere. The messenger knows (has learned) that the king is waging war in Italy. 2. . . . mīlitēs nostrōs fortiter pugnāre. The messenger is explaining that our soldiers are fighting bravely. 3. . . . exercitum ā Caesare dūcī. The messenger reports that the army is being led by Caesar. 4. . . . multōs mīlitēs capī. He writes that many soldiers are being captured. 5. . . . Caesarem oppidum oppugnāre. The messenger replies that Caesar is attacking the town.

C. 1. . . . amīcum meum Rōmae esse. I heard that my friend was in Rome. 2. . . . Appium in cūriam dūcī. I was informed that Appius was being taken into the senate house. 3. . . . Pyrrhum ex Italiā discēdere cōgī. I explained that Pyrrhus was being forced to withdraw from Italy. 4. . . . obsidēs ducī trādī. I saw that the hostages were being handed over to the leader. 5. . . . vōs cum hoste pācem facere dēbēre. I said that you ought not make peace with an enemy.

D. 1. Dīcit mīlitēs venīre, legiōnem venīre, cōpiās venīre, sē venīre. 2. Dīxit mīlitēs venīre, legiōnem venīre, cōpiās venīre, sē venīre. 3. Exīstimant castra esse magna, flūmen esse altum, fossam esse lātam, sē esse fortēs (-īs). 4. Exīstimābant castra esse magna, flūmen esse altum, fossam esse lātam, sē esse fortēs (-īs). 5. Negās nōs collēs (-īs) tenēre, eum haec facere, eōs nāvēs longās habēre. 6. Sēnsit nōs Rōmānīs esse amīcōs, nōs Germānīs esse inimīcōs, id nōbīs perīculōsum esse.

E. 1. They point out that the forces of Pyrrhus are very large. 2. They reply that they have no other way. 3. They point out that they are managing things well. 4. They inform Claudius that they are not making peace with the king. 5. They report that the troops are assembling and are not far away. 6. He warns the senators that this is dangerous to the Romans. 7. He says that some are leaving, others arriving. 8. The senators say that they are not treating with the king. 9. Of his own accord he said that he understood that he was being prevented from leaving. 10. In a loud voice he shouted that he was being driven from home.

F. 1. Vidēmus nāvēs (-īs) nostrās tempestāte frangī. 2. Vīgintī nāvēs eius generis maximō (cum) studiō cōgunt. 3. Ostendērunt cōnsulem domae suae abdere pecūniam pūblicam. 4. Nūntiant Claudium patrēs monēre rēgem esse hostem. 5. Respondet sē esse cīvem Rōmānum neque cum Pyrrhō pācem cōnfīrmāre posse. 6. Negat loca superiōra ā cōpiīs nostrīs prīmā vigiliā occupārī posse. 7. Negāvit cīvēs dē salūte dēspērāre. 8. Scrīpsī perīculum augērī. 9. Nūntius vulnerātus, ubi ad Caesarem vēnit, nūntiāvit magnās cōpiās Gallōrum convenīre. 10. Fabricius, nūntiō ad castra Pyrrhī missō, rēgem dē īnsidiīs certiōrem fēcit.

NOTES: Exercises A, B, C, and D would best be done rapidly in class in advance of homework. They will prove to be extremely valuable in fixing in the pupils' minds the essential features of the indirect statement in Latin.

Notice that in sentence 6 of Exercise F, **prīmā vigiliā** is in the ablative because the word *during* here indicates *time within which* rather than *duration of time*.

LESSON 48

Motto

These two lines furnish another example of Martial's biting satire. Point out that this writer usually withheld the sting of his epigram to the last line and that he very wisely invented names for the victims of his wit.

339   CARTHAGE

See maps on p. 64 and 156 of the text.

Regulus (Part 1)

We have shown above that the Tarentines were conquered in a war lasting almost ten years, and added to Rome's empire. With this achievement, almost all of Italy was under the rule of (*lit.* obeyed) the senate and the Roman people. But before the people of Tarentum had been conquered by the Romans, a second large and powerful city, named Carthage, had begun to extend the boundaries of its dominions. We know that, when a great war began between these two cities, for a long time neither side was victorious.

There is a tradition that Marcus Atilius Regulus, a Roman consul (and) a man of great loyalty and resolution, crossed to Africa with a large fleet, after defeating the Carthaginians in a naval battle. After he had overcome the Carthaginians there in several battles and (when) no successor was being sent by the senate, he sent a letter to the senate, for he thought that a successor should be sent and that he himself should be recalled.

Meanwhile, because the Carthaginians had not been able to achieve any degree of success (*lit.* manage things successfully), they sent for Xanthippus, a Spartan general (and) a man with a very great knowledge of military tactics. Soon the Romans were informed that Regulus had been defeated and taken prisoner.

Then the Carthaginians sent Regulus to the senate because they wanted to discuss peace and an exchange of prisoners. Regulus had sworn that, if peace or the exchange of prisoners was not effected, he would return to Carthage; and so they (the Carthaginians) were assured that he would bring back favorable peace terms.

340 Whereas it should be mentioned that the future infinitive passive is not a frequently used form, it might be better to defer any discussion of the periphrastic future, **fore (futūrum esse) ut,** until the subjunctive mood has been learned.

341 The teacher will need to emphasize that the infinitive represents an action as *going on* (present), *done* (perfect), or *yet to come* (future) at the time of the main verb.

342 Agreement of the participle should be kept constantly in the students' minds. Point out that the possible endings are **-um, -am, -um, -ōs, -ās, -a**, depending on the gender and number of the subject of the infinitive. It might be beneficial to do several sentences of this pattern before assigning any written homework.

344   EXERCISES

A.   1. He says that his mother a) is calling, b) has called, c) will call the children.   2. We believe that you a) are, b) were, c) will be sad.   3. I know that our troops a) are crossing, b) have crossed, c) will cross the river.   4. The leader said that he a) was not beginning, b) had not begun, c) would not begin battle.   5. The old men perceived that the young men a) were being influenced, b) had been influenced by their teacher.

B.   1. a) agere b) ēgisse c) āctūrōs esse.   2. a) esse b) fuisse c) futūrum esse (fore).   3. a) accēdere b) accessisse c) accessūrās esse.   4. a) comportāre b) comportāvisse c) comportātūrum esse.   5. a) līberārī b) līberātam esse

C.   1. . . . . cōnsulem Rōmānum ad Āfricam nāvigāre. The messenger said that the Roman consul was sailing to Africa.   2. . . . . equitēs impetum hostium repulsūrōs esse. I think that the cavalry will repulse the enemy attack.   3. . . . . proelium nāvāle prīmā lūce commissum esse. The officer says that a naval battle was begun at dawn.   4. . . . . frātrem nostrum rēs bene gessisse. My sister said that our brother had not managed (things) well.   5. . . . . urbem nostram circumvenīrī. The guards pointed out that our city was being surrounded.

D.   1. He said that the wisdom of this teacher would be exceptional.   2. We heard that the ditch had been filled by the slaves.   3. They were aware that the enemy had taken the middle of the city.   4. He wrote that the guards had been removed.   5. I pointed out that a new war had been started.   6. He has learned (He knows) that the soldier will demand a reward from the Romans.   7. He says that we cannot give back the money.   8. He is explaining that (the) one consul is staying in Rome (and) that the other has been sent to Africa.   9. He replies that the victors have made peace on fair terms.   10. What senators know that a naval battle has been fought?

E.   1. Dīcit līberōs ā mātre vocātōs (esse).   2. Negat mīlitēs portam clausisse.   3. Audīvimus servōs fossam complētūrōs (esse).   4. Sēnsērunt mediam urbem incēnsam (esse).   5. Scīvit (Cognōverat) mīlitem ā Rōmānīs praemium postulātūrum (esse).   6. Scit (Cognōvit) praemium ā Camillō postulātum (esse).   7. Dēmōnstrat (Ostendit) mīlitēs aegrōs in cas-

137

trīs relictōs (esse). 8. Respondet litterās ad senātum missās (esse). 9. Certior factus sum novam classem nōndum aedificātam (esse).

NOTE: Latin authors frequenty omit **esse** in the future active and perfect passive infinitives. It would be well to acquaint the students with this usage by showing the possible omission in these infinitives found in exercise E.

LESSON 49

Motto

Ask if any student can identify the literary device employed in the quotation (simile). Discuss the comparison.

346   Regulus (Part 2)

But after Regulus came to the senate at Rome, he said that, although he had been elected a consul of Rome, he was now a prisoner of the enemy and he refused to give his opinion. However, when the Romans questioned him about peace (terms), he expressed the judgment that the senate ought not make peace with the Carthaginians: (he said that) the Carthaginians were long-standing enemies of the Roman people and lasting peace could not be established with them.

Next, when they asked him his opinion about the exchange of prisoners, he replied that it was foolish to exchange them; (he said) that he was old and useless, and had been defeated by Xanthippus, but that among the Carthaginians who had been captured by the Romans, there were (some) healthy young men and good captains. Therefore, the senators refused to make peace and to exchange prisoners.

Then, although many of the Romans were opposed to the idea (*lit.* were unwilling), Regulus decided to leave Rome and set out for Carthage. To his wife, his children, and his friends, he said, "Farewell, do not weep for me, (for) I am not a Roman citizen but a prisoner of the enemy. Even though the Carthaginians are faithless enemies, I cannot break faith with them. I give my life for my country and I shall die happily. Promise that you will not despair of the safety of Rome. Farewell, Romans. Conquer!"

Although he knew (very) well that, if he failed to accomplish his mission, he would perish in pain and agony, nevertheless, with the greatest resolution he returned to Africa.

Reference: Livy, XVIII in the summary, *Periocha,* Loeb Classical Library, IV (XVIII is among the lost books of Livy's history).

347   The students will be certain to ask how the passive meanings of such verbs as *try, fear,* and *follow* are expressed in Latin. Because they already know **temptō** and **timeō,** it should not be difficult to show them that Latin, like English, has more than one verb to express an idea and that, although no two verbs in any language mean exactly the same thing, one can be used in place of another to convey essentially the same idea, namely, **sequor, succēdō; prōgredior, prōcēdō; partior, dīvidō.** (The principal parts of the model verbs should be memorized.)

350   EXERCISES

A. 1. They are afraid. 2. Follow me! 3. He (has) rejoiced. 4. We think (consider). 5. We think (believe). 6. He has died (is dead). 7. She had feared. 8. Be glad (Rejoice)! 9. They will follow. 10. I shall (a)rise.. 11. I'll try. 12. Set out (Get going)! 13. You are setting out. 14. They were advancing.

B. 1. Arbitrantur. 2. Pollicitī erāmus. 3. Gaudēbant. 4. Proficīscēminī. 5. Partītī erant. 6. Cōnābātur. 7. Gaudē (-te). 8. Prōgrediēbāmur. 9. Cōnābor. 10. Profectī sunt. 11. Revertimur. 12. Moritur. 13. Verentur. 14. Secūtus es. 15. Sequētur. 16. Audēmus. 17. Sequere (Sequiminī) mē. 18. Pollicētur. 19. Prōgrediēmur. 20. Reversa erit.

C. 1. prōgressī sunt 2. oritur 3. sē recēpērunt 4. ausī sunt (audēbant) 5. Pollicitī sunt. 6. proficīscitur 7. dabat 8. cōnābimur 9. gaudēmus 10. Sequere

NOTE: In sentence 3, the military sense, lacking in the verb **revertor,** is implied.

D. 1. He will be afraid to station the heavy baggage on top of the hill. 2. I hope you are well (*lit.* If you are well, it is well). 3. Lieutenant, do not advance too far from camp. 4. While they were wandering (about) in the forest, suddenly they were captured by the Gauls. 5. He ordered the army to proceed to port, board ship, and follow him. 6. If he is well, he will not return with his work undone. 7. Both the general who was in command of the troops and many soldiers had died. 8. As soon as he expressed his opinion, he returned to Spain with the greatest resolution.

E. 1. Ante mediam noctem ad portum pervenīre cōnātī erāmus. 2. Merīdiē profectī, nōs multa mīlia passuum sequentur. 3. Sē statim ventūram (esse) pollicētur. 4. Hī (virī) exīstimant nōs sibi inimīcōs esse. 5. Longius ā locō nōn prōgrediēmur. 6. Veritī sunt exercitūs Rōmānōs in Galliam venientēs. 7. Iuvenēs vulnerātī ad eundem locum pervenīre cōnātī erant. 8. Nostrīs cōnsiliīs cognitīs, ille rēx urbem suam dēfendere nōn est cōnātus. 9. Haec scientia ūtilis Rōmānīs, pīrātīs est inūtilis. 10. Decima legiō fidem habet; quārta dē omnibus rēbus dēspērat.

NOTE: In sentence 4 of exercise E, the reflexive pronoun refers to the subject of the main clause, rather than to the subject of the infinitive. The reflexive is used of the principal subject when reference is made to the thought or will of that subject (for example, in indirect statements, indirect questions, indirect commands, and purpose clauses).

352   WORD STUDY

agilis, able to be moved, light (agile); **docilis,** able to be taught (docile); **facilis,** able to be done, easy (facile)

cīvīlis, relating to a citizen (civil); **hostīlis,** of (by) an enemy (hostile); **iuvenīlis,** relating to a young man, youth (juvenile); **puerīlis,** relating to a boy, childish (puerile); **senīlis,** of an old man (senile)

353   SLAVES AND FREEDMEN IN ANCIENT ROME

References: Becker, pp. 199-225; Carcopino, pp. 56-61; Davis, *A Day in Old Rome,* pp. 122-143; Grant, pp. 109-119; Johnston, p. 159-182.

LESSON 50

Motto

In connection with this motto, the teacher might review the greeting Roman gladiators gave the emperor: **Avē, Imperātor, moritūrī tē salūtāmus.** This greeting emphasizes the irregular future participle of **morior.**

354   The Sibylline Books

Tarquin the Proud was the seventh king of the Romans. Once an old woman came to Tarquin the Proud carrying nine books which she insisted (*lit.* kept saying) were divine oracles. She tried to sell these books to the king. Tarquin asked the price. The woman demanded a very high price; in amazement, the king laughed at her. Suspecting a trick, he distrusted the old woman.

Then she burned three of the nine books (*lit.* three out of the nine) and offered (*lit.* wanted) to sell the remaining six at the same price. But Tarquin laughed even (*lit.* much) more and said that the old woman was mad. He said he had no desire (*lit.* did not want) to use her books. Without delay, the woman burned three more books and offered to sell the three remaining at the same price. Now Tarquin became more interested, and bought the three remaining books for a price which was not a bit lower than that which had been asked for them all. Thereafter, the Romans always guarded the three Sibylline books in the Temple of Jupiter.

NOTE: **Anus,** *old woman,* is one of the few feminine nouns of the fourth declension. **Manus, domus, nūrus** (*daughter-in-law*), **porticus** (*colonnade*), and **tribus** (*tribe*) are among others of this class.

A. 1. to wonder (at) 2. to have followed 3. to use 4. to be about to speak 5. to demand. 6. to protect 7. to have pointed out 8. to be going to destroy 9. to have been led out 10. to have delayed

B. 1. The left wing is about to set out. 2. We saw the legion trying to defend itself. 3. The enemy are going to share the booty. 4. The soldier who had been wounded (wounded soldier) was exhausted. 5. After waiting a long time, finally he moved. 6. The old man demanding money is ill. 7. I. was watching the children (who were) amazed at the show. 8. After saying this, the senators left. 9. After these statements had been made, the senators went away. 10. After advancing at daybreak, the soldiers came into view of the enemy.

C. 1. We saw the legion a. as they disembarked. b. after they had disembarked. c. about to disembark. 2. He is walking with young men who a. dare (to do) many things. b. have dared (to do) many things. c. intend to dare (to do) many things. 3. a. The marching soldiers neared the boundaries of Gaul. b. After making a march, the soldiers neared the boundaries of Gaul. c. About to make a march, the soldiers neared the boundaries of Gaul.

D. 1. cōnfīsī 2. fugientēs (-īs) 3. tuentēs (-īs) 4. morātī 5. Comportātō

E. 1. mīrārī 2. secūtūrōs esse. 3. reversūrōs esse 4. cōnātam esse 5. audēre

F. 1. She promised that she would go with you. 2. They were informed that the leader was dead. 3. Fearing a shortage of grain, he decided to advance farther. 4. Because of the deep shadow(s) they did not dare (to) linger in the forest. 5. They hope that they will reach camp very easily. 6. We cannot use swords; under my leadership, the Romans will not declare war. 7. The Britons attacked the Romans while their ships were being repaired. 8. Are these young men who are rejoicing those (*lit.* the same) who were very sad yesterday? 9. We know that the defeated inhabitants tried to reach the shore safely. 10. Regulus was informed that the enemy were following our army; he did not think that they would dare (to) attack us.

G. 1. Mīles negāvit sē verērī. 2. Duōs lēgātōs loquentēs audīvimus. 3. Cognōvimus imperātōrem mortuum esse. 4. Tempestāte ortā, multae nāvēs frāctae sunt. 5. Nōlīte gaudēre, amīcī, rē īnfectā. 6. Imperium dīvīnum veritus, ante merīdiem profectus est. 7. Hīs rēbus dictīs (Haec locūtus), abiit. 8. Negāvit parvum exercitum arcem tuērī posse. 9. Ōrāculum esse dīvīnum suspicantēs (suspicātī), imperiīs pāruimus. 10. Fortis iuvenis vulnerātus fugā salūtem petere cōnātus est.

361 Ask the students to suggest meanings for the italicized words in the following phrases, basing their answers on words learned in the most recent vocabularies: a *loquacious* woman; *reverence* for the gods; the *consequences* of rash behavior; a *moribund* political party; a religion of the *Orient; stultify* our efforts; a *sententious* remark; Board of *Arbitration;* suffer from *claustrophobia; inception* of the idea; *admirable* restraint.

REVIEW LESSON EIGHT

II.   FORMS AND SYNTAX

A.   Participles

	Active		Passive
Pres.	**dēmōnstrāns,** pointing out	*Perf.*	**dēmōnstrātus,** having been pointed out
Fut.	**dēmōnstrātūrus,** about to point out		
Pres.	**dēdēns,** surrendering	*Perf.*	**dēditus,** having been surrendered
Fut.	**dēditūrus,** going to surrender		
Pres.	**sentiēns,** feeling	*Perf.*	**sēnsus,** having been felt
Fut.	**sēnsūrus,** going to feel		
Pres.	**claudēns,** closing	*Perf.*	**clausus,** having been closed
Fut.	**clausūrus,** about to close		
Pres.	**trahēns,** dragging	*Perf.*	**tractus,** having been dragged
Fut.	**tractūrus,** about to drag		

B.   Infinitives

	Active		Passive
Pres.	**crēdere**	*Pres.*	**crēdī**
Perf.	**crēdidisse**	*Perf.*	**crēditus esse**
Fut.	**crēditūrus esse**	*Fut.*	**crēditum īrī**
Pres.	**incipere**	*Pres.*	**incipī**
Perf.	**incēpisse**	*Perf.*	**inceptus esse**
Fut.	**inceptūrus esse**	*Fut.*	**inceptum īrī**
Pres.	**sentīre**	*Pres.*	**sentīrī**
Perf.	**sēnsisse**	*Perf.*	**sēnsus esse**
Fut.	**sēnsūrus esse**	*Fut.*	**sēnsum īrī**

Pres. **polliceri**   *Perf.* **pollicitus esse**
Fut. **polliciturus esse**

Pres. **proficisci**   *Perf.* **profectus esse**
Fut. **profecturus esse**

NOTE: If the future passive infinitive has not been learned, the students will not be expected to give that form.

C.   **progredior   progredi   progressus   sum**

Pres. **progrediuntur**   *Perf.*   **progressi sunt**
Imper. **progrediebantur**   *Pluperf.*   **progressi erant**
Fut. **progredientur**   *Fut. Perf.* **progressi erunt**

D. 1. exercitui 2. exercitui 3. imperatori (duci) 4. auxilio 5. imperatori (duci) 6. imperatori (duci) 7. gloriae 8. nobis

E. 1. (de)monstrare 2. (de)monstrare 3. (de)monstravisse 4. (de)-monstravisse 5. sequi 6. secutos esse 7. secuturos esse

III. A. 1. Thinking that such terms would not be useful to the Romans, Claudius said that the senate ought not make peace with Pyrrhus. 2. Though the soldiers were bravely resisting the enemy, they could not withstand the assault of their attackers. 3. We saw the boys running to meet their father as he was returning home in the evening. 4. The king thought that he ought not to pardon those (who were) trying to harm him. 5. He was glad because he knew that his mother had returned to Rome at (during) the third hour. 6. We know that Carthage, a mighty and powerful city, (has) waged war with the Romans for many years.

IV. A. 1. harmful; destructive 2. change of penalty to a lesser one 3. meetings for the purpose of reaching a settlement 4. habits; customs; manners 5. expressing endeavor or effort 6. made young again 7. order of occurrence 8. a settlement of dispute by a party chosen or legally appointed to resolve differences. 9. excessive display 10. beginning; early

B. 1. suffix **-ilis**, *able to be;* **facilis**, able to be done; *facile*, easily accomplished 2. suffix **-ilis**, *able to be;* **credibilis**, able to be believed; *credible*, believable 3. suffix **-ilis**, *pertaining* or *belonging to;* **iuvenilis**, pertaining to a youth; *juvenile*, youthful or a young person.

V. 4; 3; 5; 7; 1; 6

VI. 1. They had escaped by rapid flight. 2. He wanted to be made their king. 3. He promised to protect them from every danger. 4. He exercised authority harshly (*lit.* with cruel claws) and ate his victims one by one. 5. One dove said they deserved their fate.

143

LESSON 51

362   A Scene from Roman Life: The Fire (Part 1)

In Rome were large buildings in which many families lived. The Romans used to call these buildings "islands"; for just as in certain regions there are islands in the middle of the river, so these buildings were surrounded by streets. In the Subura, which was a valley between the hills of the city of Rome, there were many high "islands." They had several stories; in the bottom story were shops, in the higher (ones) families lived.

Marcus runs up to his mother on the street.

Marcus.   Oh Mother, look, look; an "island" is on fire!

Cluentia.   Be quiet, Marcus, I'm busy. Now, first I shall buy the vegetables for dinner; then I shall take you to the barber for your hair is too long. Let's get along (*lit.* advance) quickly. Let's not dawdle.

Marcus.   Mother, Mother, do look! There's a big (*lit.* tall) apartment house on fire in the Subura.

Cluentia.   What are you saying, son? Oh! It's our apartment house and the children are home. Run to your father's shop and tell him everything. Have him come at once.

Marcus quickly runs to his father's shop, which is in the Argiletum. Cluentia runs up to two senators.

Cluentia.   Oh, most illustrious sirs, please help us; I implore your protection. Save my dear children. We are poor, we shall all perish. Where are my children!

Then Cluentia goes home.

References: Becker, p. 232; Cowell, *Everyday Life in Ancient Rome*, pp. 16, 17, 26-28 and pp. 126-127; Davis, *A Day in Old Rome*, pp. 34-39; Showerman, *Eternal Rome*, pp. 66-75; Treble and King, p. 30.

368   EXERCISES

A. 1. Let's work here. 2. Tell me everything.   3. Have them come back. 4. Let us follow. 5. Let's not lose the money. 6. Let us ask them. 7. Follow me! 8. Help us! 9. Let the plan be adopted. 10. The plan will be adopted. 11. Let them be gone. 12. Let's not delay. 13. Let the senators dare. 14. Let them advance to that place. 15. They will be heard. 16. Let us inform them. 17. Be quiet, (my) daughter. 18. Let him buy the shop. 19. Let them teach the children. 20. Let us increase the property.

B. 1. Gaudeāmus. 2. Fac hoc (haec) (hās rēs)! 3. Nē nāvis incendātur. 4. Hīc maneāmus. 5. In vallem currat. 6. Exercitus prōgrediātur. 7. Legiō proficīscētur. 8. Legiō proficīscātur. 9. Nē collis circumveniātur. 10. In arcem impetum faciāmus. 11. Loquiminī nōbīscum. 12. Ea frūmentum emat. 13. Sīmus occupātī (-ae). 14. Pollicēmur. 15. Polliceāmur.

C. 1. Let's try to win (gain) a victory today. 2. Don't let them advance farther from the city. 3. Let us rejoice because we have won (gained) a victory. 4. Let the poor have grain because they can't buy it. 5. Let's run to father's shop; he will help us; let's rely on (trust) him. 6. Have him leave camp and set out for Rome after noon. 7. We cannot save everyone; let us save the children and the old people. 8. Have the citizens break down the bridge; if they destroy the bridge, the Etruscans will not be able to cross. 9. Let the enemy make an end to their wrongdoing (the wrongs they are committing); then we'll be able to make peace.

D. 1. Puerī in vallem celerrimē currant. 2. Senātōrēs auxilium rogent. 3. Nē pontem frangere dubitēmus. 4. Suōs līberōs cārōs iuvet. 5. Prīmā lūce omnēs proficīscantur. 6. Pater dormit; omnēs taceāmus. 7. Nē ille vir crūdēlis servum miserum pūniat. 8. Sī urbs expugnāta erit, hostēs repellere cōnēmur. 9. Nōn sōlum iuvenēs sed etiam senēs sē nōbīs (nōbīscum) iungent.

SUPPLEMENTARY EXERCISES

A.   Present Subjunctive

Active		Passive	
līberem	līberēmus	līberer	līberēmur
līberēs	līberētis	līberēris (-re)	līberēminī
līberet	līberent	līberētur	līberentur
videam	videāmus	videar	videāmur
videās	videātis	videāris (-re)	videāminī
videat	videant	videātur	videantur
audiam	audiāmus	audiar	audiāmur
audiās	audiātis	audiāris (-re)	audiāminī
audiat	audiant	audiātur	audiantur

B.   Present Indicative

Active		Passive	
cōnspiciō	cōnspicimus	cōnspicior	cōnspicimur
cōnspicis	cōnspicitis	cōnspiceris (-re)	cōnspiciminī
cōnspicit	cōnspiciunt	cōnspicitur	cōnspiciuntur
laudō	laudāmus	laudor	laudāmur
laudās	laudātis	laudāris (-re)	laudāminī
laudat	laudant	laudātur	laudantur

145

C.

Present

Indicative		Subjunctive	
moror	morāmur	morer	morēmur
morāris (-re)	morāminī	morēris (-re)	morēminī
morātur	morantur	morētur	morentur
vereor	verēmur	verear	vereāmur
verēris (-re)	verēminī	vereāris (-re)	vereāminī
verētur	verentur	vereātur	vereantur
proficīscor	proficīscimur	proficīscar	proficīscāmur
proficīsceris (-re)	proficīsciminī	proficīscāris (-re)	proficīscāminī
proficīscitur	proficīscuntur	proficīscātur	proficīscantur
gaudeō	gaudēmus	gaudeam	gaudeāmus
gaudēs	gaudētis	gaudeās	gaudeātis
gaudet	gaudent	gaudeat	gaudeant

LESSON 52

370   A Scene from Roman Life: The Fire (Part 2)

While the mother, mindful of her children, returns home running and Marcus hurries as fast as he can to his father's shop, much is transpiring at home. For meanwhile, on the third floor of the "island," the sons and daughters of Cluentia are terrified by the flames. The house is full of smoke.

Aulus.   Oh Tertia, bring (some) water. What are we to do? I wish that Father and Mother would come home. I hope they won't be long (*lit.* May they not delay). Let's wait for them here. For Mother didn't give us permission to go out. She said, "Children, don't leave the house (*lit.* go out)."

Tertia.   If only they were here now. We don't have any water now. Secunda, run down to the fountain and bring this jar back full of water. The smoke is coming up through the floor boards.

Secunda.   I can't carry the jar; you are big, you carry it. I'm frightened. I hope that the staircase won't burn (*lit.* May the staircase not burn). There is no hope for help. Oh, Mother, come!

Publius enters.

Publius.   Girls, let us all run down at once. Where is Aulus? I can't see him. The smoke is so thick.

Tertia.   He is under the table. Come, Aulus.

Publius.   Let us join hands. Come, Secunda; don't cry, be brave. Let's proceed fearlessly.

146

372-373   Although it is difficult to generalize, the following observations may enable the student to grasp more clearly the nature of the subjunctive.

The subjunctive is used for the unreal, the hypothetical, and the uncertain, as opposed to the indicative, which is the mood of fact. The subjunctive expresses something willed, but not necessarily attained (*hortatory* and *jussive*), something wished (*optative*); something only possible or *potential*. It is in these *independent* uses that the essential nature of the subjunctive mood is most easily seen.

The subjunctive is used in conditions that express an uncertainty or hypothesis. Future less vivid (*should—would*) conditions are related to the potential subjunctive, and contrary to fact conditions are often labelled "unreal."

Some dependent uses of the subjunctive suggest its basic nature. Purpose shows *intention,* indirect command expresses *will,* and indirect quotation may imply *uncertainty.* In other cases, such as the **cum**-clauses, it is difficult to discover the element of uncertainty and a result clause seems very factual indeed.

It is important to remind the student that he must not memorize a translation for the subjunctive. (See Section 365). The temptation is to use *should, would, may,* or *might* at all times for the subjunctive. One must know *why* Latin uses the subjunctive and then translate accordingly.

375   EXERCISES

A.   1. We shall depart.   2. Don't give orders.   3. What am I to do?
4. Bring the soldiers.   5. He is away.   6. May this not happen to us.   7. I wish you would try (*lit.* May you try).   8. May the state not be destroyed.
9. Let us not run to meet them.   10. What were they to say?   11. If you would only try.   12. Let them live here.   13. Let the city be stormed.   14. O that the affair were not being entrusted to him.   15. Look (Watch)!

B.   1. Quid dīcerēmus?   2. Prōgredientur.   3. Prōgrediantur.   4. Emātur.
5. Nē lacrimēmus.   6. Gaudeant.   7. Nē vulnerētur.   8. Utinam adesset.
9. Quid faciam?   10. Rogā causam mortis (eius).   11. Utinam arcem expugnāre possēmus.   12. Agmen prōgrediātur.   13. Pāreāmus rēgī malō?
14. Eāmus domum.   15. Possit pugnae fīnem facere.

C.   1. Surely these merchants aren't greedy for money?   2. I hope these woods aren't full of the enemy.   3. Meanwhile the smoke of the fires could be seen in the distance.   4. To what town were we to proceed without a leader?   5. Let us choose a leader wise and skilled in military science.
6. May our troops not turn (I hope that our troops will not turn) and flee at the approach of the enemy.   7. If only the king were not unmindful of you.   8. Because they were not familiar with this type of fighting, they could not rout the enemy.

D. 1. Legiō celeriter accēdēbat (appropinquābat). Quid facerēmus?
2. Proficīscāmur quam celerrimē ūnā cum equitibus et ad reliquum exercitum pervenīre cōnēmur. 3. Utinam mātrem nostram accēdentem vidēre
possēmus. 4. Fūmum ignium vidēre possumus. Putēmus auxilia adesse?
5. Quod fossa est plēna aquae, trānsīre nōn possunt. 6. Intereā sub lūcem
ab hōc locō proficīscantur. 7. Sub noctem proficīscantur; hōc factō, nōbīs
prīmā lūce sē coniungere poterunt.

SUPPLEMENTARY EXERCISE
Present Subjunctive

Active		Passive	
vulnerem	vulnerēmus	vulnerer	vulnerēmur
vulnerēs	vulnerētis	vulnerēris (-re)	vulnerēminī
vulneret	vulnerent	vulnerētur	vulnerentur

Imperfect Subjunctive

vulnerārem	vulnerārēmus	vulnerārer	vulnerārēmur
vulnerārēs	vulnerārētis	vulnerārēris (-re)	vulnerārēminī
vulnerāret	vulnerārent	vulnerārētur	vulnerārentur

NOTE: Only the first person singular of the conjugation will be given from
this point on. Since the conjugation is completely regular, it is deemed un-
necessary to give the complete conjugation.

Pres. Act.	Pres. Pass.	Imp. Act.	Imp. Pass.
iubeam	iubear	iubērem	iubērer
expellam	expellar	expellerem	expellerer
cōnspiciam	cōnspiciar	cōnspicerem	cōnspicerer
inveniam	inveniar	invenīrem	invenīrer
	morer		morārer
	pollicear		pollicērer
	proficīscar		proficīscerer
sim		essem	
possim		possem	

377 WORD STUDY

amō—amor, amōris, love; clāmō—clāmor, clāmōris, loud shouting, cry;
teneō—tenor, tenōris, course, continued movement; terreō—terror, terrōris,
fear, fright, dread
clāmor, loud shouting, cry; clāmātor, one who shouts, shouter; amor,
love, passion; amātor, one who loves, lover

148

LESSON 53

378   A Scene from Roman Life (Part 3)

On the street the watchmen are already trying to extinguish the fire with pumps. A rich senator is urging them on. Cluentia is crying; she wants to go into the "island" and can scarcely be held back by the others.

Cluentia. My children! Where are you? Let me go, men; why are you holding me back? Why won't you let me enter the house? I will save my children or I will perish.

At this moment Marcus Accius, Cluentia's husband, enters quickly and pushes through the crowd with his son. At the entrance of her husband, Cluentia cries out.

Cluentia. Oh, Marcus, what are we to do? Help the children.

Accius. Where are the children, Cluentia?

Cluentia. I told them not to go out.

Accius. I will go in; no one will stop me.

Marcus. Me, too.

They run to the door of the apartment house. But at this very moment the children come out almost choked with smoke and holding one another by the hand. They can hardly see.

Accius. Let us praise the gods. We are all here. May such a thing never happen again. We will sacrifice to the gods.

Cluentia. If only the "island" had not burned. (How I wish the "island" had not burned). Where, dear husband, are we to live now?

Marcus. Look! The watchmen are extinguishing the flames with their pumps. Oh father, I wish I were a fireman. Our house is (*lit.* has been) saved.

Senator. Accius, come here. I have always found you a trustworthy client. Come with your wife and children and live at my house until yours is repaired.

Cluentia. We are most grateful to you, patron. You have relieved us of a great worry (*lit.* removed a great burden from us).

Accius and Cluentia thank their patron and sacrifice in the temple to the gods who have saved their dear children.

NOTE: Before 6 A.D., Rome had no fire fighting force. At that time, Augustus created the **Cohortēs Vigilum,** a combination police force and fire brigade. (See Cowell, *Everyday Life in Ancient Rome,* pp. 15-16.)

385   EXERCISES

A. 1. If only my friend were here. 2. Let us encourage them. 3. Do not wander too far. 4. If only they had come home. 5. What am I to do? 6. Encourage the soldiers. 7. May the Romans always conquer. 8. I

wish that he were coming back. 9. You are trying to learn (Try to learn).
10. Let us try to learn. 11. O that it had not been destroyed. 12. Let's
not hold her back. 13. What were they to say? 14. I wish that he had
cried out. 15. Let them live here. 16. Tell me everything. 17. If only
the ships had been repaired. 18. Let us rejoice. 19. Let golden armor
be given (to) him. 20. May this not happen to us.

B. 1. Utinam Rōmam vēnissent. 2. Utinam nē mortuus esset. 3. Sit
semper memor nostrī. 4. Tacēte. 5. Nōlī īre. 6. Clientēs nostrī līberentur.
7. Quid dīcās? 8. Nē timeāmus (vereāmus). 9. Utinam nē essēmus
pauperēs. 10. Quid facerēmus? 11. Signum dētur. 12. Utinam essem
dīves. 13. Utinam nē remissī essēmus. 14. Redī (Redīte) statim. 15. Prō-
grediminī sub collem (ad īmum collem). 16. Discere cōnēmur.

C. 1. Quid cōnsiliī 2. satis tēlōrum 3. Quantum frūmentī? 4. nimis
discordiae 5. minus pecūniae

D. 1. Paucī dē (ex)cīvibus 2. Duo ex mīlitibus 3. Ūnus ex adulēscentibus 4. Paucī vestrum 5. Ūnus ex nōbīs

E. 1. If only the general had sacrificed to the gods before the battle. 2. I
wish that the same law which pertains to the wife pertained to the husband.
3. Let them all leave just before dawn; let them not delay. 4. Shout loudly
and run to the citadel; don't delay. 5. How much money am I to give this
crowd of young men? 6. Let us send 2000 infantry (men) to guard the
camp. 7. Ask everyone for help for the weeping children. 8. Let him not
be greedy for money, because it is the root (beginning) of all evil. 9. Let
us promise to buy the rest of the books. 10. Let the wicked citizens leave
our city; encourage the good ones; have them all gather in one place.

F. 1. Quid cōnsiliī caperet rēx? 2. Signō datō clāmor sublātus est. 3. Imperātor ad fīnitimōs vīcōs lēgātōs mittat. 4. "Utinam uxōrēs nōs omnēs
habērēmus," dīxit ūnus ē iuvenibus. 5. Nē ex spectāculō lacrimantēs fu-
giant. 6. Utinam nē ad spectāculum vestrum vocātī essēmus.

SUPPLEMENTARY EXERCISES

A.   Subjunctive

	Active	Passive	Active	Passive
Pres.	līberent	līberentur	retineant	retineantur
Imperf.	līberārent	līberārentur	retinērent	retinērentur
Perf.	līberāverint	līberātī sint	retinuerint	retentī sint
Pluperf.	līberāvissent	līberātī essent	retinuissent	retentī essent
Pres.	expellant	expellantur	cōnspiciant	cōnspiciantur
Imperf.	expellerent	expellerentur	cōnspicerent	cōnspicerentur
Perf.	expulerint	expulsī sint	cōnspēxerint	cōnspectī sint
Pluperf.	expulissent	expulsī essent	cōnspēxissent	cōnspectī essent

Pres.	inveniant	inveniantur
Imperf.	invenīrent	invenīrentur
Perf.	invēnerint	inventī sint
Pluperf.	invēnissent	inventī essent

Deponents

Pres.	hortētur	polliceātur	revertātur
Imperf.	hortārētur	pollicērētur	reverterētur
Perf.	hortātus sit	pollicitus sit	reversus sit
Pluperf.	hortātus esset	pollicitus esset	reversus esset

Pres.	moriātur	audeat
Imperf.	morerētur	audēret
Perf.	mortuus sit	ausus sit
Pluperf.	mortuus esset	ausus esset

B. Erat Rōmae satis virōrum, sed inopia fēminārum. Rōmulus volēbat virōs habēre uxorēs; itaque lēgātōs ad prīncipēs fīnitimī vīcī mīsit. Nūntium Rōmulī dedērunt, "Fīliae vestrae dentur in mātrimōnium Rōmānīs meīs." Prīncipēs hoc (haec) facere nōlēbant. Quid faceret Rōmulus?

(Is) auxiliō suōrum (virōrum) hoc cōnsilium, cēpit. Fīnitimōs (suōs) (ūnā) cum uxōribus līberīsque vocāvit ad spectāculum quod maximā cum cūrā parāverat. Multī vīsūrī spectāculum Rōmam vēnērunt.

Subitō clāmor tollitur (sublātus est); signō datō, turba (multitūdō) iuvenum multās virginēs pulchrās raptās in arcem sustulērunt. Quod parentēs fīliās suās iuvāre nōn poterant, lacrimantēs Rōmā fūgērunt. Ā cēterīs incolīs Italiae auxilium petīvērunt et multōs mensēs (-īs) cum Rōmānīs bellum gerēbant. Tandem, (modo) parvā parte aestātis reliquā, pāx facta est.

TEACHER'S NOTES

BIBLIOGRAPHY

Although some of the books in the following list may no longer be in print, their value as reference works merits their inclusion. Books found by the authors to be especially useful are indicated by an asterisk.

FOR THE STUDENT

I. Roman History, Daily Life and Customs, Literature

BOTSFORD, GEORGE WILLIS. *Ancient History*. New York: The Macmillan Co., 1913.

*CHURCH, ALFRED J. *Roman Life in the Days of Cicero*. New York: Biblo & Tannen Booksellers & Pubs., Inc., 1940.

COOLIDGE, OLIVIA. *Roman People*. Boston: Houghton Mifflin Co., 1959.

FOSTER, GENEVIEVE. *Augustus Caesar's World*. New York: Charles Scribner's Sons, 1947.

GUERBER, H. A. *The Story of the Romans*. New York: American Book Co., 1924.

HALL, JENNIE. *Buried Cities*. New York: The Macmillan Co., 1964.

KIRTLAND, G. B. *One Day in Ancient Rome*. New York: Harcourt, Brace & World, Inc., 1961.

MOORE, R. W. *The Roman Commonwealth*. Port Washington: Kennikat Press Corp., 1969.

*SHUMWAY, EDGAR S. *A Day in Ancient Rome*. Boston: D. C. Heath and Co., 1885.

*TREBLE, H.A., and KING, K. M. *Everyday Life in Rome in the Time of Caesar and Cicero*. Oxford: Oxford University Press, 1930.

WINER, BART. *Life in the Ancient World*. New York: Random House, Inc., 1961.

II. Mythology and Legend

COLUMN, PADRAIC. *Adventures of Odysseus*. New York: The Macmillan Co., 1918.

COLUMN, PADRAIC. *The Golden Fleece*. New York: The Macmillan Co., 1920.

COOLIDGE, OLIVIA. *Greek Myths*. Boston: Houghton Mifflin Co., 1949.

*HERZBERG, MAX S. *Classical Myths*. Boston: Allyn and Bacon, Inc., 1935.

HUTCHINSON, W. M. L. *Orpheus with His Lute*. New York: Longmans, Green & Co., Inc., 1931.

KINGSLEY, CHARLES. *The Heroes*. New York: The Macmillan Co., 1954.

LOWREY, JANETTE SEBRING. *In the Morning of the World*. New York: Harper & Bros., Publishers, 1944.

REES, ENNIS, trans. *The Odyssey of Homer*. Indianapolis: Bobbs-Merrill Co., Inc., 1977.

DeSÉLINCOURT, AUBREY. *Odysseus the Wanderer*. New York: Criterion Books, Inc., 1956.

FOR THE TEACHER

I. Roman History, Daily Life and Customs, Literature

ABBOTT, FRANK FROST. *A History and Description of Roman Political Institutions*. New York: Biblo & Tannen Booksellers & Pubs., Inc., 1911.

BOAK, ARTHUR E. R. *A History of Rome to 565 A.D.* 3rd ed. New York: The Macmillan Co., 1943.

BOTSFORD, GEORGE WILLIS. *The Roman Assemblies*. New York: The Macmillan Co., 1909.

*ROBATHAN, DOROTHY. *The Monuments of Ancient Rome*. Rome: L'Erma di Bretschneider, 1950.

II. Mythology and Legend

FRAZER, SIR JAMES GEORGE. *The New Golden Bough, A New Abridgment of the Classical Work*. Edited by Dr. Theodor H. Gaster. New York: S. G. Phillip's Inc., 1959.

GRAVES, ROBERT. *The Greek Myths*. New York: George Braziller Inc., 1959.

*ROSE, H. J. *A Handbook of Greek Mythology*. New York: E. P. Dutton & Co., Inc., 1959.

FOR BOTH STUDENT AND TEACHER

I. Roman History, Daily Life and Customs, Literature

ABBOTT, FRANK FROST. *The Common People of Ancient Rome*. New York: Biblo & Tannen Booksellers & Pubs., Inc., 1911.

ALLEN, WILLIAM F. *A Short History of the Roman People*. Boston: Ginn and Co., 1898.

*BECKER, W. A. *Gallus or Roman Scenes of the Time of Augustus*. 2nd ed. Translated by the Reverend Frederick Metcalfe. New York: Longmans, Green & Co., Inc., 1915.

CARCOPINO, JÉRÔME. *Daily Life in Ancient Rome*. Edited by Henry T. Rowell. Translated by E. O. Lorimer. New Haven: Yale University Press, 1960.

CHURCH, ALFRED J. *Pictures from Roman Life and Story*. New York: Appleton-Century-Crofts, Inc., 1907.

COWELL, F. R. *Cicero and the Roman Republic*. New York: Random House, Inc., 1948.

*COWELL, F. R. *Everyday Life in Ancient Rome*. New York: G. P. Putnam's Sons, 1961.

DAVENPORT, MILLIA. *The Book of Costume*. New York: Crown Publishers, Inc., 1964.

DAVIS, WILLIAM STEARNS. *Rome and the West*. Boston: Allyn and Bacon, Inc., 1913.

DAVIS, WILLIAM STEARNS. *A Day in Old Rome*. New York: Biblo & Tannen Booksellers & Pubs., Inc., 1925.

DUFF, J. WRIGHT. *A Literary History of Rome, From the Origins to the Close of the Golden Age*. London: T. Fisher Unwin, Ltd., 1920.

EVANS, MARY. *Costume Throughout the Ages*. Philadelphia: J. B. Lippincott Co., 1950.

FRANK, TENNEY. *A History of Rome*. New York: Henry Holt & Co., Inc., 1923.

GEER, RUSSEL M. *Classical Civilization: Rome*. Englewood Cliffs, N.J.: Prentice-Hall, Inc., 1941.

GRANT, MICHAEL. *History of Rome*. New York: Charles Scribner's Sons, 1978.

HADAS, MOSES. *A History of Latin Literature*. New York: Columbia University Press, 1952.

HADAS, MOSES. *A History of Rome from its Origins to 529 A.D*. Magnolia: Peter Smith Publisher Inc., 1956.

HAMILTON, EDITH. *The Roman Way*. New York: W. W. Norton & Co., Inc., 1932.

HASKELL, H. J. *This Was Cicero*. New York: Alfred A. Knopf, Inc., 1942.

HOUSTON, MARY G. *Ancient Greek, Roman and Byzantine Costume and Decoration*. Totowa: Barnes & Noble Books, 1977.

HUS, ALAIN. *The Etruscans*. Westport: Greenwood Press, 1975.

*JOHNSTON, MARY. *Roman Life*. Chicago: Scott, Foresman and Co., 1957.

JUDSON, H. P. *Caesar's Army*. New York: Biblo & Tannen Publishers, Inc., 1888.

LESTER, KATHERINE MORRIS. *Historic Costume*. Peoria: Charles A. Bennett Co., Inc., 1977.

LISSNER, IVAR. *The Living Past*. New York: G. P. Putnam's Sons, 1957.

MACKAIL, J. W. *Virgil and His Meaning to the World of Today*. Totowa: Cooper Square Pubs., Inc., 1939.

MAIURI, AMEDEO. *Pompeii*. Novara, Italy: Istituto Geografico de Agostini, S.P.A., 1957.

MOMMSEN, THEODOR. *A Literary History of Rome from the Origins to the Close of the Golden Age*. Abridged by C. Bryans and F. J. Hendy. New York: Philosophical Library, Inc., 1959.

MUNROE, DANA CARLETON. *A Source Book of Roman History*. Boston: D. C. Heath and Co., 1904.

MYERS, PHILIP VAN NESS. *Rome: Its Rise and Fall*. Philadelphia: Richard West, 1901.

PLUTARCH. *The Lives of the Noble Grecians and Romans*. Modern Library Edition. Edited by Arthur Hugh Clough. Translated by John Dryden. New York: Random House, Inc.

ROBINSON, CHARLES ALEXANDER. *Ancient History*. 2nd ed. Edited by A. L. Boegehold. New York: Macmillan Publishing Co., Inc., 1967.

SELLAR, W. Y. *The Roman Poets of the Augustan Age: Virgil*. New York: Biblo & Tannen Booksellers & Pubs., Inc., 1908.

SHOWERMAN, GRANT. *Eternal Rome*. New Haven: Yale University Press, 1925.

*SHOWERMAN, GRANT. *Rome and the Romans*. Totowa: Cooper Square Pubs., Inc., 1934.

STRACHAN-DAVIDSON, J. L. S. *Cicero and the Fall of the Roman Republic*. New York: Arno Press, 1972.

SWAIN, J. W., and ARMSTRONG, W. H. *Peoples of the Ancient World*. New York: Harper & Bros., 1959.

WILCOX, R. TURNER. *The Mode in Footwear*. New York: Charles Scribner's Sons, 1948.

II. Mythology and Legend

ASIMOV, ISAAC. *Words from the Myths*. Boston: Houghton Mifflin Co., 1961.

BULFINCH, THOMAS. *Bulfinch's Mythology*. New York: Thomas Y. Crowell Co., 1970.

BULFINCH, THOMAS. *The Age of Fable*. New York: E. P. Dutton, 1969.

*GAYLEY, CHARLES MILLS. *The Classic Myths in English Literature and in Art*. Kennebunkport: Longwood Press, Ltd., 1977.

*HAMILTON, EDITH. *Mythology*. New York: New American Library, 1971.

MURRAY, ALEXANDER. *Manual of Mythology*. New York: Tudor Publishing Co., 1936.

SCHMIDT, JOEL. *Larousse Greek and Roman Mythology*. New York: McGraw-Hill Book Co., 1980.

III. Dictionaries

ERNOUT, A., and MEILLET, A. *Dictionnaire Etymologique de la Langue Latine*. Paris: Librairie C. Klincksieck, 1939.

LEWIS and SHORT. *New Latin Dictionary*. Edited by E. A. Andrews. Darby: Arden Library, 1979.

SIMPSON, D. P., ed. *Cassell's Latin Dictionary*. New York: Macmillan Publishing Co., Inc., 1977.

SMITH, WILLIAM and LOCKWOOD, J. F., eds. *Chambers Murray Latin-English Dictionary*. 3rd ed. Totowa: Barnes & Noble Books, 1976.

IV. Grammars

ALLEN and GREENOUGH's *New Latin Grammar*. Edited by G. L. Kittredge et al. New Rochelle: Caratzas Brothers, Pubs., 1975.

BENNETT, CHARLES E. *New Latin Grammar*. Boston: Allyn and Bacon, Inc., 1960.

GILDERSLEEVE, B. L. and LODGE, G. *Latin Grammar.* 3rd ed. New York: St. Martin's Press, Inc., 1895.

GREEN, JOHN C., JR. *Ritchie's First Steps in Latin.* New York: Longman Inc., 1978.

LANE, GEORGE M. *Latin Grammar for Schools & Colleges.* New York: AMS Press, Inc., 1970.

2 3 4 5 6 7 8 9 10 11 12 13 14 15 — 89 88 87 86 85 84 83